THEN & NOW

MEREDITH

In memory of Mr. and Mrs. Jessie Allen, whose rare collection of Meredith photographs has made this book possible.

THEN & NOW

MEREDITH

Bruce D. Heald, Ph.D.

ARCADIA PUBLISHING

ISBN 978-0-7385-3768-9

Published by Arcadia Publishing
Charleston, South Carolina

Printed in the United States of America

Library of Congress Catalog Card Number: 2004116275

For all general information, contact Arcadia Publishing:
Telephone 843-853-2070
Fax 843-853-0044
E-mail sales@arcadiapublishing.com
For customer service and orders:
Toll-free 1-888-313-2665

Visit us on the Internet at www.arcadiapublishing.com

Contents

Acknowledgments

Special thanks are extended to the following individuals for their willingness to contribute to this volume: William Allen; Robert and Barbara Bennett; Steven Bennett; Wayne Chase; Dawn Dever and the Meredith Historical Society; the *Meredith News*; Ingunn Gardner; Hart's Turkey Farm Restaurant; Inter-Lakes Junior Senior High School; Rusty McLear; Aaron Ober; Jan Phillips and the Meredith Village Savings Bank; Sandra L. Quinney; and Brent Summers.

Introduction

Meredith, known as the "Latchkey to the White Mountains," is nestled in the Lakes Region of New Hampshire. This community of superb scenery is uniquely clustered with many lakes and rivers, streams and meadows, and islands and bays. It is truly considered the sentinel to the North Country.

Formed as a corporate town in the mid-18th century, Meredith is one of the oldest towns in this section of the state. In its earlier years, it was considered one of the best farming towns in New Hampshire. Today Meredith attracts visitors from all over the world and is regarded as one of the finest resort communities in New England.

In 1748, the first settlement, Palmer's Town, was established. It was soon renamed Salem, and that name was later changed to New Salem. The town (consisting of only 17 families) grew slowly until a petition for town privileges was granted. Meredith was incorporated on December 30, 1768. Since the mid-19th century, Meredith Village has served as the town's civic, industrial, commercial, and residential center. The village is peacefully nestled on a narrow neck of land bordered by lakes on either side, and its streets are gracefully lined with 19th- and 20th-century buildings. Stunning vistas of Lake Winnipesaukee are afforded from many vantage points across the landscape.

Located 36 miles from New Hampshire's capital city of Concord, Meredith is bounded by Center Harbor to the north; by Lake Winnipesaukee to the north and northeast; by Laconia to the southeast; by Sanbornton to the south; and by New Hampton to the west and northwest.

Meredith Village's beginnings stem from the construction of a sawmill in 1795, and later, a gristmill along the outlet of Lake Waukewan into Lake Winnipesaukee. The outlet provided early industries with a great supply of waterpower. An 1822 account of the village mentions five stores, a tannery, a cloth dresser, and a manufacturer. The arrival of the Boston, Concord and Montreal Railroad at Meredith Village in 1848 was a key to the town's continued growth. By the 1880s, a small village had taken shape with the addition of stores and homes.

Early settlers in Meredith were men and women of a most sturdy character. They were pioneers of an extraordinary kind, and they took an active part in the formation of the Granite State. Over the past 200 years, the town has witnessed a steady and substantial growth. This thriving resort community has continued to reflect the values of its earlier settlers. Its history is that of ordinary people who lived in self-sufficiency.

The purpose of this volume is to compare the past with the present. Here is a way of life that we will not know again. In retrospect, it seems a little touch of heaven, and that is how we should remember the people who lived then and those who live now. With the generosity of the Meredith Historical Society and many friends who wished to preserve our heritage, a rare set of photographs has been assembled to capture the legacy and spirit of the "Latchkey to the White Mountains."

—Bruce D. Heald, Ph.D.

The *Sophie C.* is shown at the Meredith town dock *c.* 1946. The sign over the small building reads, "Don't Miss It! 3 1/2 hour Round Trip $1.50. 10:00 am & 1:00 pm. Buy tickets on the boat." In the distance is the new location of the St. Charles Catholic Church. Today that property is known as Church Landing. Meredith Village, located on Meredith Bay, has become a magnet for the tourist. The Native Americans marked this spot as a favorite campsite; there were sandy beaches where they could land canoes, and a spring where they could get clear, cold water. Today there are many town docks to welcome visitors to Meredith.

Chapter 1
The Lakes, Islands, and Bays

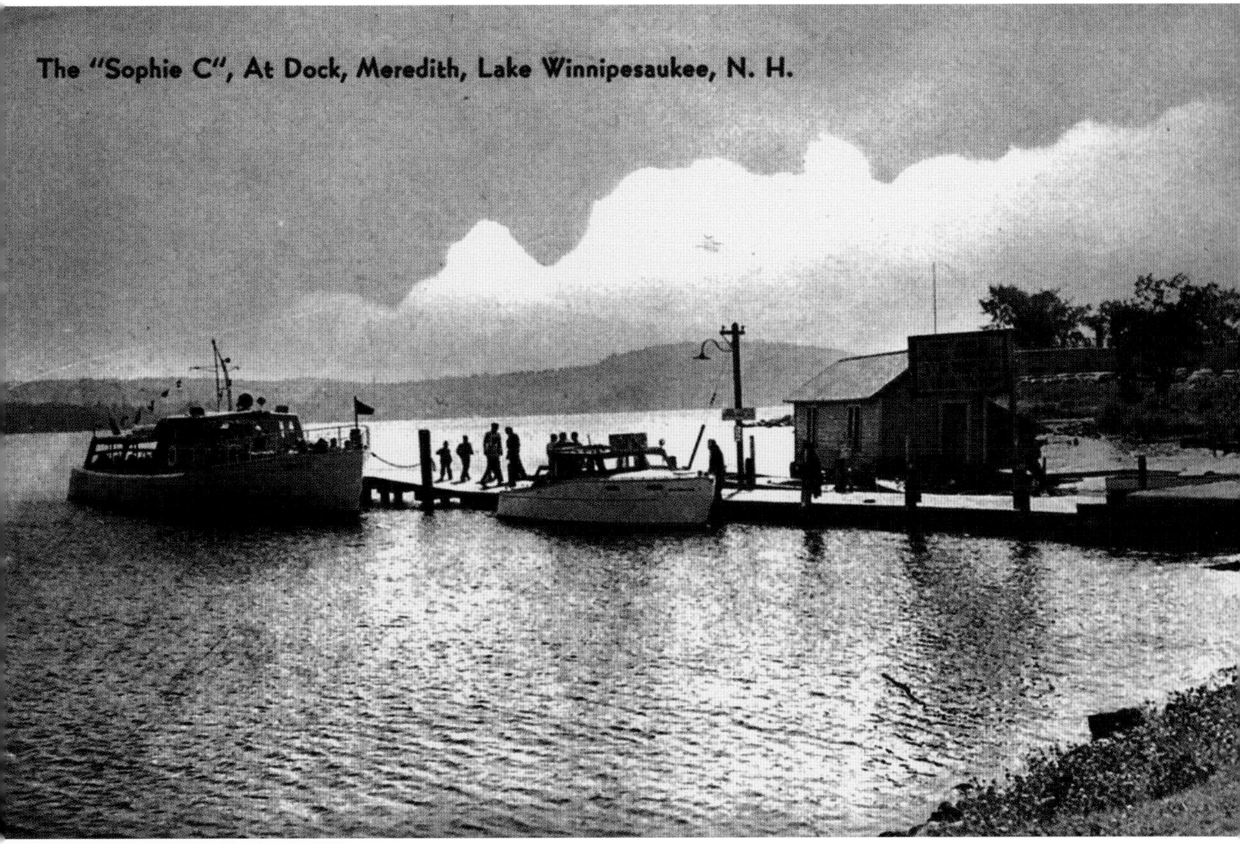

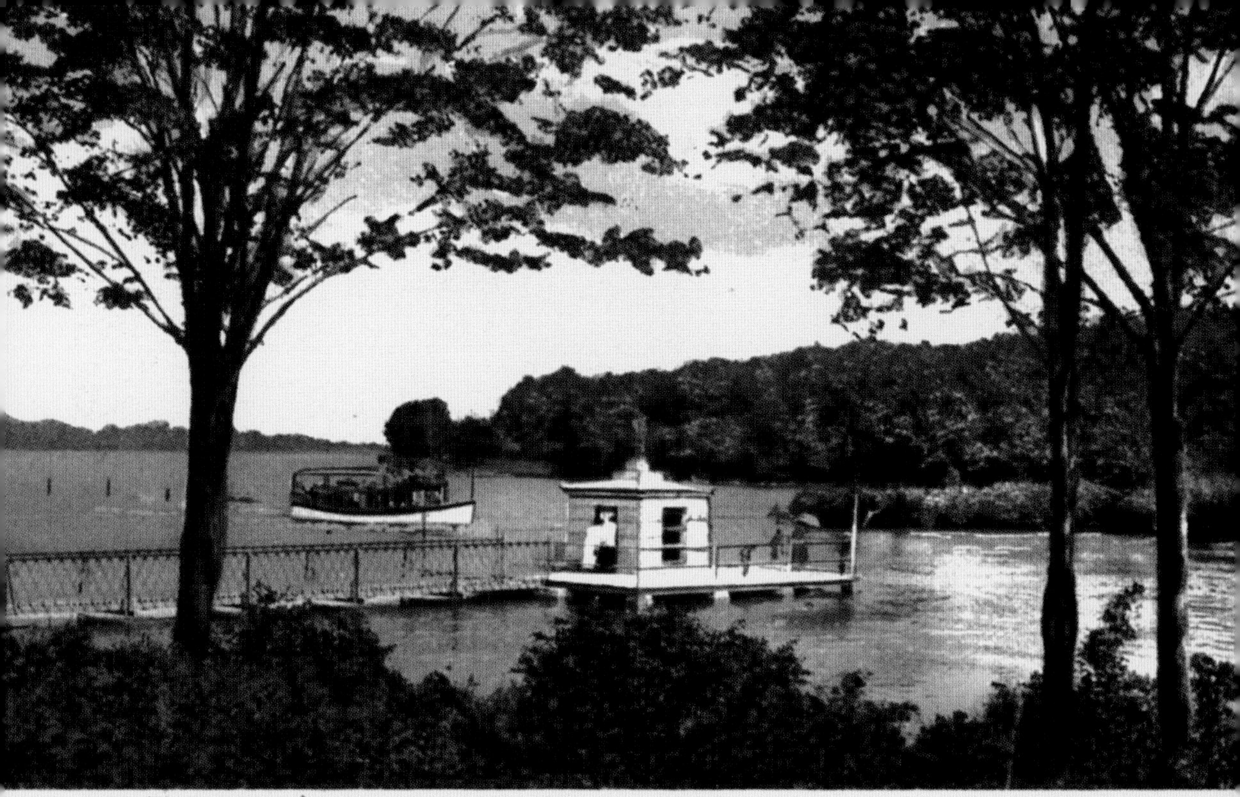

MAIL BOAT "UNCLE SAM," PASSING ENDICOTT ROCK, WEIRS, LAKE WINNEPESAUKEE, N. H.

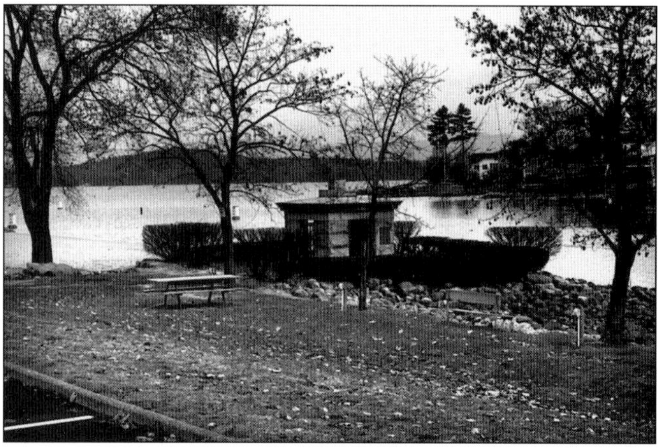

In 1652, the Massachusetts Bay Colony sent a delegation to learn the northernmost boundary of the territory. The members of the delegation chiseled the name of Gov. John Endicott on a large round-topped boulder near the mouth of the Lake Winnipesaukee outlet. For 181 years, the boulder was apparently forgotten. It was rediscovered in 1833, and the state enclosed it in a granite structure in 1892. The Endicott Rock Monument, located at the Weirs, is also an old boundary for Meredith Bridge. In the earlier image, a steamer is seen entering the Weirs Channel. Today the monument's site is enclosed by filled land.

This is how Meredith Village appeared from Center Harbor in the late 1800s. The traveler into this picturesque and rural scene would certainly find a sense of peace in these natural surroundings. In 1850, the new road to Center Harbor was built. Guide boards were made and erected at the road intersections. Today this a major highway (Route 25) that proceeds east to Center Harbor and Moultonboro, and Portland, Maine.

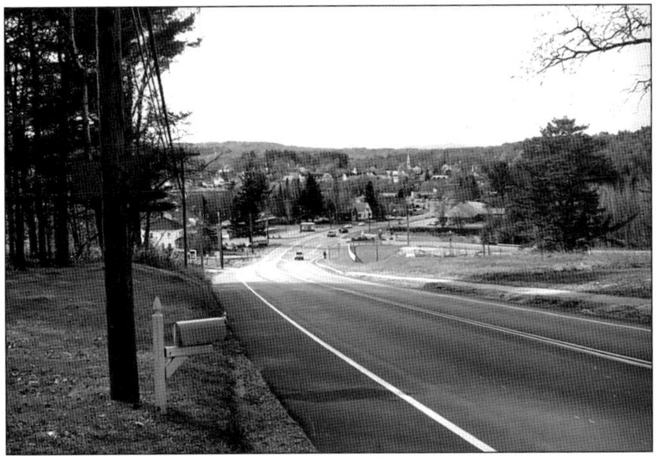

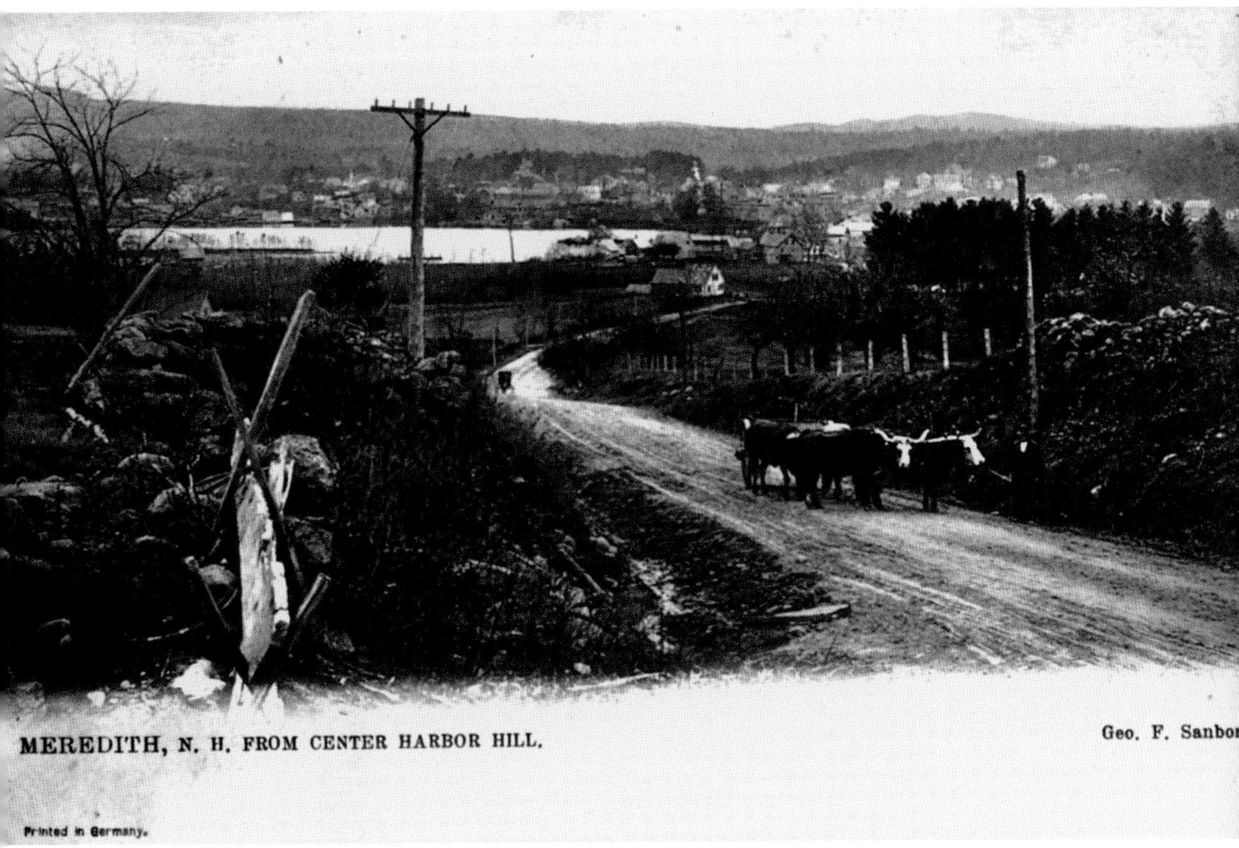

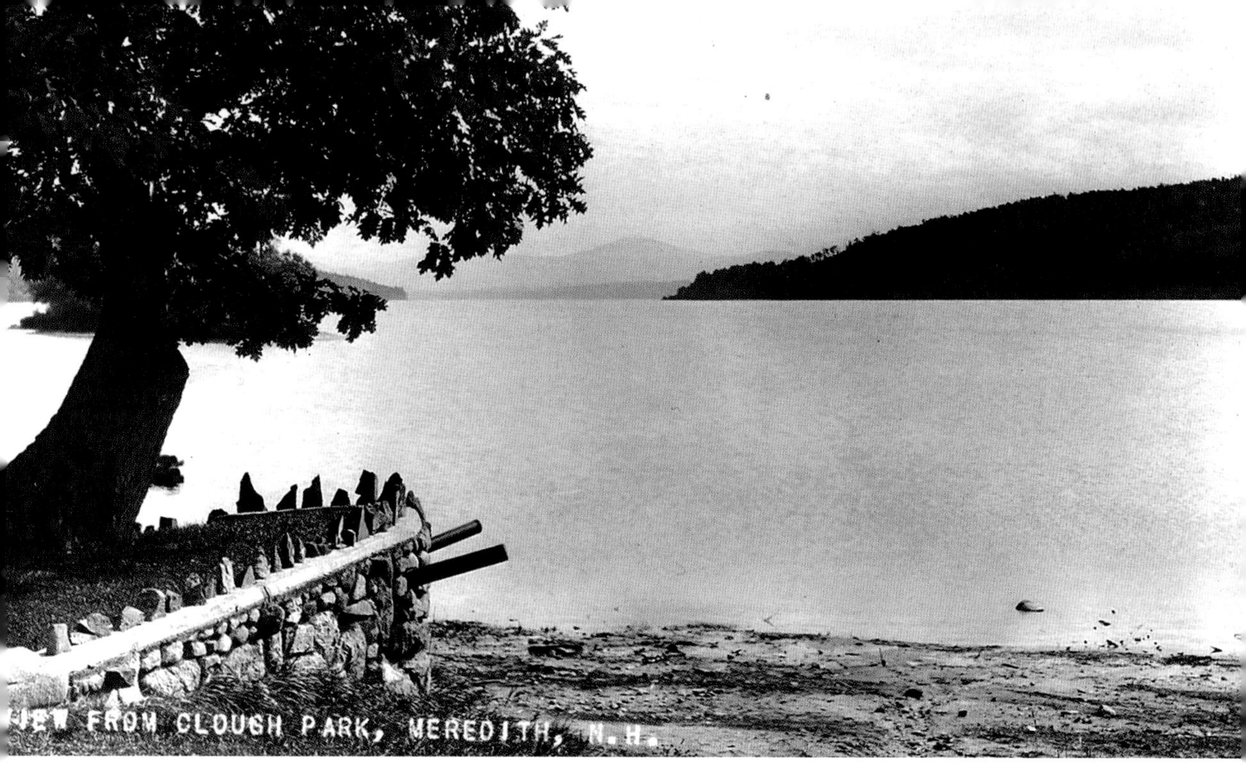

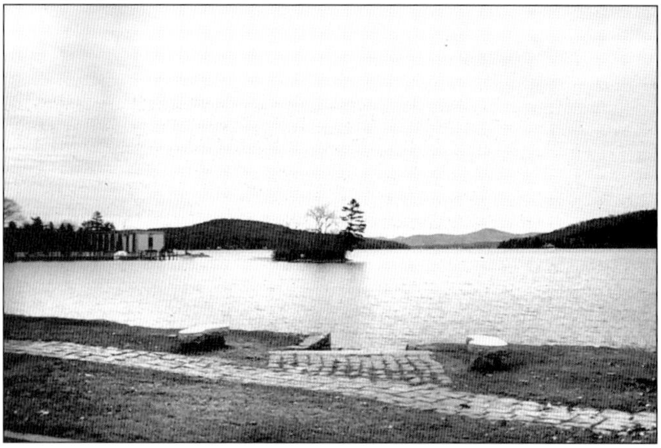

We are looking at an early landmark on Meredith Bay—the Old Oak. In the early 1900s, Clough Park underwent many renovations, and the oak stood here as a landmark for Meredith. At some point, however, the oak disappeared and an open view of the bay is now seen from the park. Meredith Bay rightfully boasts of its scenic attraction, as seen here from Clough Park, with Meredith Bay commanding as it does the mountains, lakes, and island views. Today this natural vista is maintained by preserving the reasonable, well-planned growth of the town's shore.

This distant southeasterly view of Lake Winnipesaukee overlooks the Broads. The scene was photographed from Pinnacle Park on Meredith Neck and Col. Charles H. Cummings's 350-acre Spindle Point estate. Lake Winnipesaukee, one of the largest freshwater lakes entirely situated within the borders of one state, has a perimeter of about 186 miles, a water surface of about 72 square miles, and a length of about 23 miles. The origin of the point may be traced to a 500-acre farm owned by John Eaton, which was later sold to his son John Morton Eaton. During the late 1800s, the younger Eaton sold the land to Cummings. In the distance is the Belknap Mountain Range. In 1859, there was no Pinnacle Park road, as exists today. Today a fine summer estate is located near the spot where the early photograph was taken, but now vegetation has replaced the farming pastures. The present-day picture was taken from the third floor of the estate.

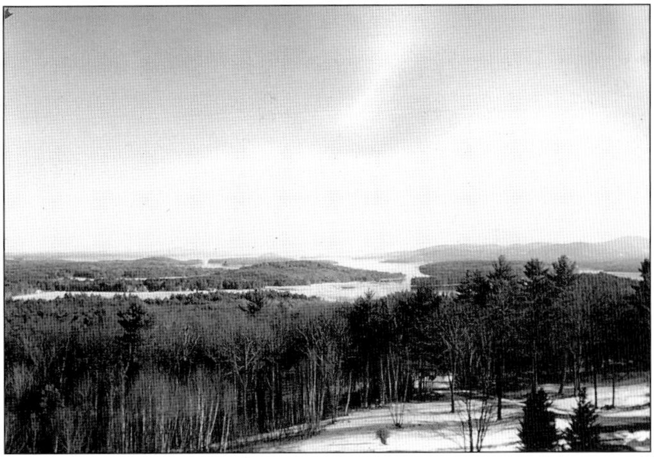

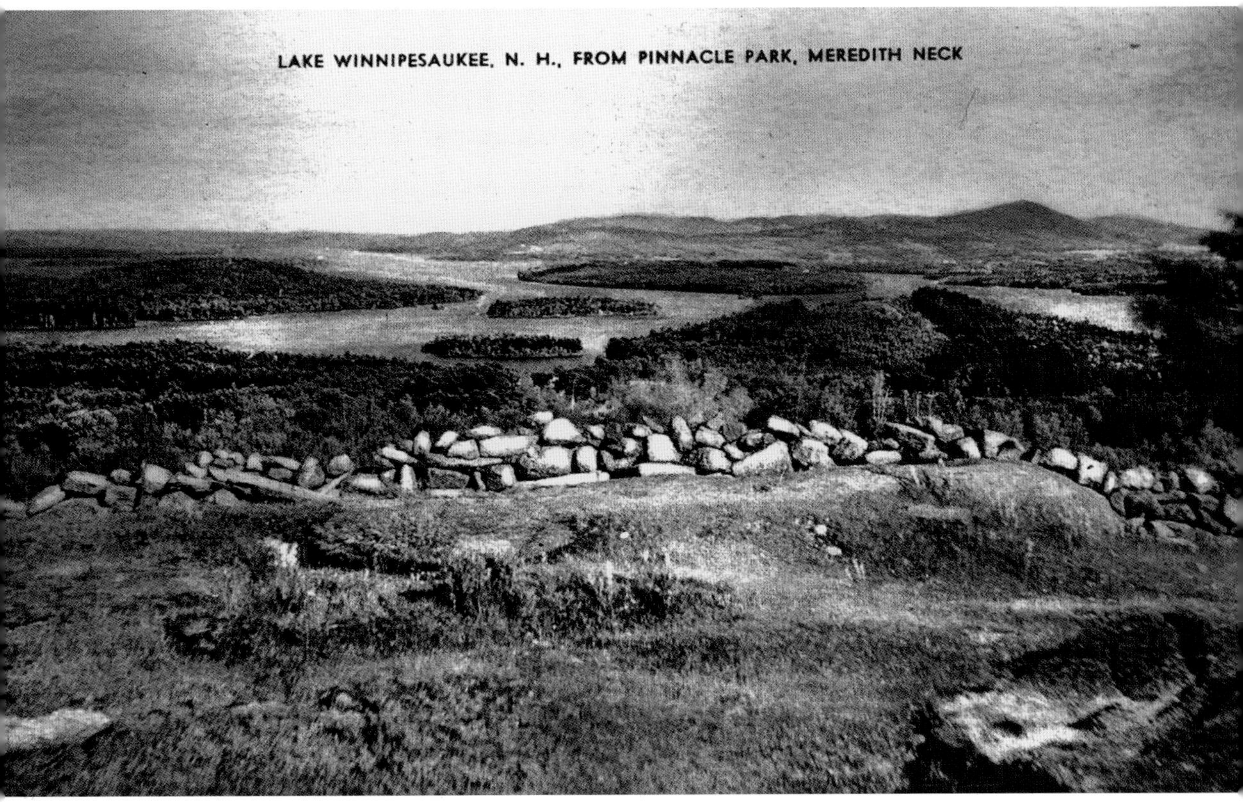

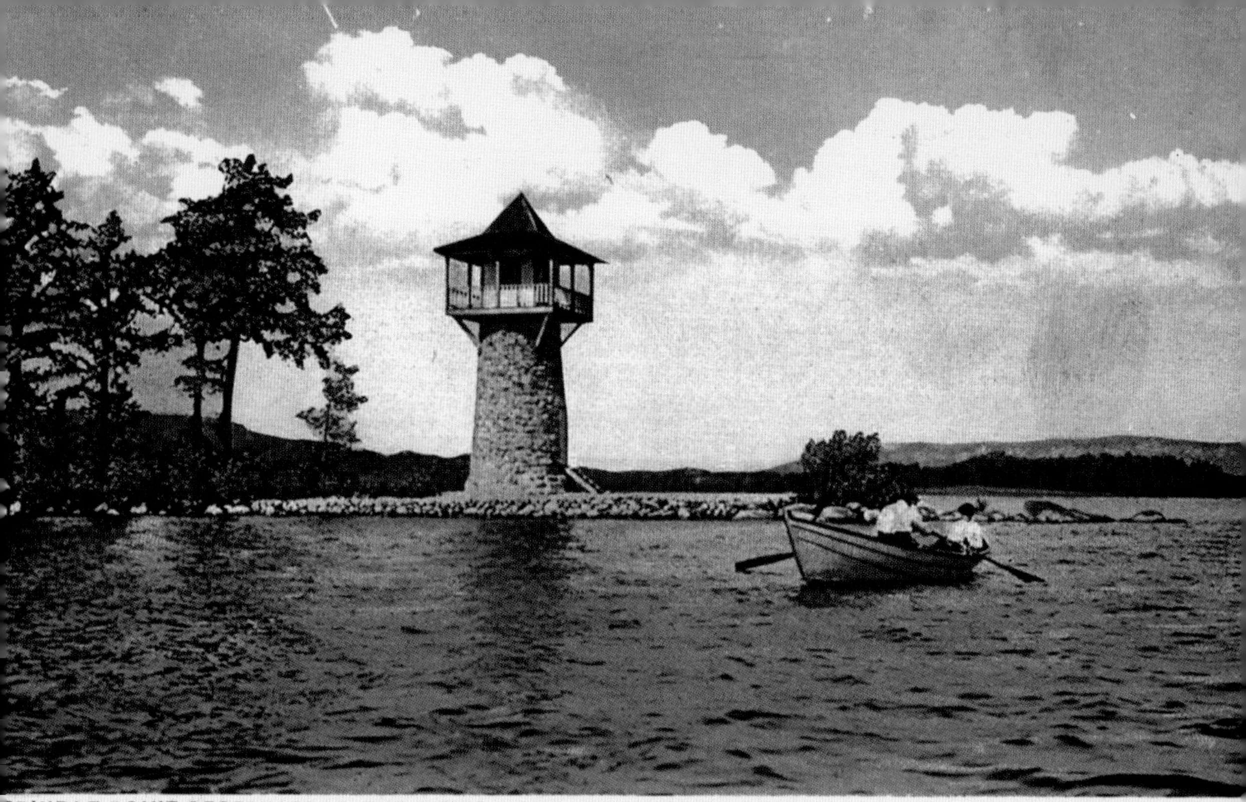

SPINDLE POINT OBSERVATORY, THE WEIRS, LAKE WINNEPESAUKEE, N. H.

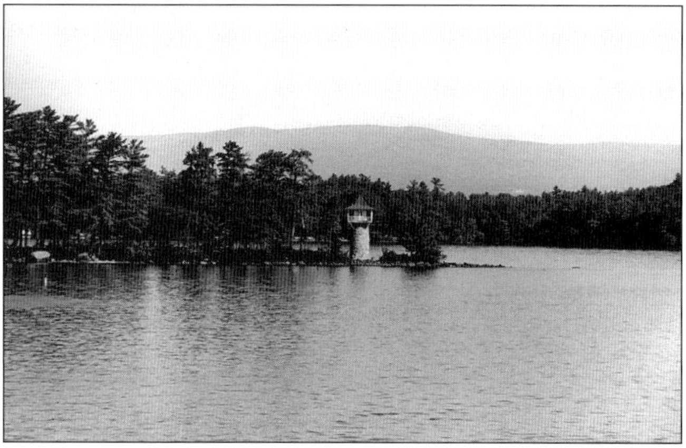

At the north point of Weirs Bay, between Meredith Bay and Center Harbor, lies Meredith Neck, which extends into Lake Winnipesaukee. The first division of Meredith Neck, sloping from the Pinnacle, is known as Spindle Point. It is recognized by its lighthouse, which was constructed by Col. Charles Cummings as an art studio for his daughter. From this vantage point, we have an excellent view of the Belknap Mountain Range, the vast expanse of the Broads, and (to the east) the Ossipee Mountains, with Mount Shaw in full view. Today we see Lighthouse Point, which extends off Observatory Road on Meredith Neck as a beacon for navigators and tourists alike.

Lake Wicwas is seen from Smith's Corner in Meredith Center. This beautiful sheet of water has similar charms as Lakes Winnipesaukee and Winnisquam. Note the landscape change, from cultivated pastures to forest growth today.

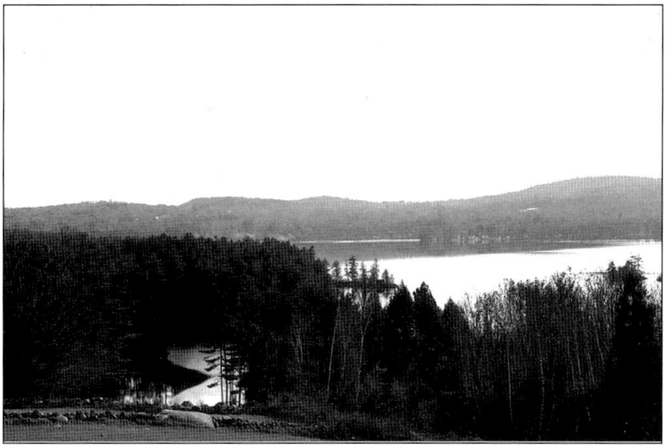

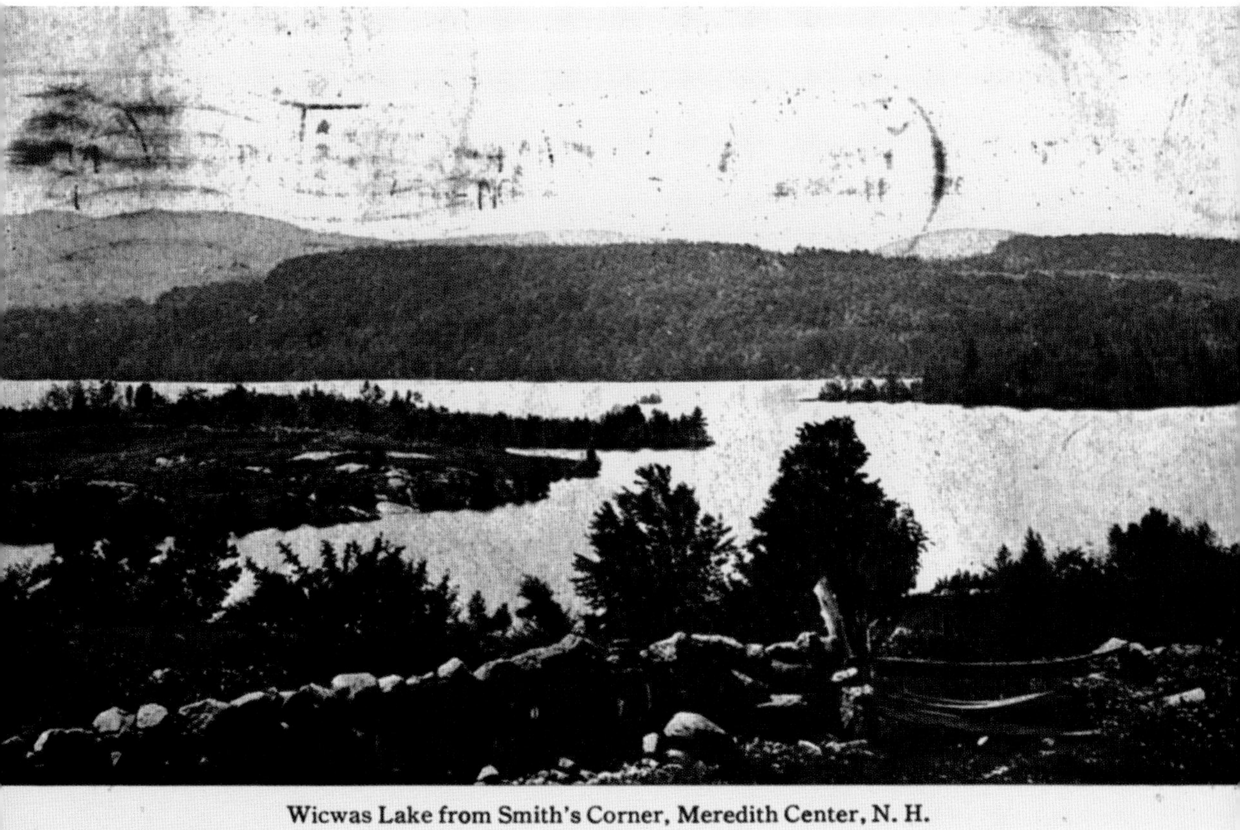

Wicwas Lake from Smith's Corner, Meredith Center, N. H.

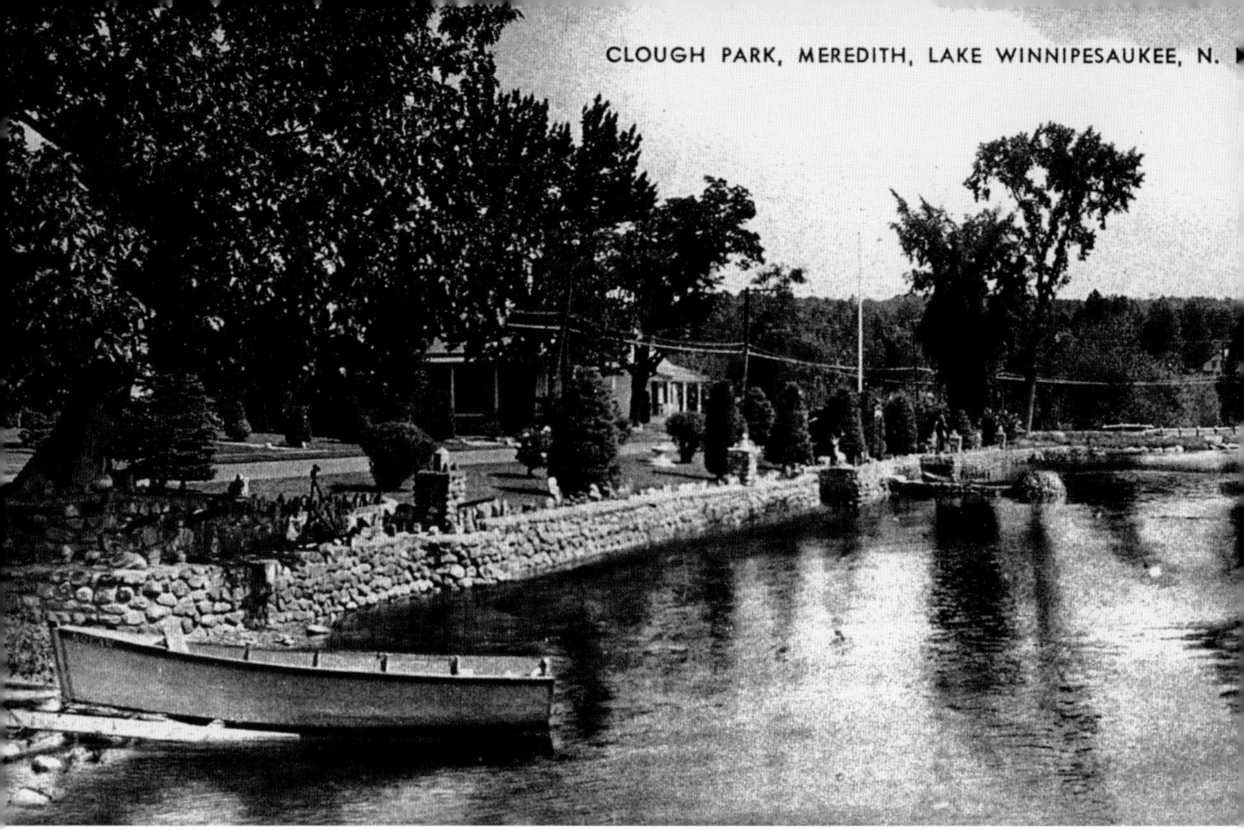

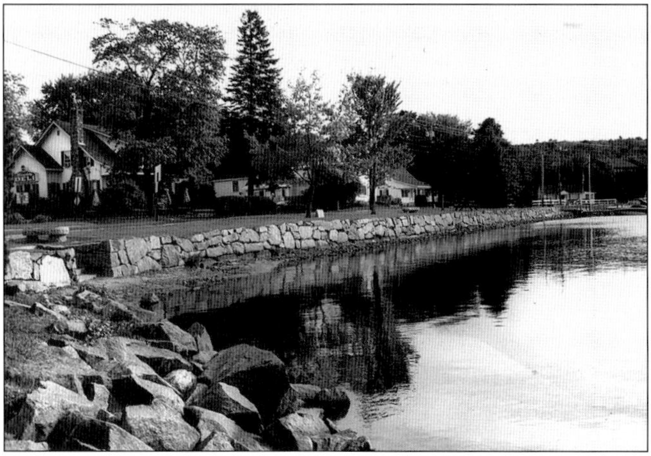

Few changes have transpired at Clough Park on Meredith Bay over the past 50 years. This picture shows the view looking east on Winnipesaukee Street. The rocks that make up the wall were collected or donated from all over the world.

In 1940, Indian Island exhibited this fine statue of Chief Chocorua, seen here from Scenic Park. For many years, this statue was missing from the island, until the efforts of many concerned citizens raised funds to erect a new statue. Today we see the statue proudly standing as a sentinel to the bay and village.

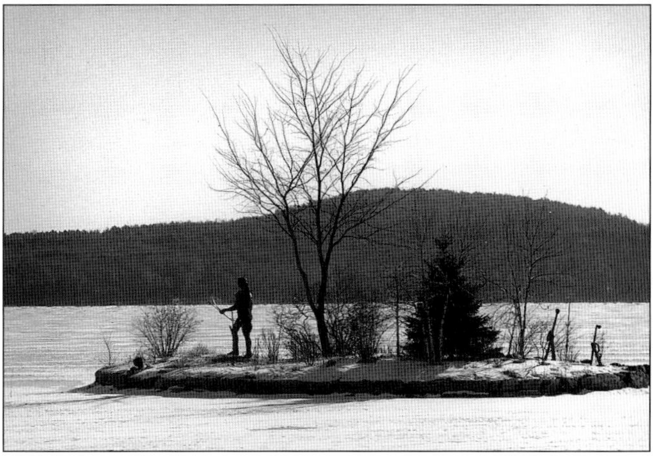

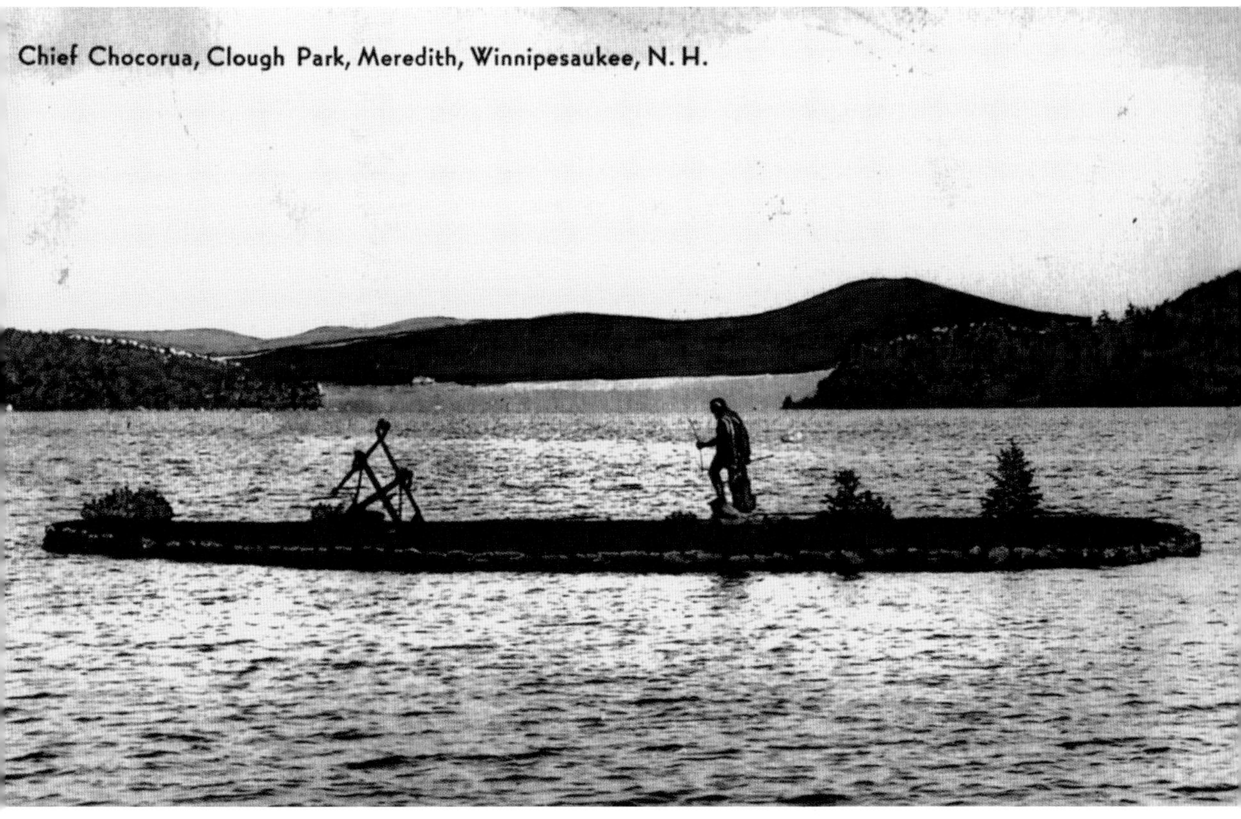

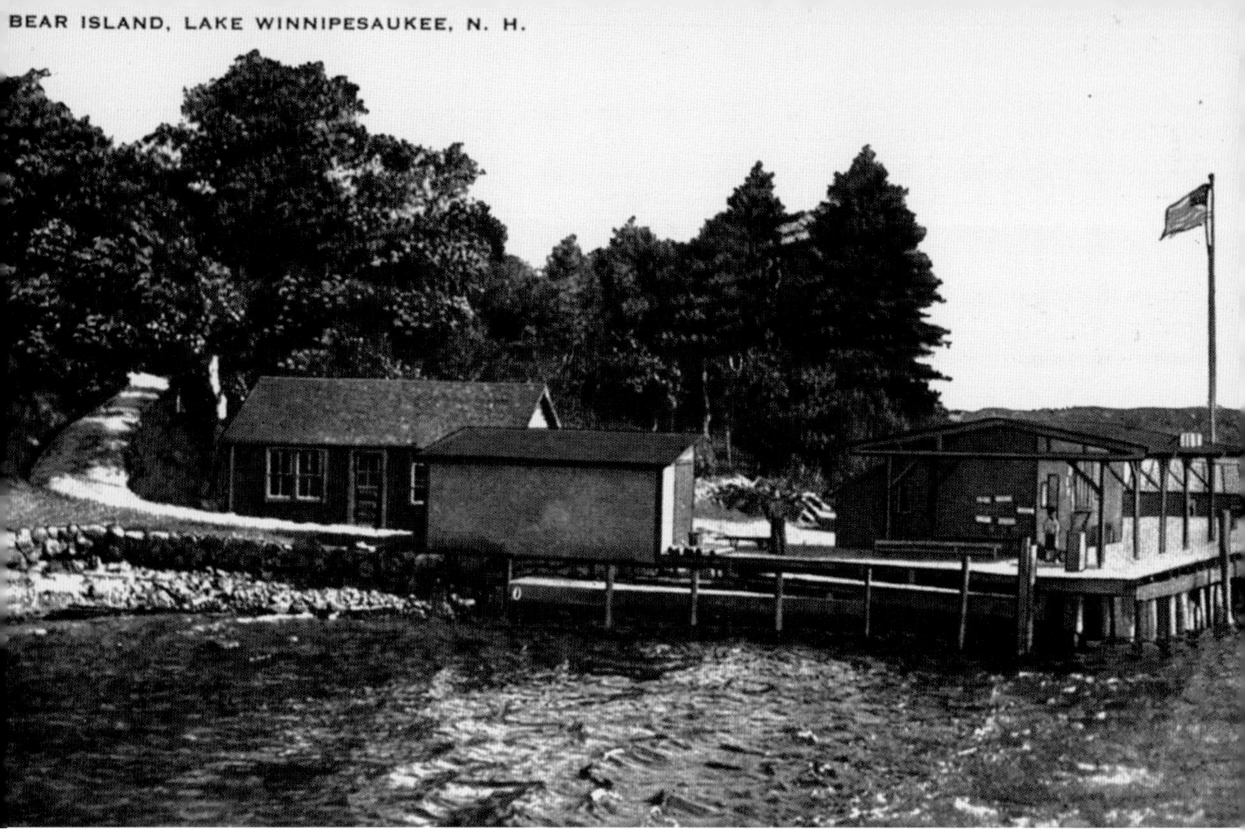

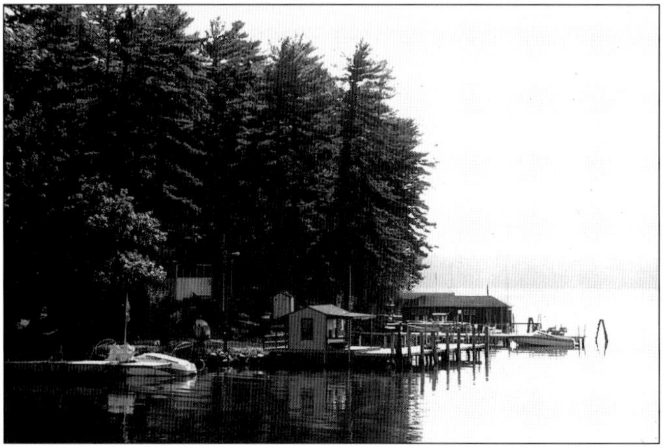

The Bear Island dock and the post office are pictured in the early 1900s. The dock was originally called the Bear Island Wharf and served as the mail dock "port of entry." The mail boat *Uncle Sam* made daily mail runs to this and the many other islands in the lake. Today the mail delivery continues the tradition of making Bear Island one of the mail-delivery stops for the mail boat *Sophie C.* Bear Island is the second-largest island in Lake Winnipesaukee. It is quite thickly populated and is the only island that still maintains its own church. Some idea of the size of Bear Island may be gained from the fact that it has a shoreline of about eight and a half miles. Today the new post office has been established in order to provide better service for the Bear Island residents.

The two most popular mail boats to sail among the islands in Meredith were the *Sophie C.* and the *Uncle Sam*, both of which were officially licensed to carry and cancel mail. The first address (RFD No. 7, Laconia) was established in 1892, when the first mail vessel was put upon the lake. In 1916, an act of Congress made this the only floating post office on an inland body of water in the United States, and it has remained so to this day. The original *Uncle Sam* was built in 1903. The vessel was 65 feet long, had a 14-foot beam, and was capable of carrying 100 passengers. In 1962, *Uncle Sam II* made its appearance on the lake. This vessel was a converted PT boat. In 1969, the mail franchise was placed with the *Sophie C.* This boat is not strictly a post office, however, for tourist passengers are more than welcome to ride aboard the *Sophie C.* to explore the lake and the inlets. The *Sophie C.* was launched at Center Harbor in August 1945 for the sole purpose of serving as a shuttle service between Wolfeboro and the Weirs during the period that the *Mount Washington* was out of commission. The *Sophie C.* measures 76 feet in length and 16 feet at the beam, and has a capacity of 150 passengers. When this vessel was commissioned, it was christened *Sophie C.* after the owner's mother. The boat is now owned by the Winnipesaukee Flagship Corporation.

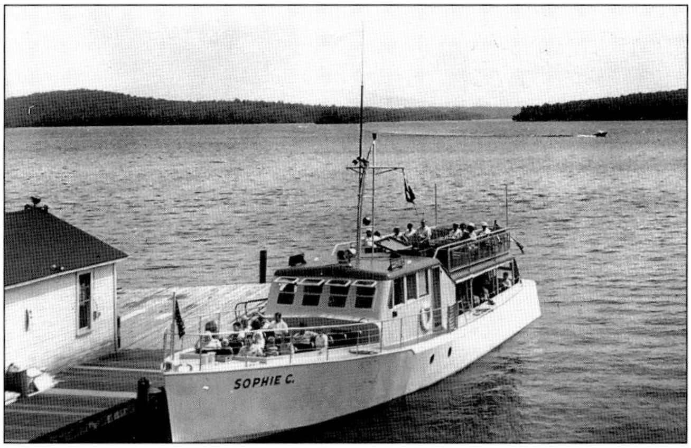

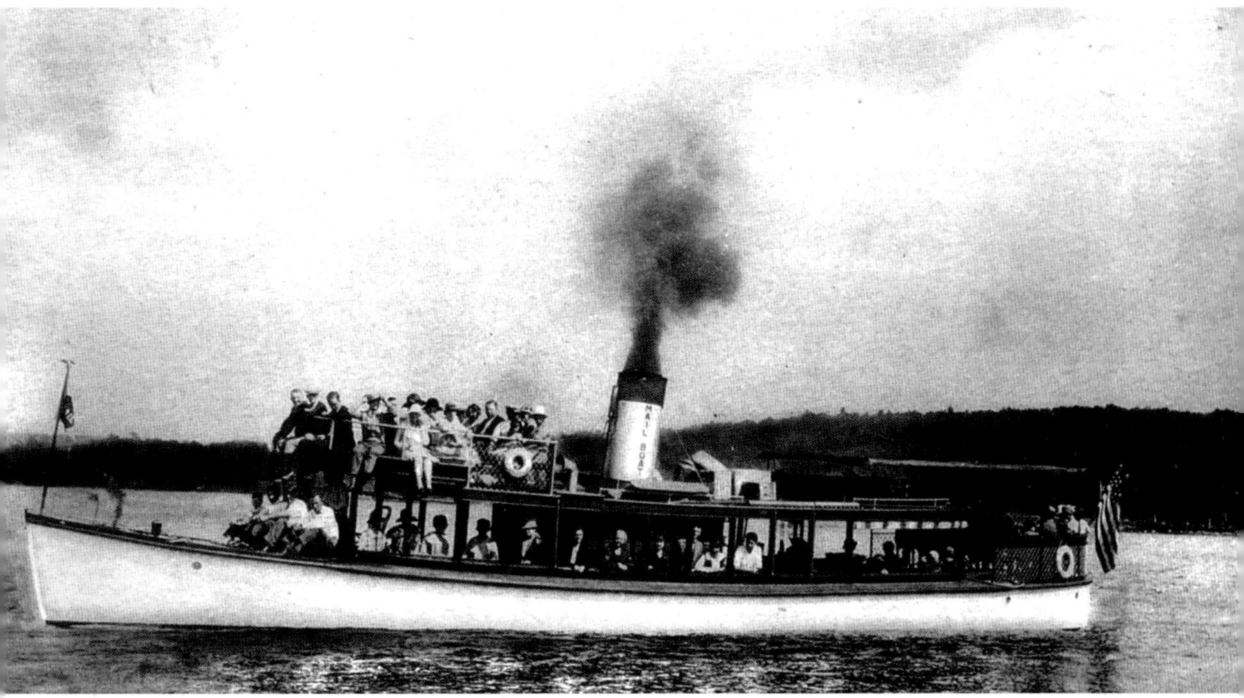

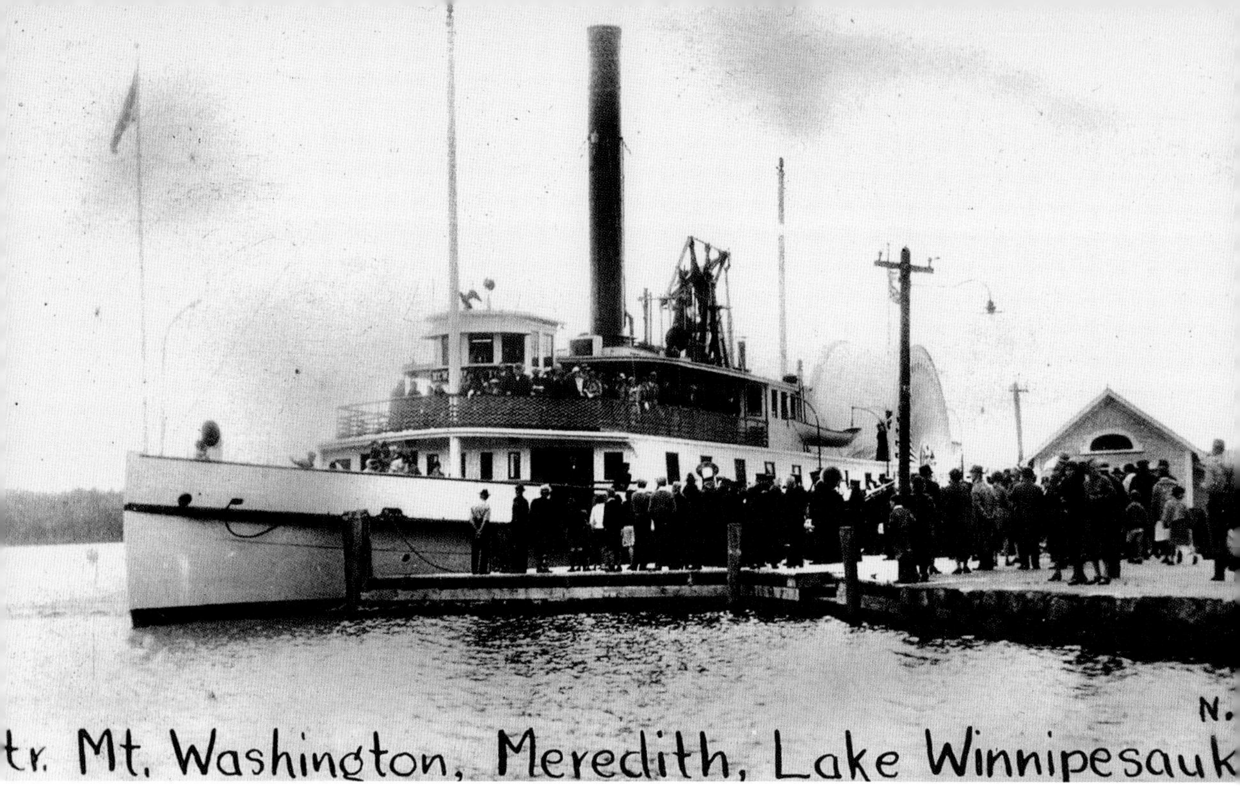

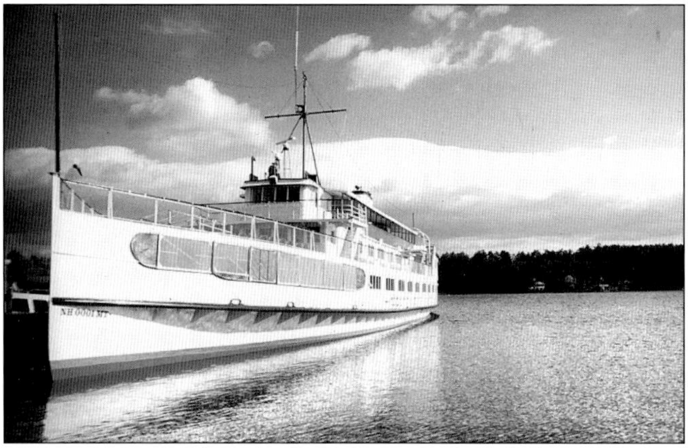

The side-wheeler *Mount Washington*, a prominent feature of the Lakes Region since 1872, is seen here in Meredith Bay during the early 1900s. The *Mount Washington* made Meredith a regular port of call during the summer. Originally, the *Mount Washington* was an extension of the Boston & Maine Railroad Company, which built the vessel and offered lake transportation for its rail passengers. Today the *Mount Washington* makes a stop at Meredith each Monday throughout the season. After the original *Mount Washington* burned on December 23, 1939, it was replaced with a new and larger vessel, which continues the tradition of making Meredith a weekly stop during the season.

People entering the town of Meredith by Route 3 are welcomed to the "Latchkey" to the White Mountains. Nestled in the foothills of the White Mountains, this community features many lakes, rivers, meadows, islands, and bays. Directly below the Meredith sign was the site of Aaron Clark's Dairy Farm.

Chapter 2
MAIN STREET AND VILLAGE SCENES

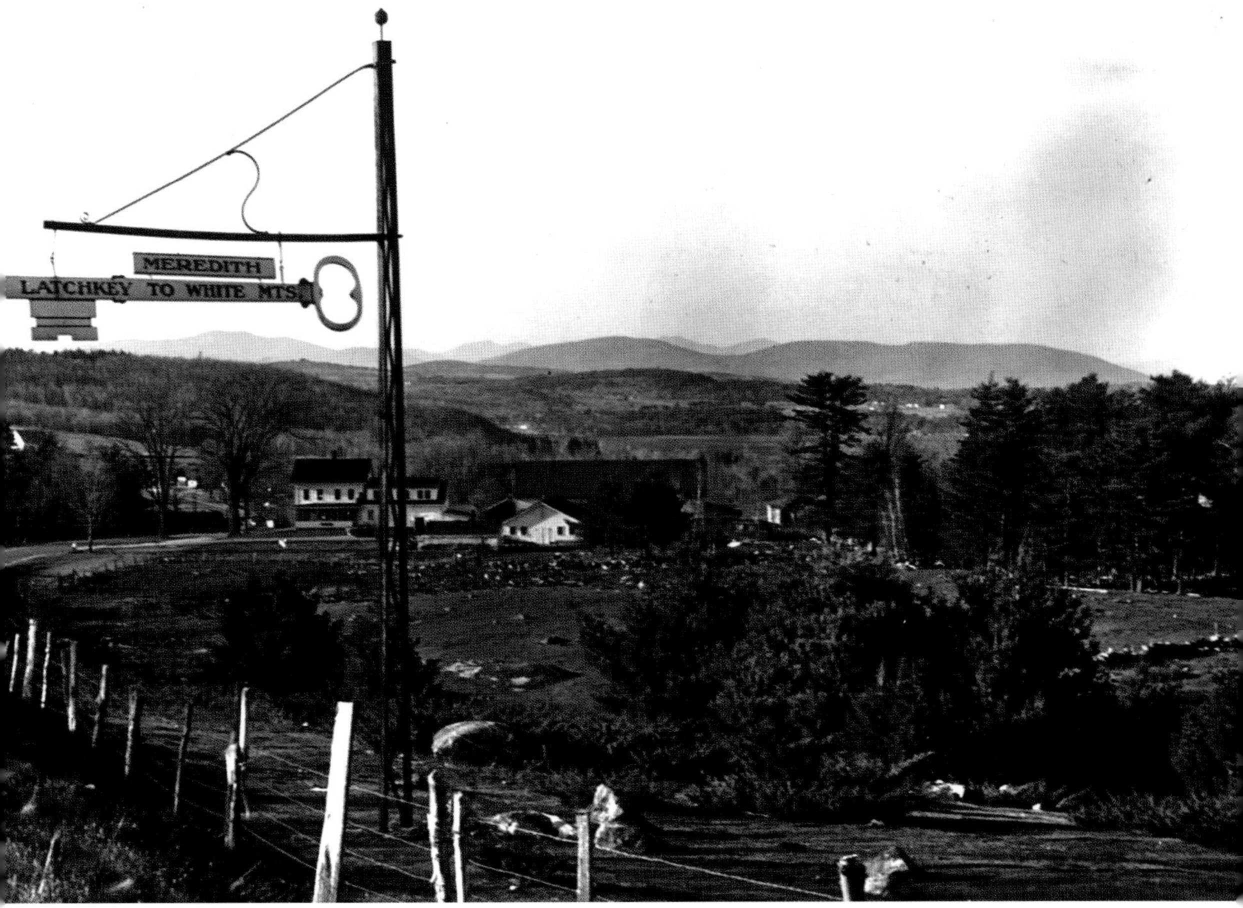

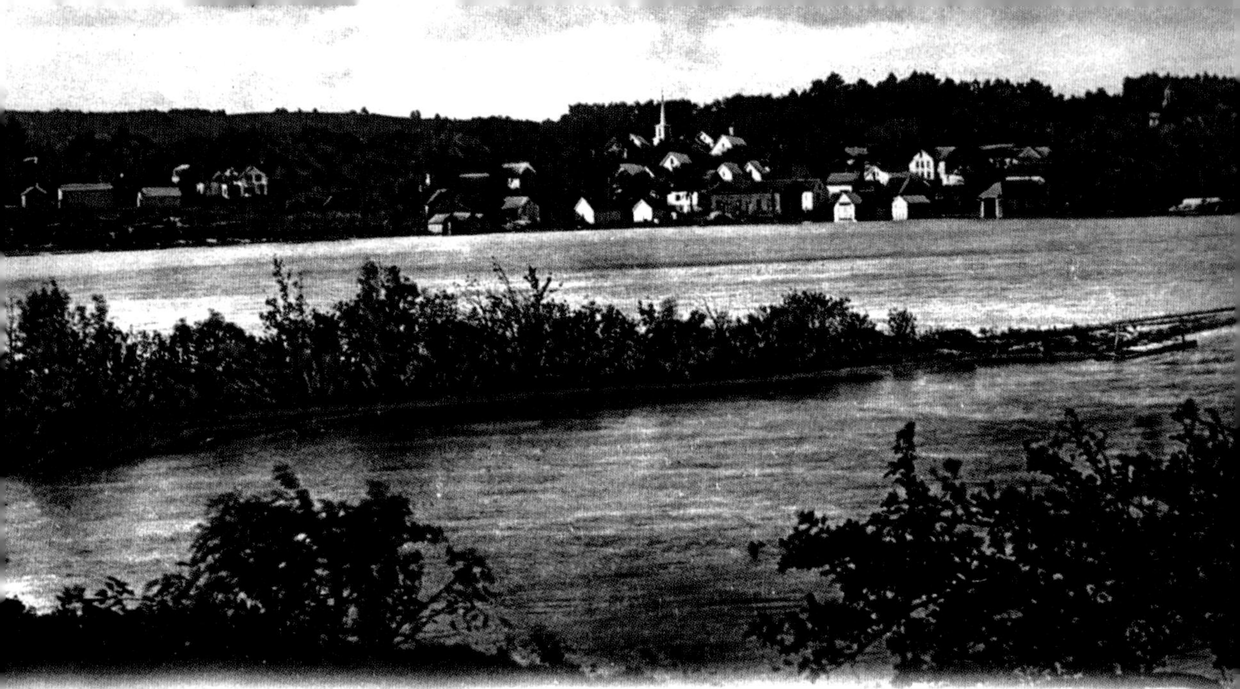

MEREDITH, N.H. FROM MOSES POINT, LAKE WINNIPESAUKEE. Morrison the Druggist

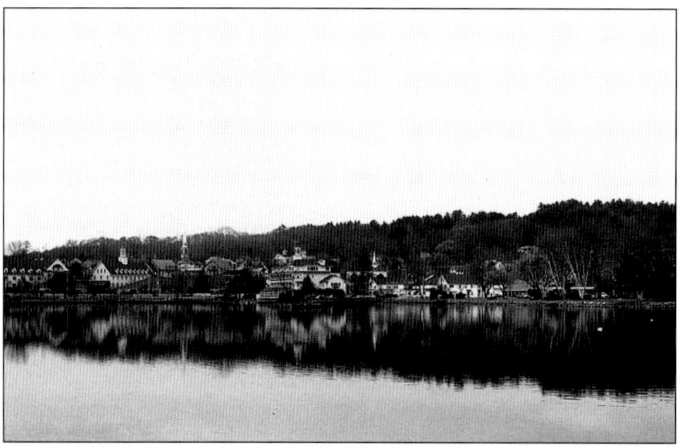

Meredith Village is seen from Moses Point in the 1940s. This area, which is where most of the town's business is transacted, is bounded on the north by Center Harbor and Lake Winnipesaukee, on the northeast by Lake Winnipesaukee, on the southeast by Laconia, on the south by Sanbornton, and on the west and northwest by New Hampton. Today this thriving resort community on Meredith Bay maintains a much-desired country atmosphere, as evident in the elegance of the white building with the spire in the center of the village.

Over the past 100 years, Meredith Village has witnessed many changes. The factories and mills of years past have gradually been replaced by fine hotels, eating establishments, and well-designed parks along the shores of the area's many lakes.

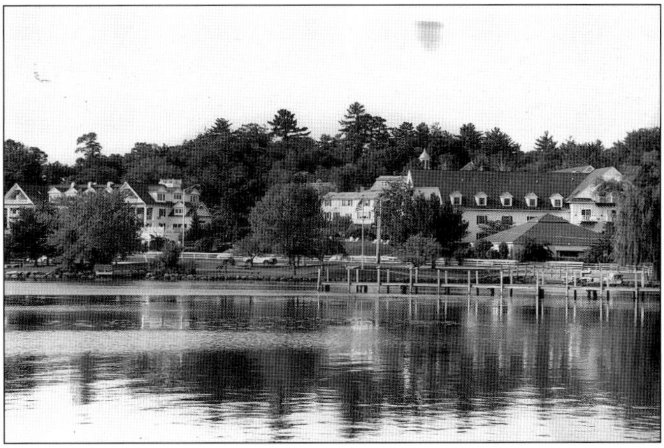

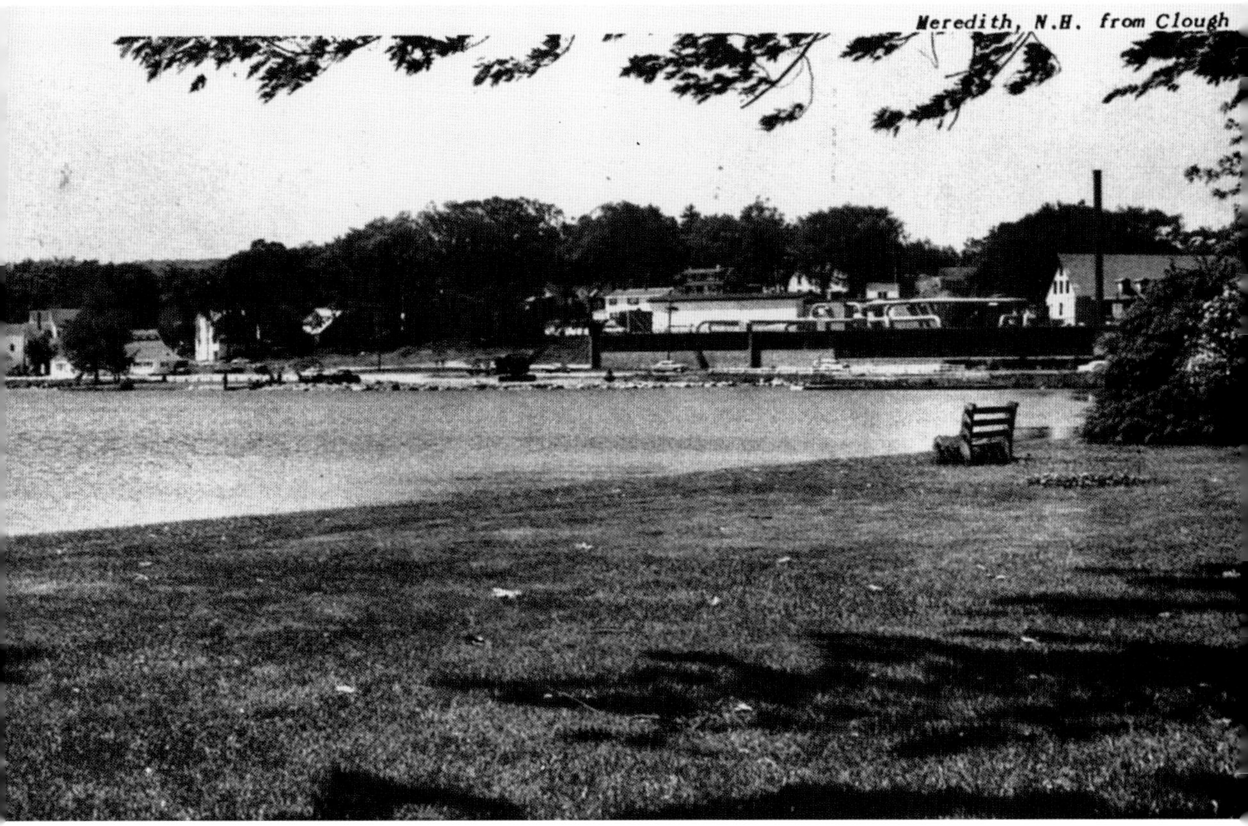

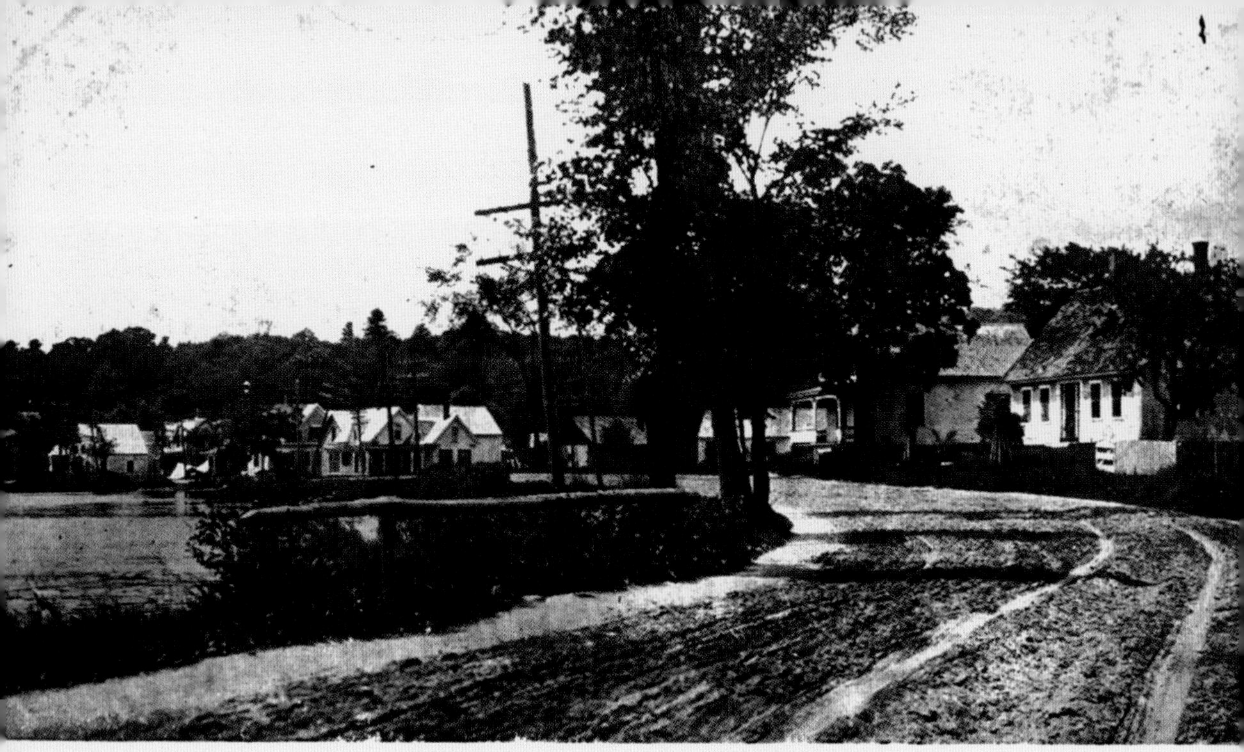

"The Flats" from the Neck Road, Meredith. N. H.

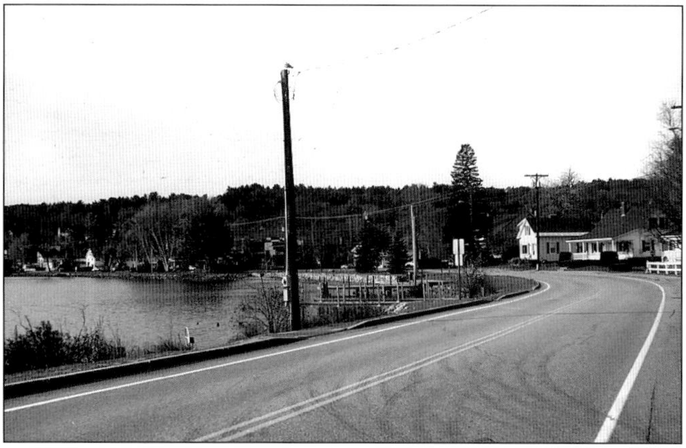

The area known as "the Flats" of Winnipesaukee Street, seen here from the Meredith Neck Road, hugs the shoreline of Meredith Bay and the village homes in the distance. Scenic Park and Clough Park, located along the northern shore of Meredith Bay, date from the 1920s. The rocks adorning the top of the stone wall were collected from all over the world. Clough Park was named for Edward H. Clough, who revived the Old Oak, a landmark that later became the town emblem.

The Estes Gulf station, located on Winnipesaukee Street, at the intersection of Route 25 and Pleasant Street is pictured in 1947. (Pleasant Street is also known as the Meredith Neck Road.) This station remained in business until it was purchased by the Meredith Village Savings Bank in the late 20th century.

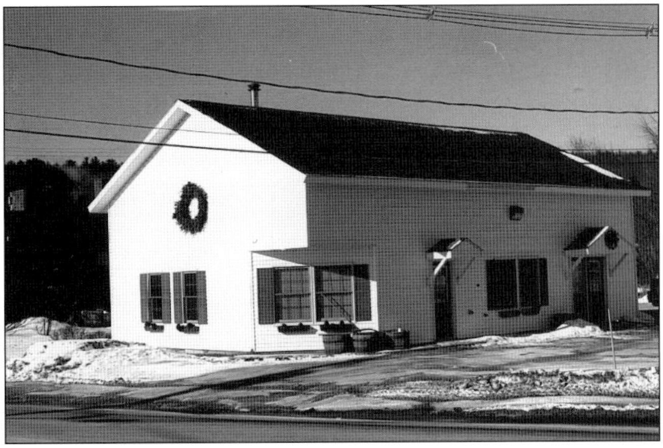

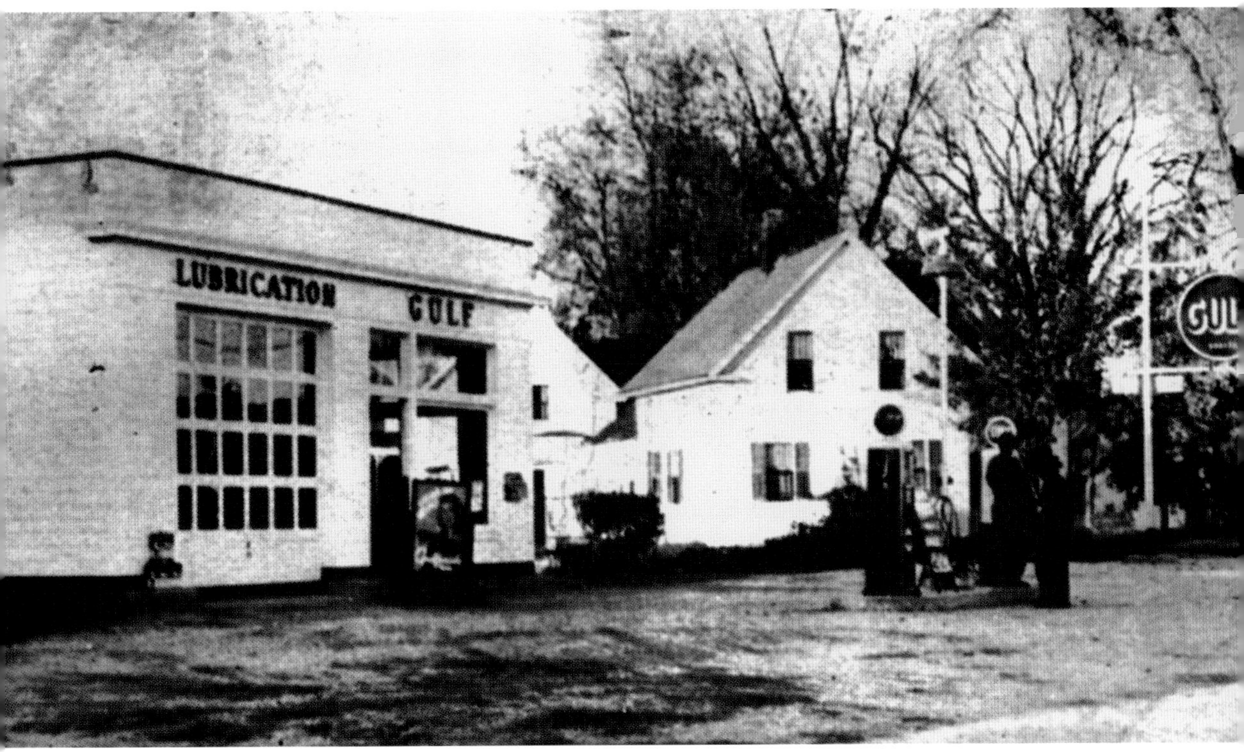

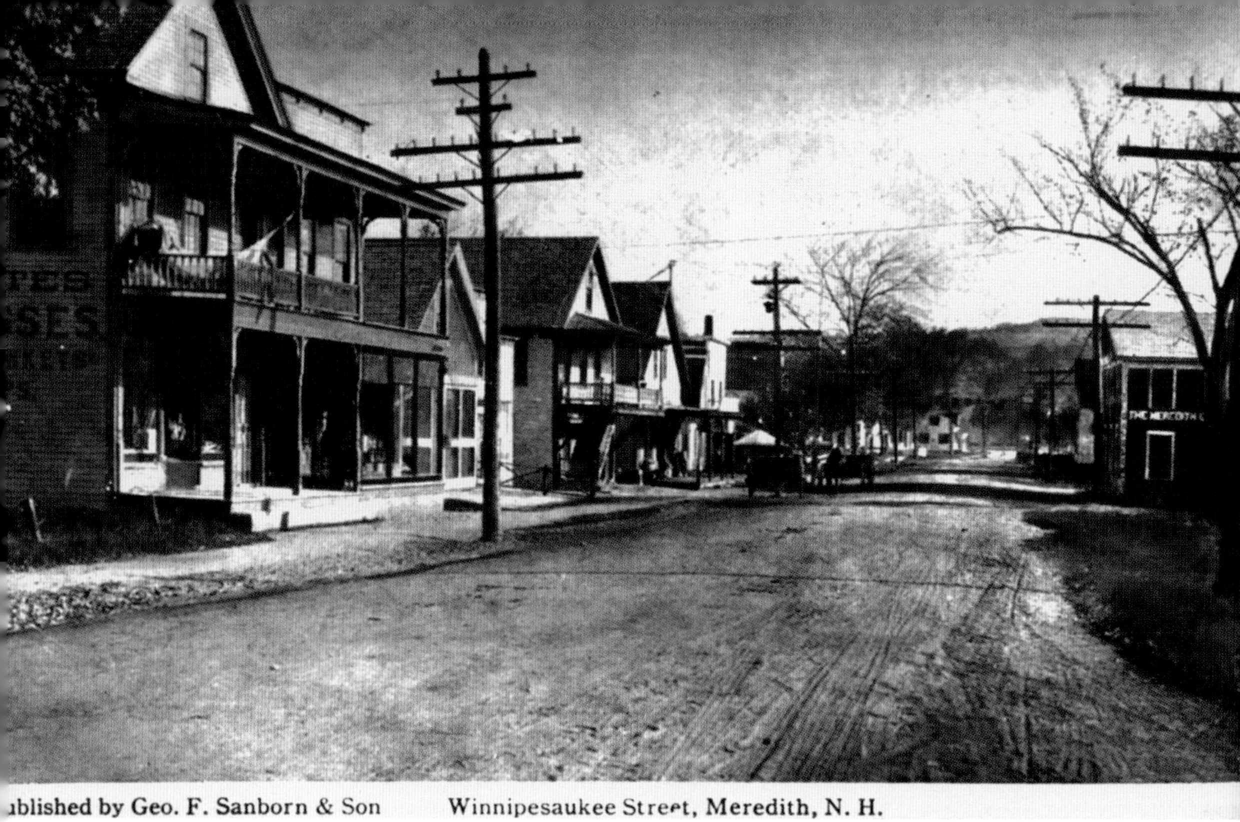

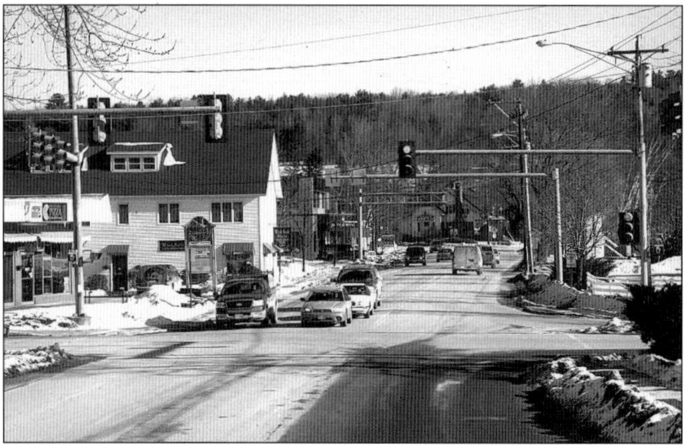

Winnipesaukee Street, seen in a view looking east, was an extension of Main Street. At the very end of the street now is the intersection of Route 25 and Pleasant Street (Meredith Neck Road). Before Route 3 was established in 1948, many stores and restaurants lined the northwestern side of the street. On the right is Meredith Bay. The buildings on the left include the Estes harness and leather shop, Montana's Restaurant, Robert's Market, a pizza restaurant, a gas station, and a bowling alley. Today Winnipesaukee Street has become Route 25. Many of the original buildings have disappeared. The gas station on the right has been replaced by the Inn at Bay Point, while most of the other buildings on the street have been supplanted by the Meredith Village Savings Bank.

Winnipesaukee Street is shown in a view looking west. At the very end of the street is the present restaurant known as Sunshine and Pa's. Previously this was the site of the Meredith Garden Florist. All the old businesses and buildings on the right are long gone. We are looking at the intersection of Route 25 and Route 3. The building on the corner is owned by Bootleggers Footwear Center.

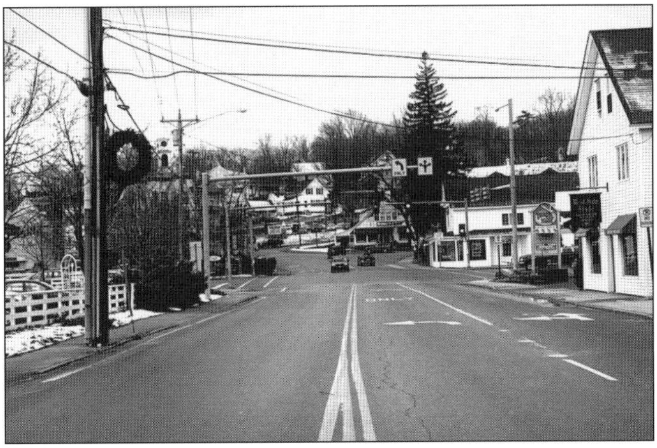

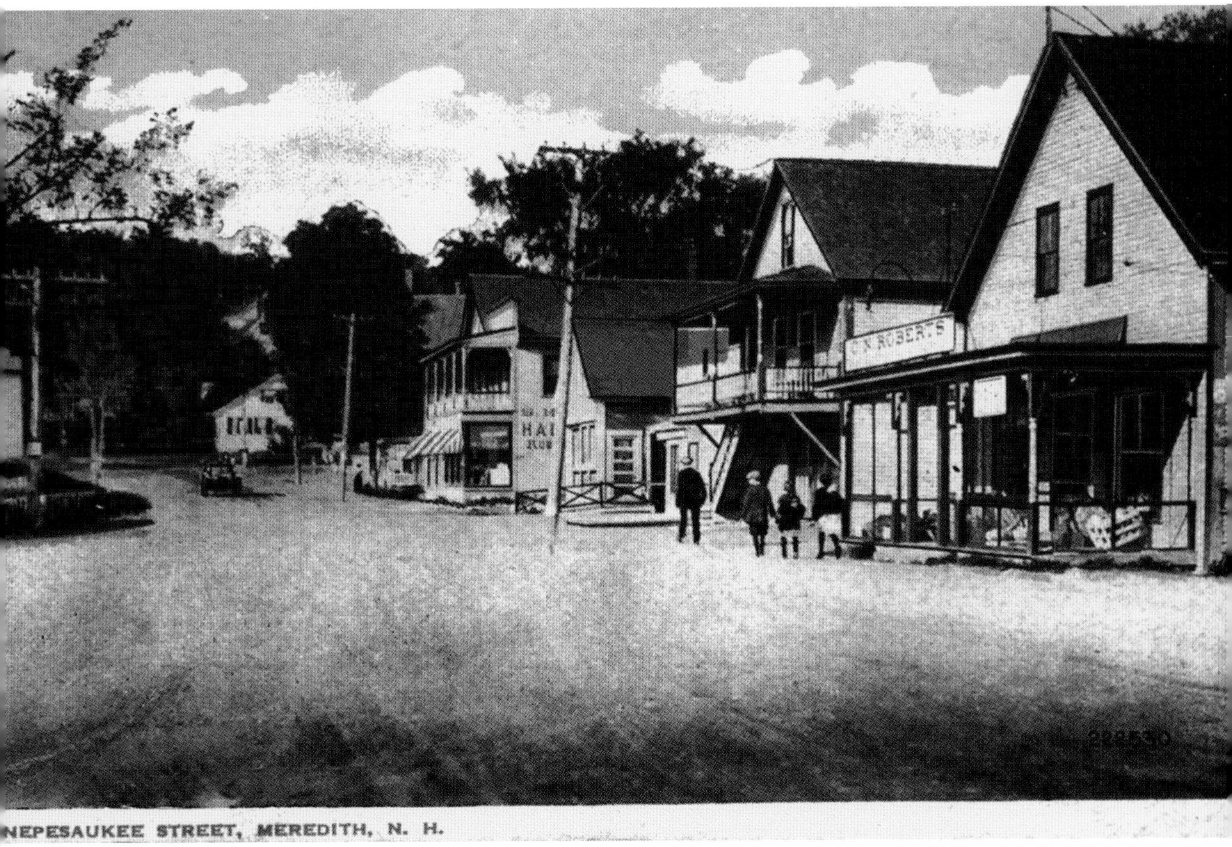

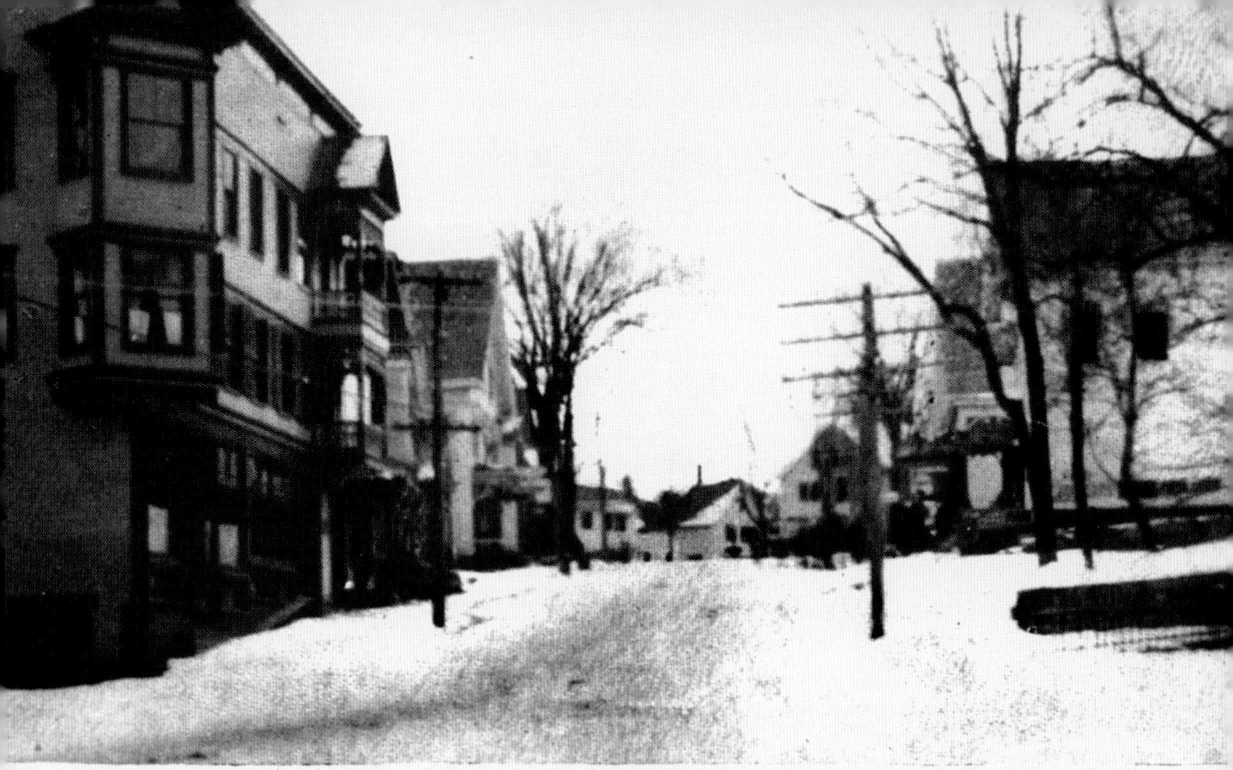

Main Street, looking West, Meredith, N. H.

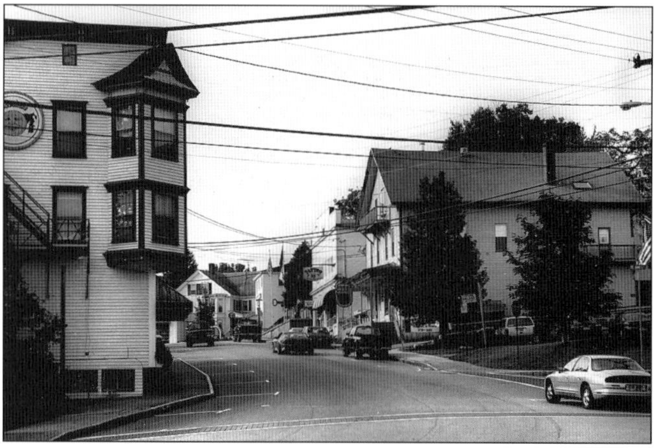

This area was the principal business district of Meredith in 1860. The diverse concerns in the district included dry goods, grocery, and apothecary stores, as well as a barbershop, a millinery, a tailor, and a billiard parlor. The large building to the left, on Main Street, was one of Meredith's largest commercial buildings. It was constructed in the 1890s by husband and wife Dr. Newell Nutting and Dr. Mary Nutting. After Newell's death in 1947, the block was purchased by Guy U. Horne and his wife, Dr. Edith (Bushway) Horne, Meredith's first chiropractor. Horne continued her practice well into the 1990s. Today the first floor is occupied by two establishments—Dick's Barber Shop (once the home of Ruel's Barber Shop) and Castle Bails and Spa.

Seen in a view looking west is the corner of Plymouth and Main Streets. The home in the photograph belonged to a Mrs. Herley. Frank Prescott later bought the property for the American Legion, which still occupies the building. In the background is a red-brick home that is now Mame's Restaurant.

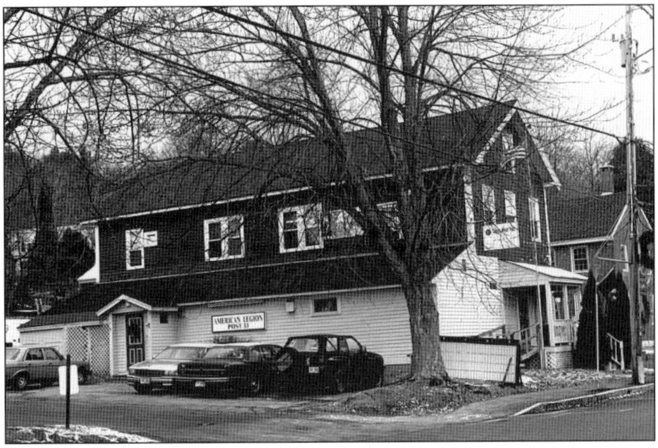

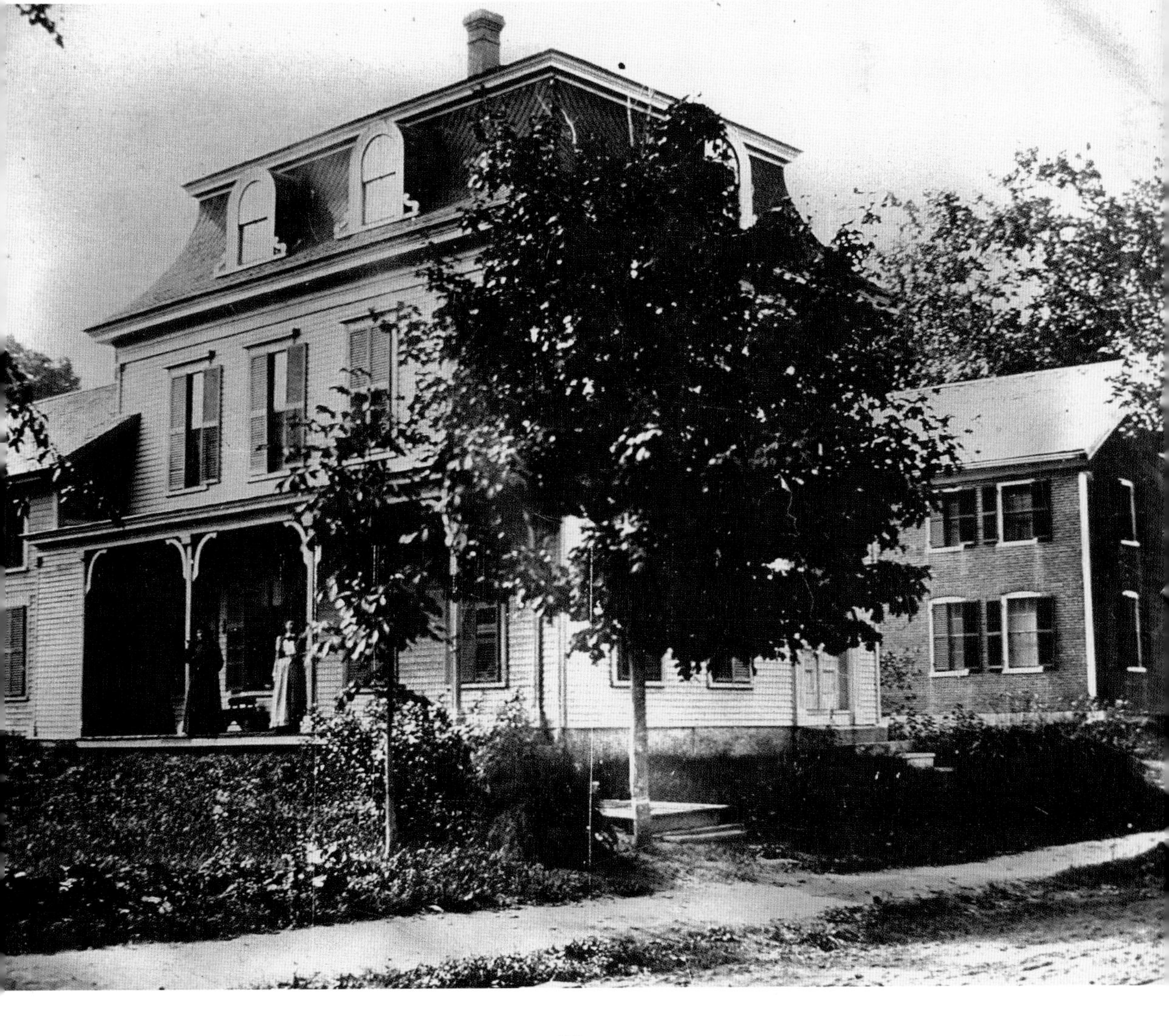

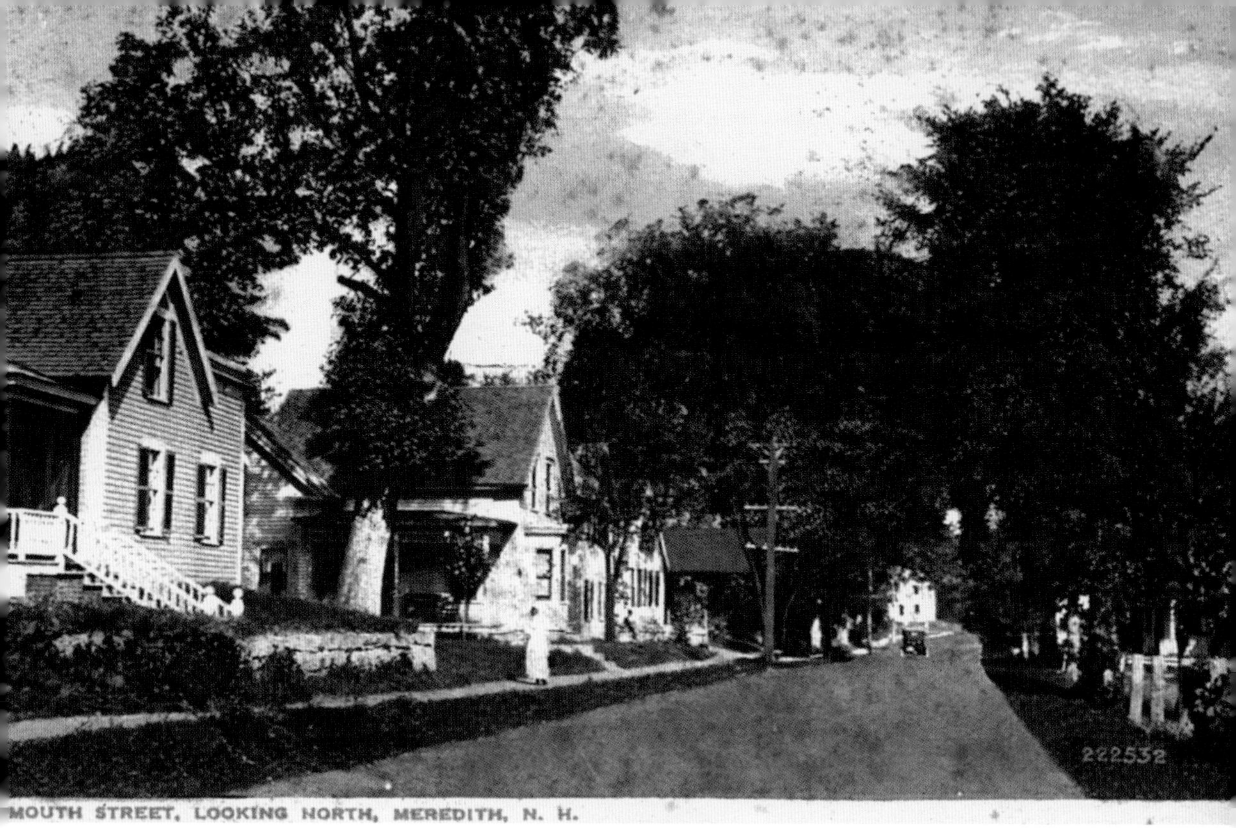

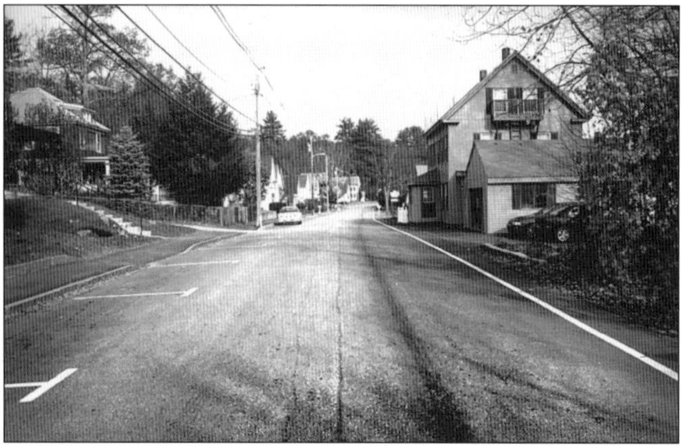

Plymouth Street is pictured in a view looking north. This residential street was so named because it was the main route to Plymouth. There were clusters of small businesses and private homes along the road. Today the area retains its residential atmosphere with the fine trees that border the street.

Seen in this view looking west up Main Street is the old establishment known as N. C. Prescott (on the left). At the top of the hill is Post Office Square. The building on the right is the Key Theatre; today it is an apartment building. Farther up the street is Seneca Ladd's home (the second building from the right), which later became the municipal building.

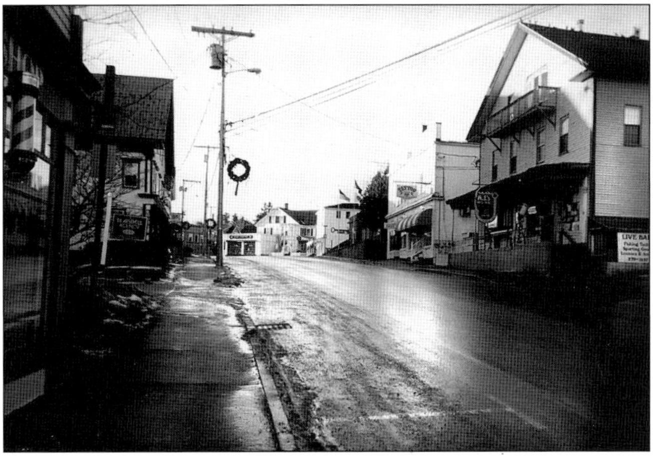

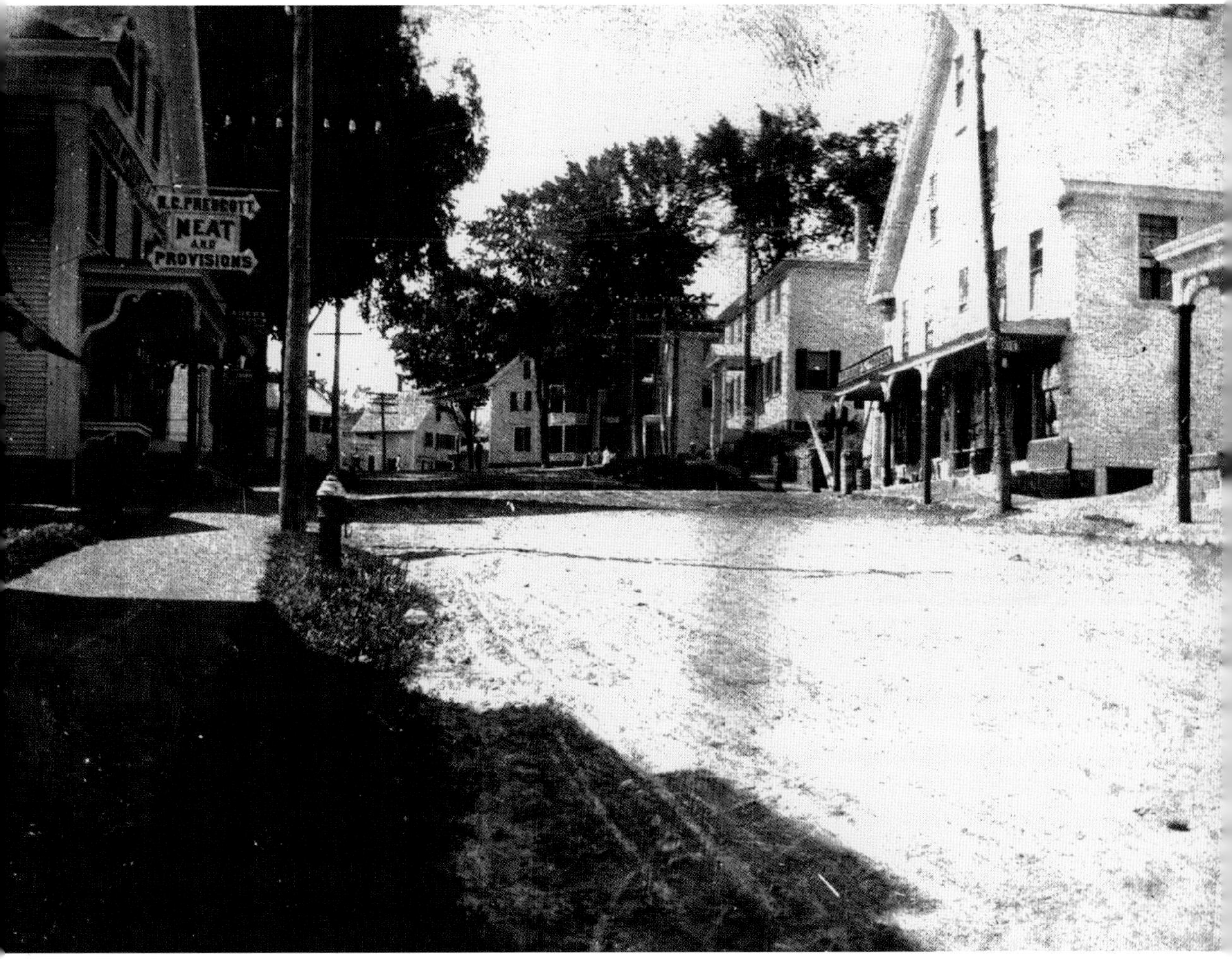

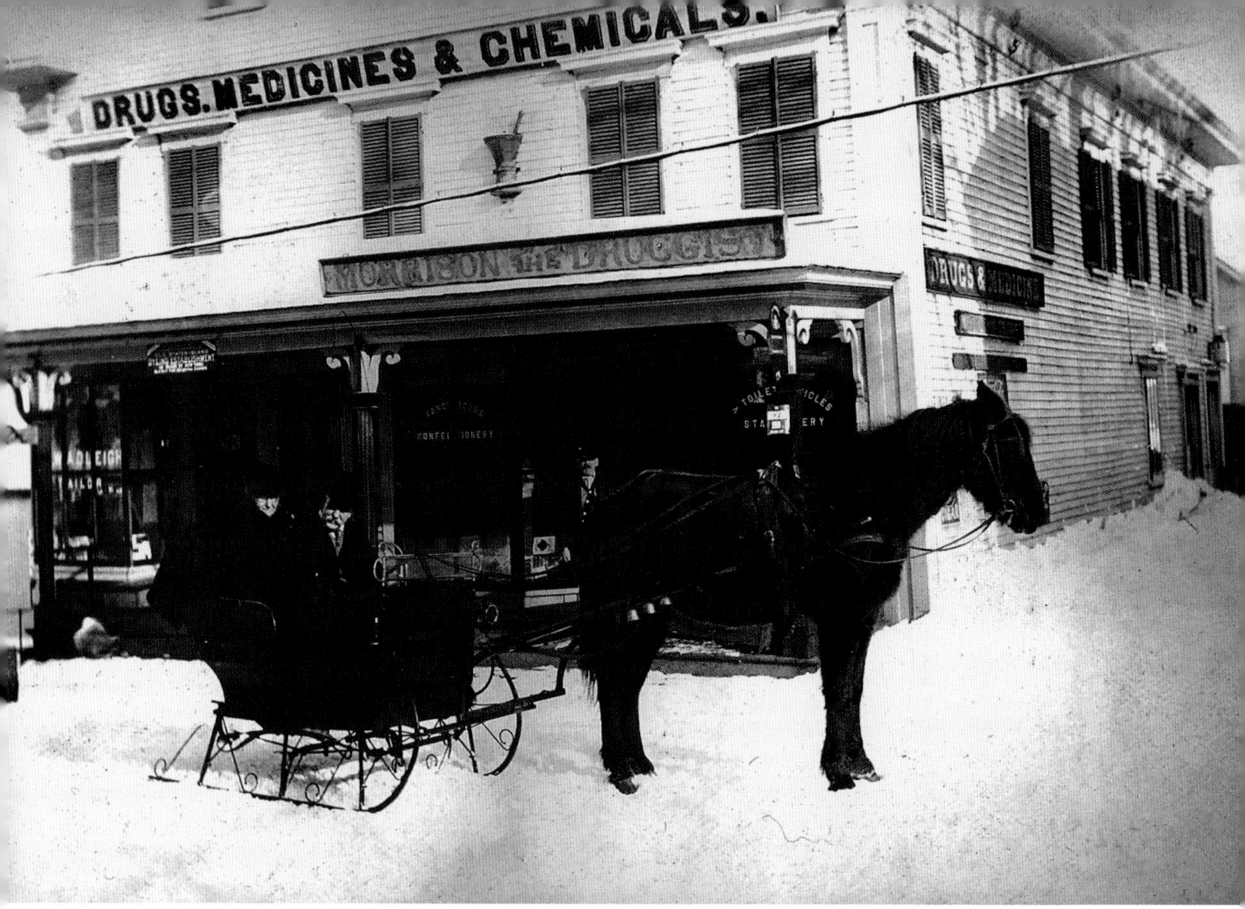

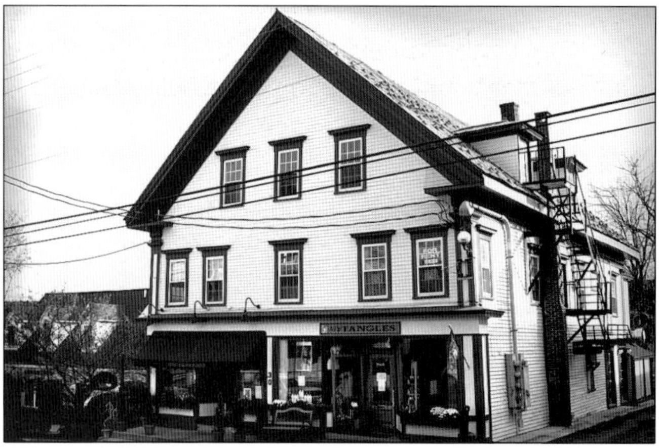

The Morrison drugstore was located in the Wadleigh (Wiggins) Building on Main Street during the mid-1800s. Located beside the Blaisdell Insurance Agency, this building later served as the Odd Fellows hall. The structure has been remodeled, while its exterior has been kept as near as possible to the original design. Riding in the sleigh are Alma Blake and Charles Morrison. Two stores now occupy the first floor of this building.

Directly across the street from the Nutting Block was this stately home, seen in the early 1900s. This site later became the parking lot for the Advent Christian Church. Down on the right is the corner of Main and Plymouth Street.

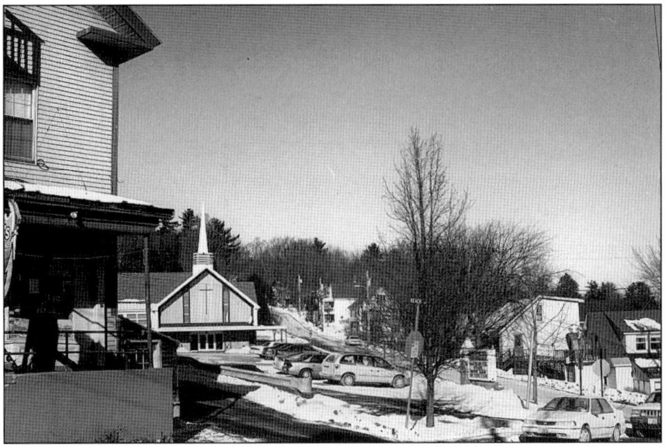

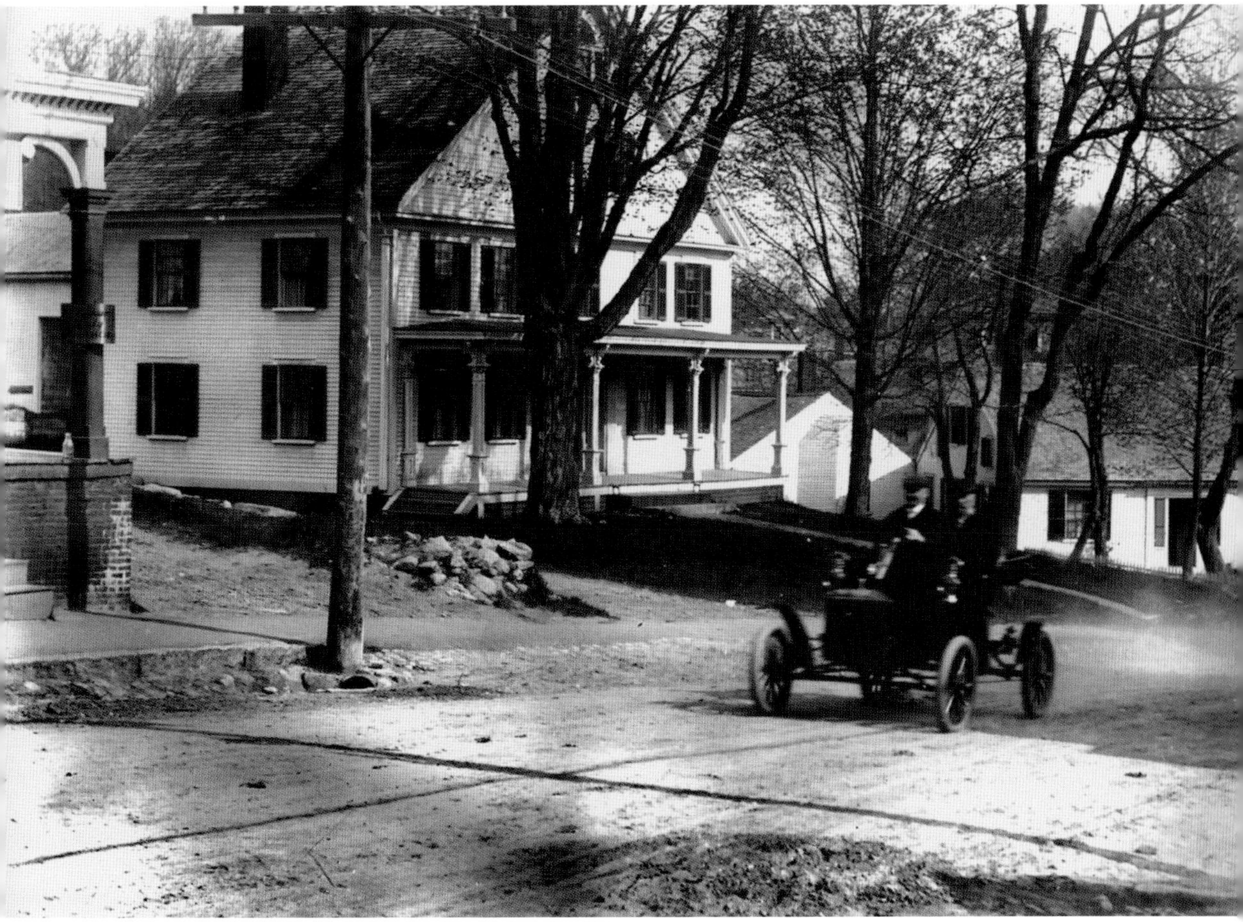

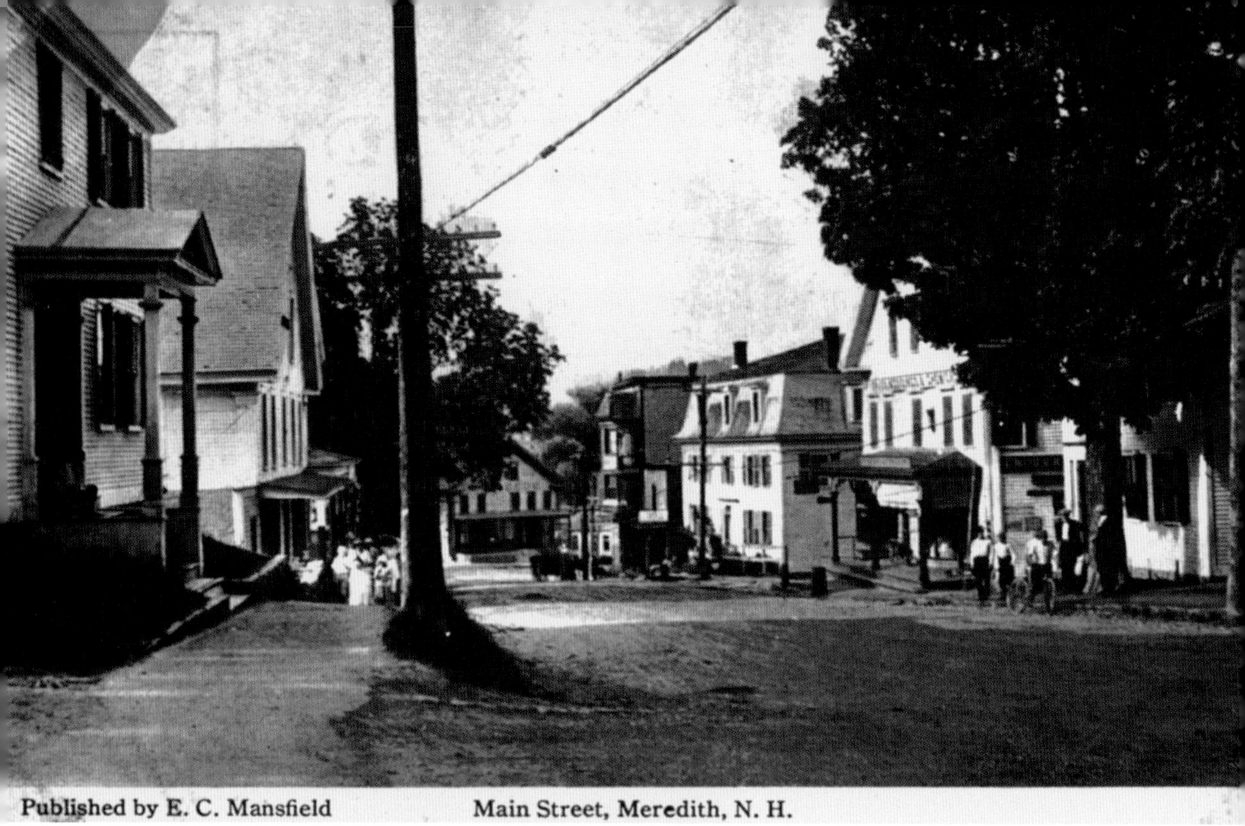

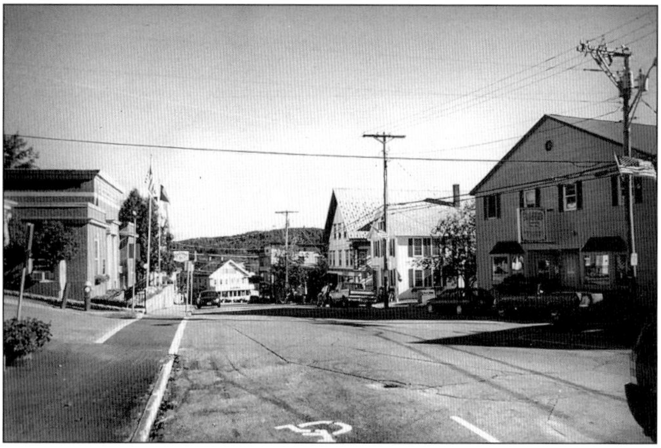

Looking east down Main Street from Post Office Square, we notice the changing face of the village. During the 1880s, several homes and business buildings intermingled here, but at the beginning of the 20th century, the area gave way to the modern model of the business district. The brick building on the left replaced the home of Seneca Ladd. It became the Meredith Village Savings Bank and is now the municipal building. On the right is the Guy Horne home, the Morrison drugstore, and the building that was once the Monroe boardinghouse. At the far end on the right of Lower Main Street is the Horne Block. The area is now occupied by Patricia's Specially for You, the Once New Antique Shop, and an Italian restaurant.

It is evident from this *c.* 1880s view (looking from Post Office Square down South Main Street) that many changes have transpired over the years. A wooden structure known as Sanborn's Drug Store was replaced in 1911 with a brick structure known as the Hawkins Block (right). Farther down on the right is a large white building belonging to Thadeus and Emily Moses. On the left is Edward C. Mansfield's Ready Made Clothing Store. Capt. Joseph Lang, who owned this building, started a dry goods business there in 1838. Lang was better known as the captain of the 12th New Hampshire Volunteer Regiment in the Civil War. The hall above his store was used as a recruiting site for soldiers. During the early 1900s, this building housed the Weeks and Smith store. From the 1950s to the present, many of the buildings have survived the test of time in Post Office Square, but some have disappeared from the village. The Moses home has been replaced with a park. The Ready Made Clothing Store has changed hands several times; today it is the site of Vintage Gourmet Coffee and Pastries. On the corner of Water and Main Streets, the Hawkins Block has become the home of Phu Jee Chinese Cuisine and Waukewan Antiques. Note also that the trough pictured here has since been removed.

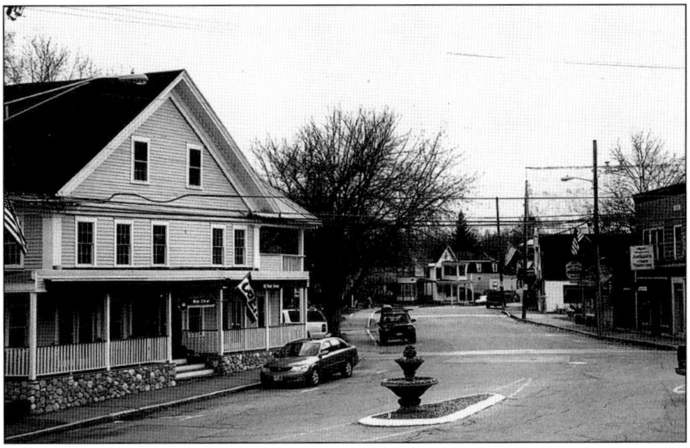

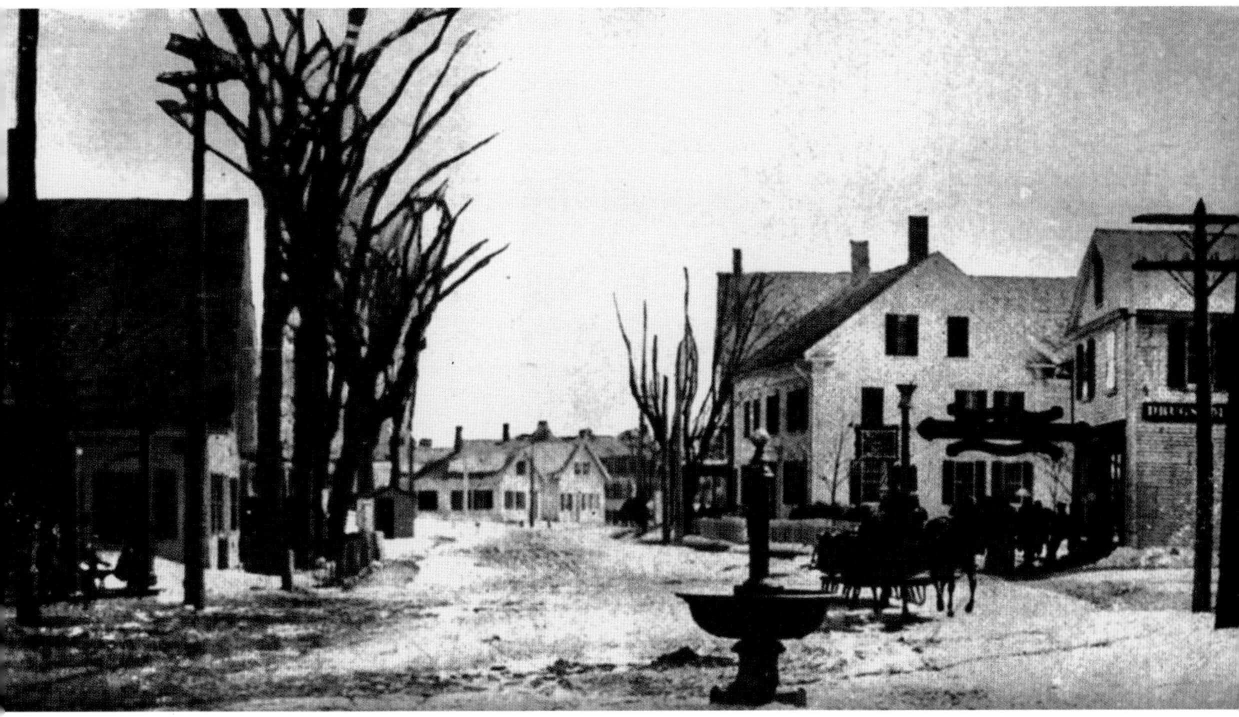

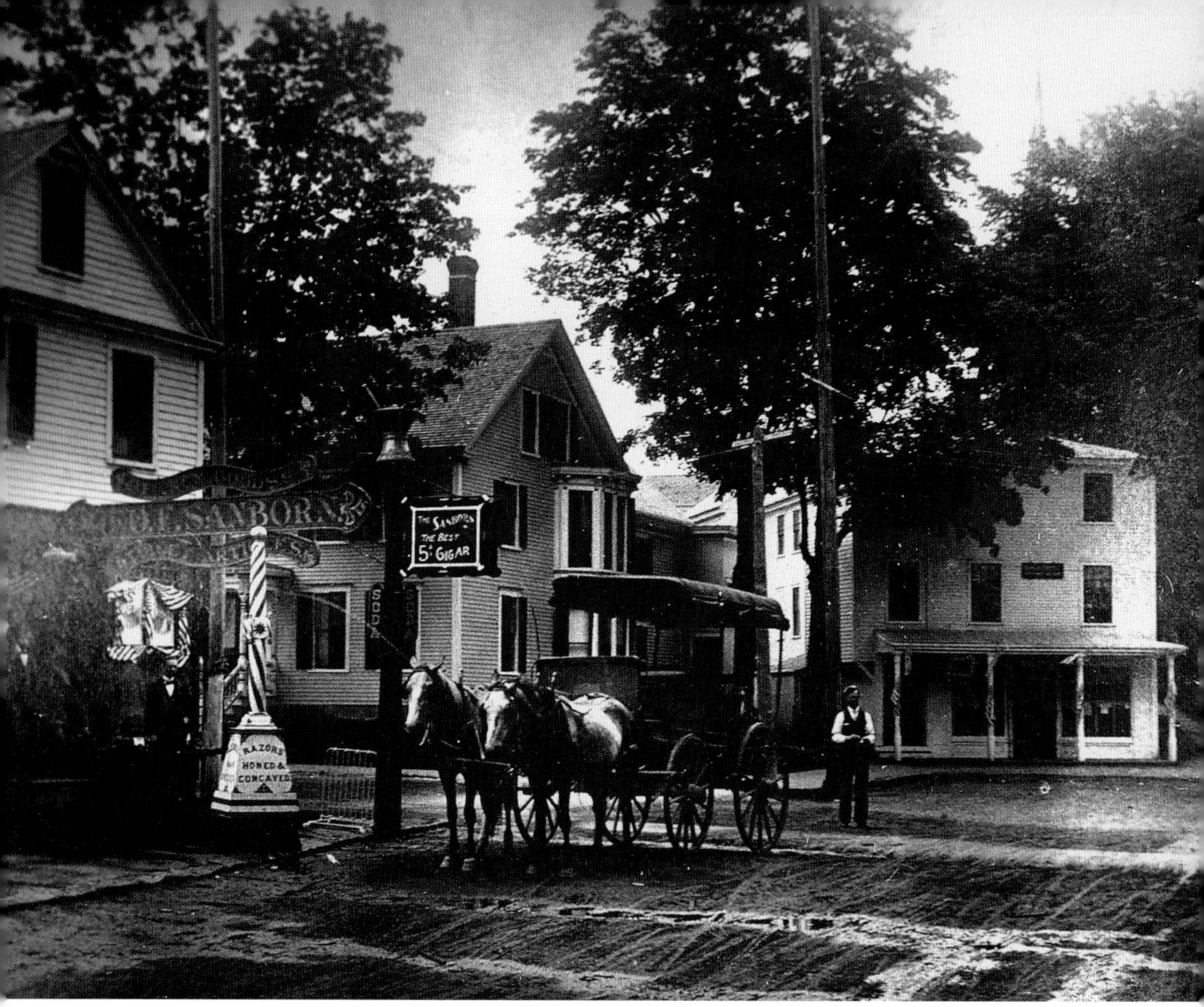

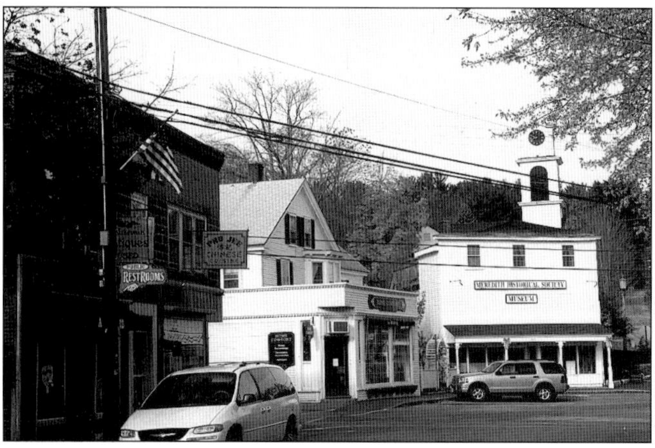

The *c.* 1880s Sanborn Block was known as a center of social and economic activity in the village for well over a century. The building represented the gradual conversion of a house into commercial use. Dr. George Sanborn was the principal town physician in the late 1800s, and he ran his practice from this building. Seen in the photograph are drugstore clerks Bert Sloane (standing on left) and Clarence Greene (at the rear of the carriage on right). The carriage, which brought the mail, belonged to Ed Cox.

In 1884, George Sanborn opened a drugstore at Water and Main Streets, on the corner opposite the buildings in the previous photograph. In 1909, he added the projecting storefront to his home and made this his store. Notice that on either side of the diagonal entrance, he installed stained-glass pharmacy symbols, which still decorate the entrance. Today this building is occupied by Home Comfort. Seen to the right and center is the Ladd building, in Post Office Square. The Ladd building was the first home of the Meredith Village Savings Bank.

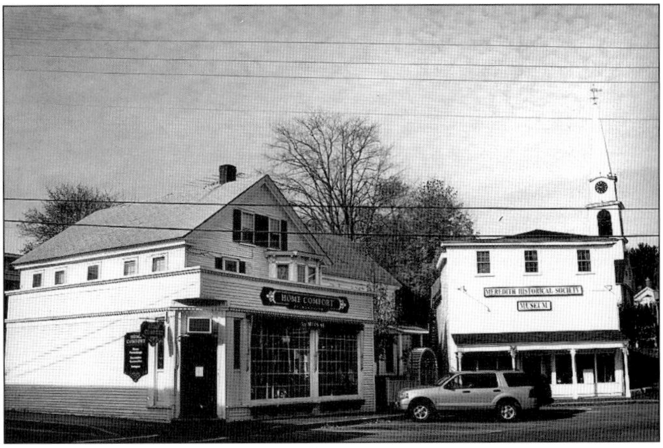

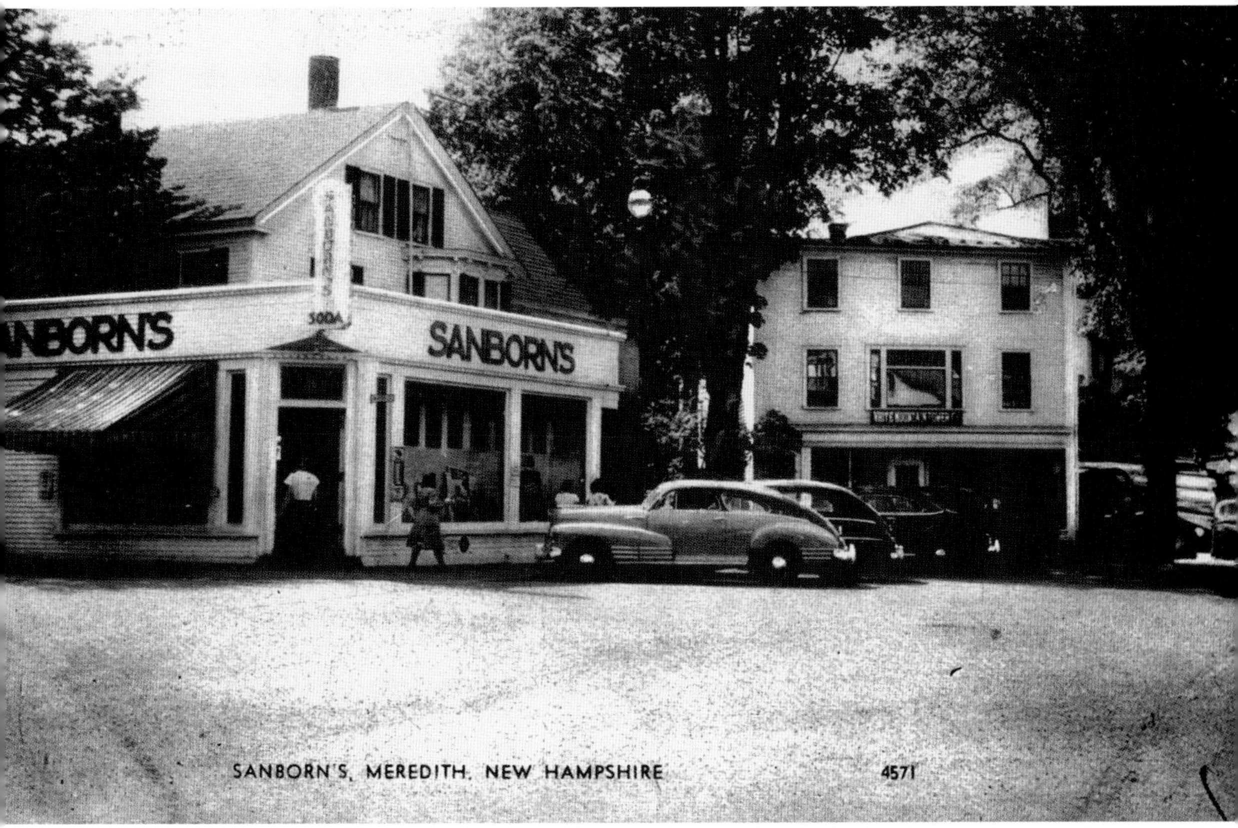

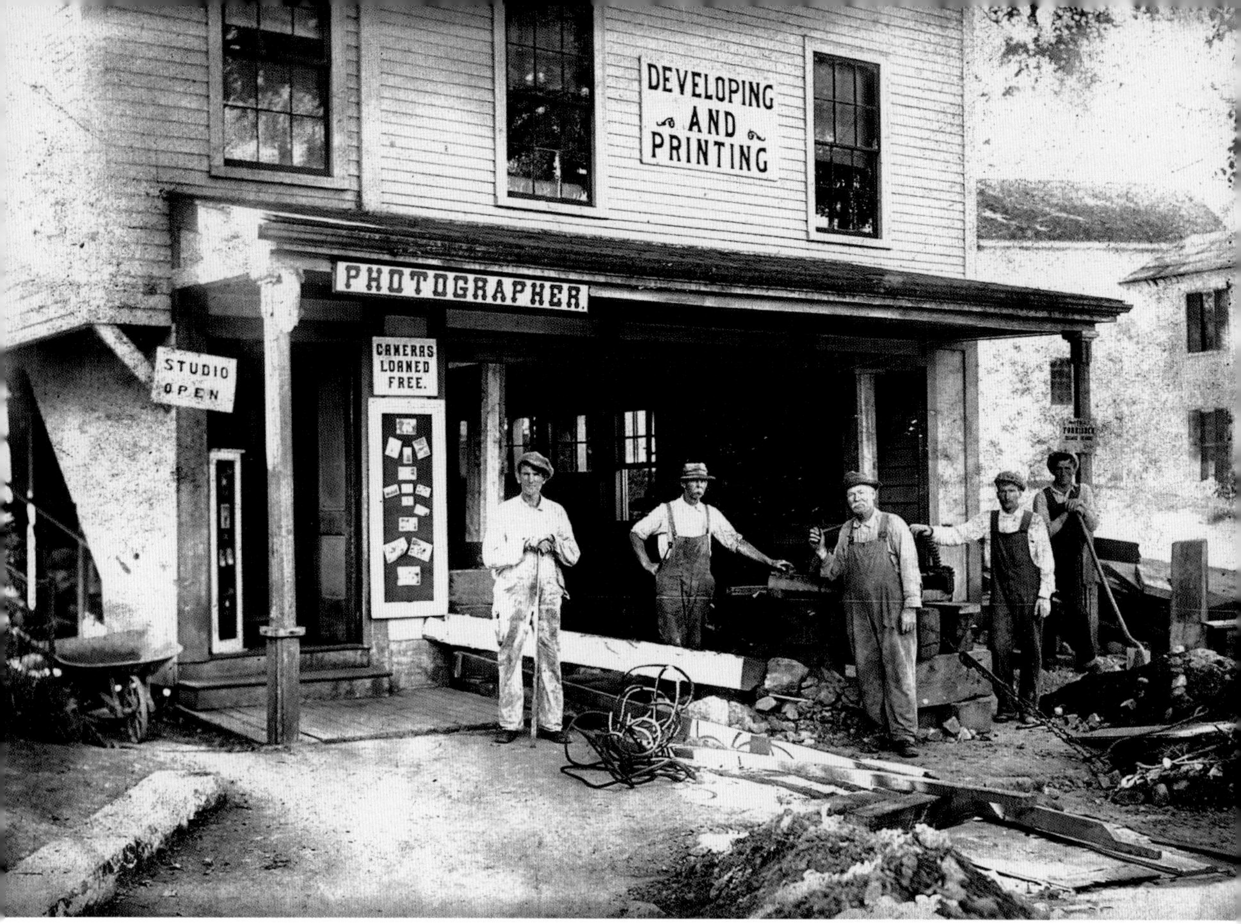

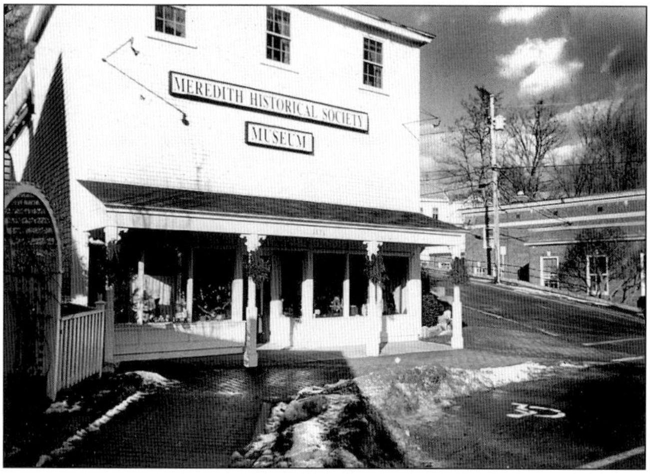

The Ladd Block is shown in the early 1900s, when it was a photographic studio. Standing in front of the building are, from left to right, T. H. Batchelder, Colby Cox, W. G. Cox, Fred Perkins, and George Batchelder. It appears that these men are remodeling the structure. Today this handsome building, which has served many uses over the years (including a post office, a bank, and other businesses), is the home of the Meredith Historical Society.

The Ladd Block was built *c.* 1820 as a store and residence. At various times over the years, it housed a library, a funeral parlor, a law office, a post office, and the town's first bank. In 1854, Seneca Ladd bought the building and moved his piano business there. For the next 18 years, Ladd was engaged in the manufacture of pianos and melodeons. In 1869, he gave up that business and decided to open a savings bank.

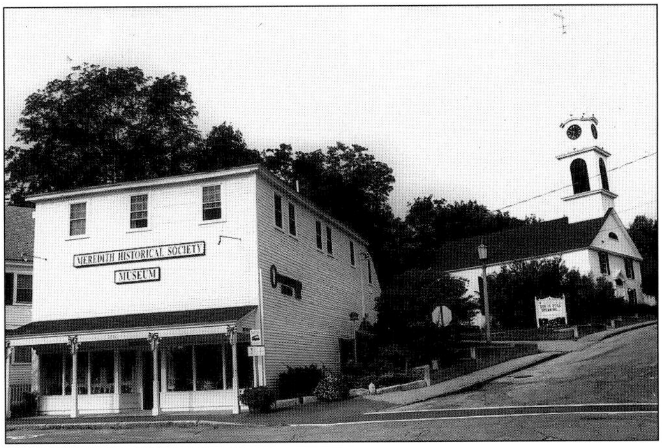

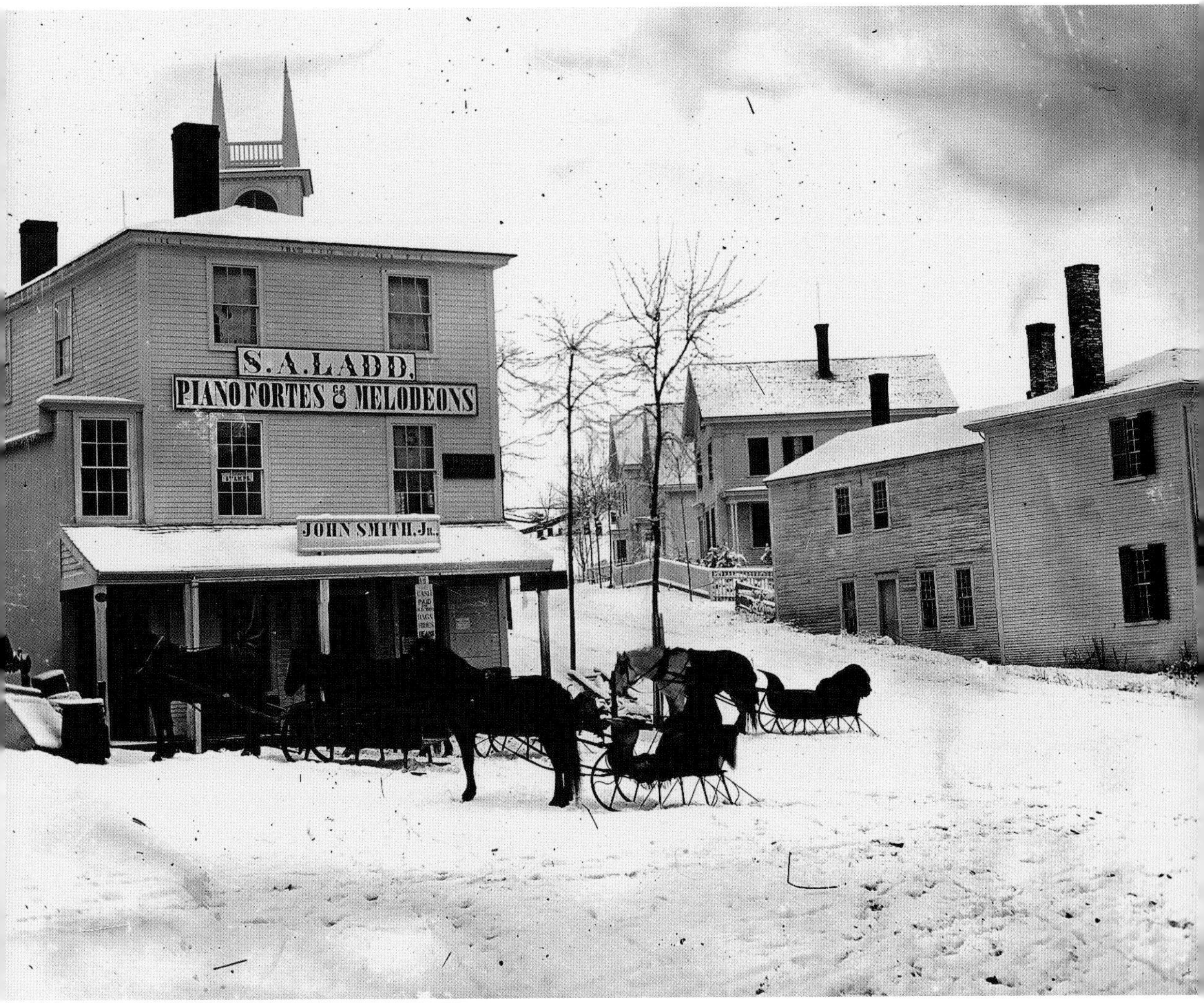

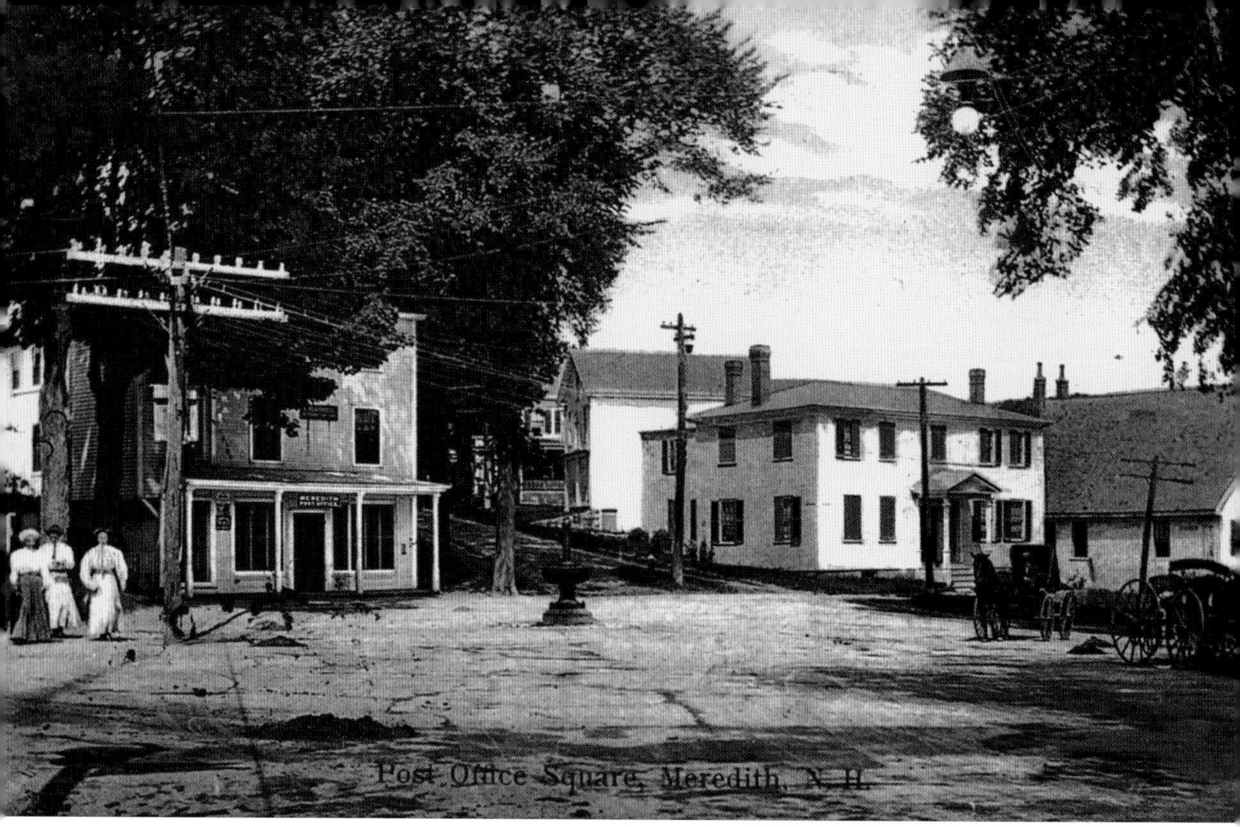

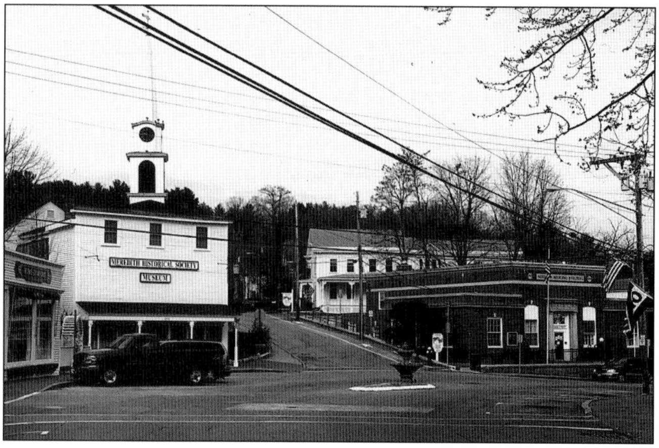

The Ladd Block (left) was the first home of the Meredith Village Savings Bank. The entrance to the bank office was located on the right side, just above the post office. Another well-known occupant of the building's lower level was the Meredith Village post office. The office remained in this building until 1935, when a permanent post office was built. Another tenant of the building was the Meredith Public Library (1888–1901). In 1994, this building was acquired by the Meredith Historical Society as a historical museum. The house to the right, on the corner of Highland and Main Streets, was the home of Seneca Ladd, who sold it to the Meredith Village Savings Bank in 1924.

When the Meredith Village Savings Bank moved into this building in 1924, it was joined there by its associate bank, the Meredith Trust Company. In 1941, two wings were added to the existing bank, thus doubling the available space. In 1958, the building was purchased by the town of Meredith, and it now houses the municipal offices.

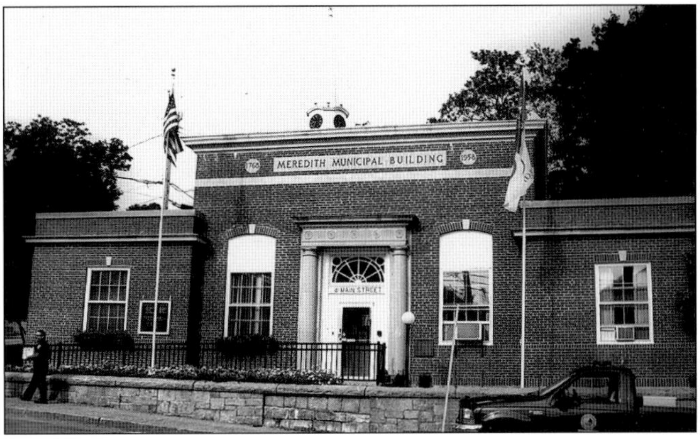

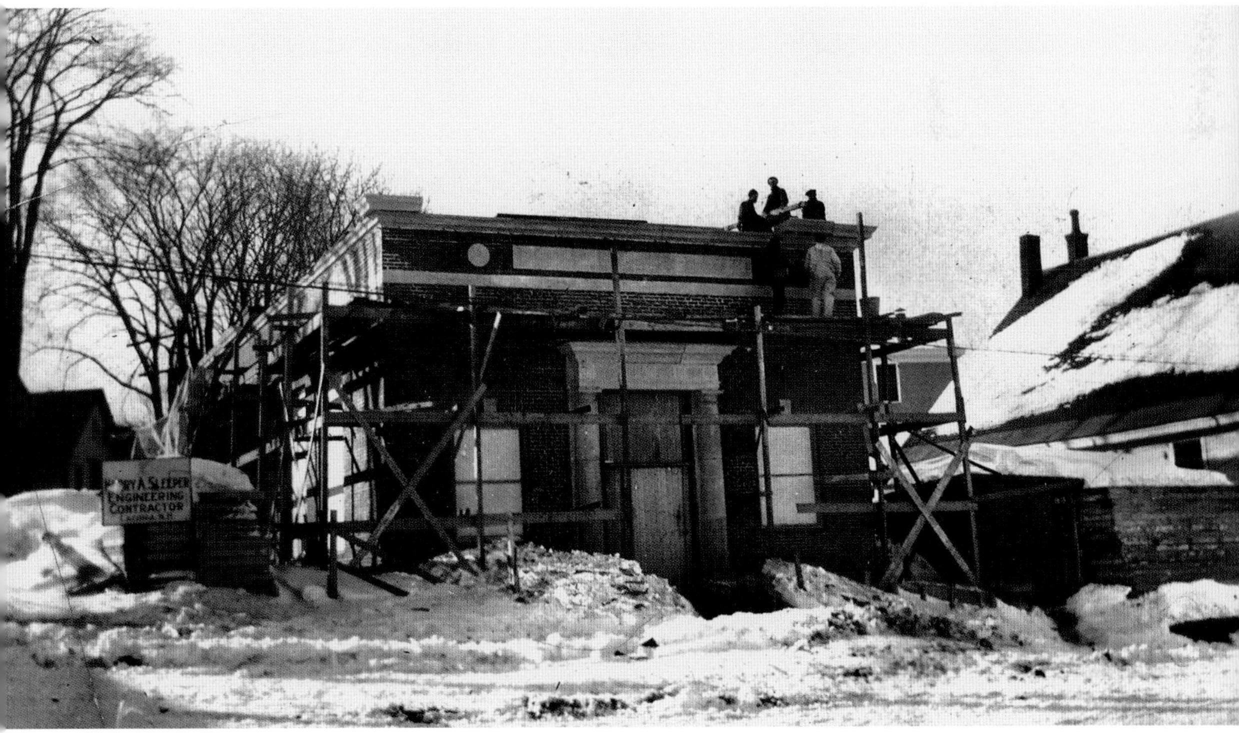

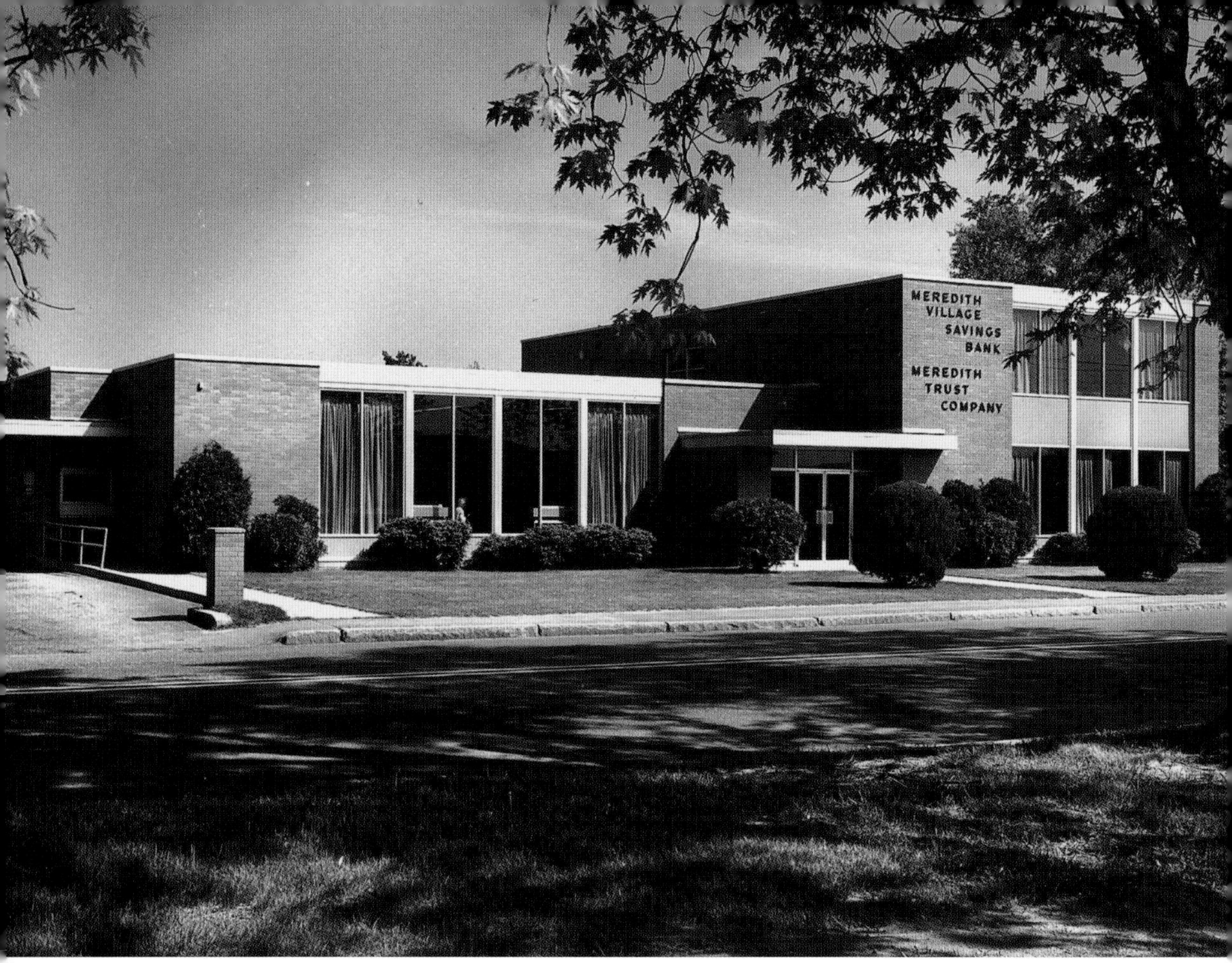

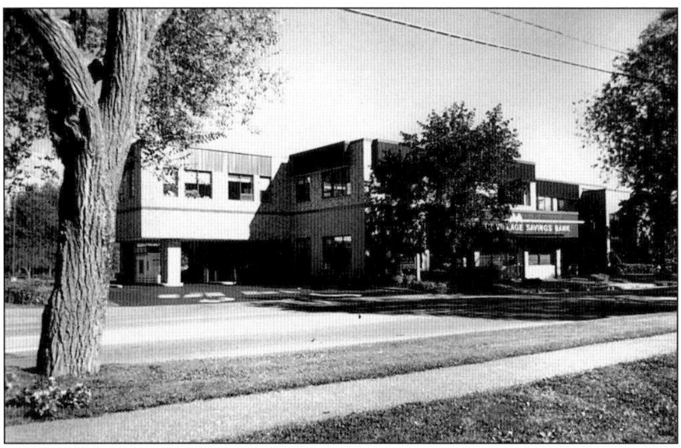

In 1958, the Meredith Village Savings Bank and the Meredith Trust Company moved into a new building at the top of Meredith Bay on Route 25. In 1998, the bank added an extension to the building to accommodate the needs of a growing banking institution.

Another notable building found in the village on Highland Street is the Beede House. An outstanding example of Italianate architecture, the home was completed in 1867. From its octagonal cupola are stunning views toward the village and east toward Lake Winnipesaukee. The elaborate entry portico, corner quoins, and graciously landscaped grounds enclosed by a Victorian wooden fence complete one of Meredith's finest homes. John W. Beede and his wife lived in the elegant house for many years.

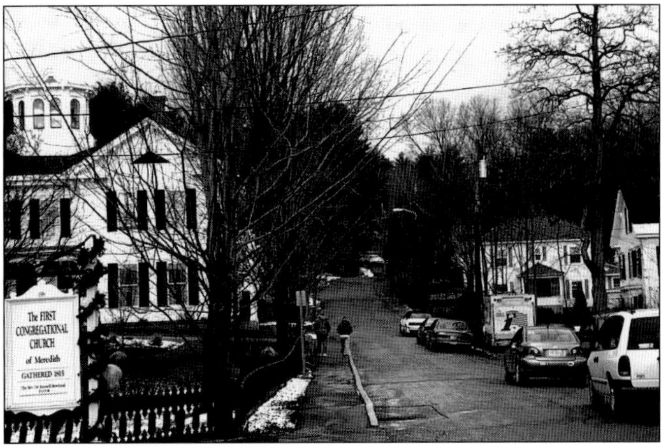

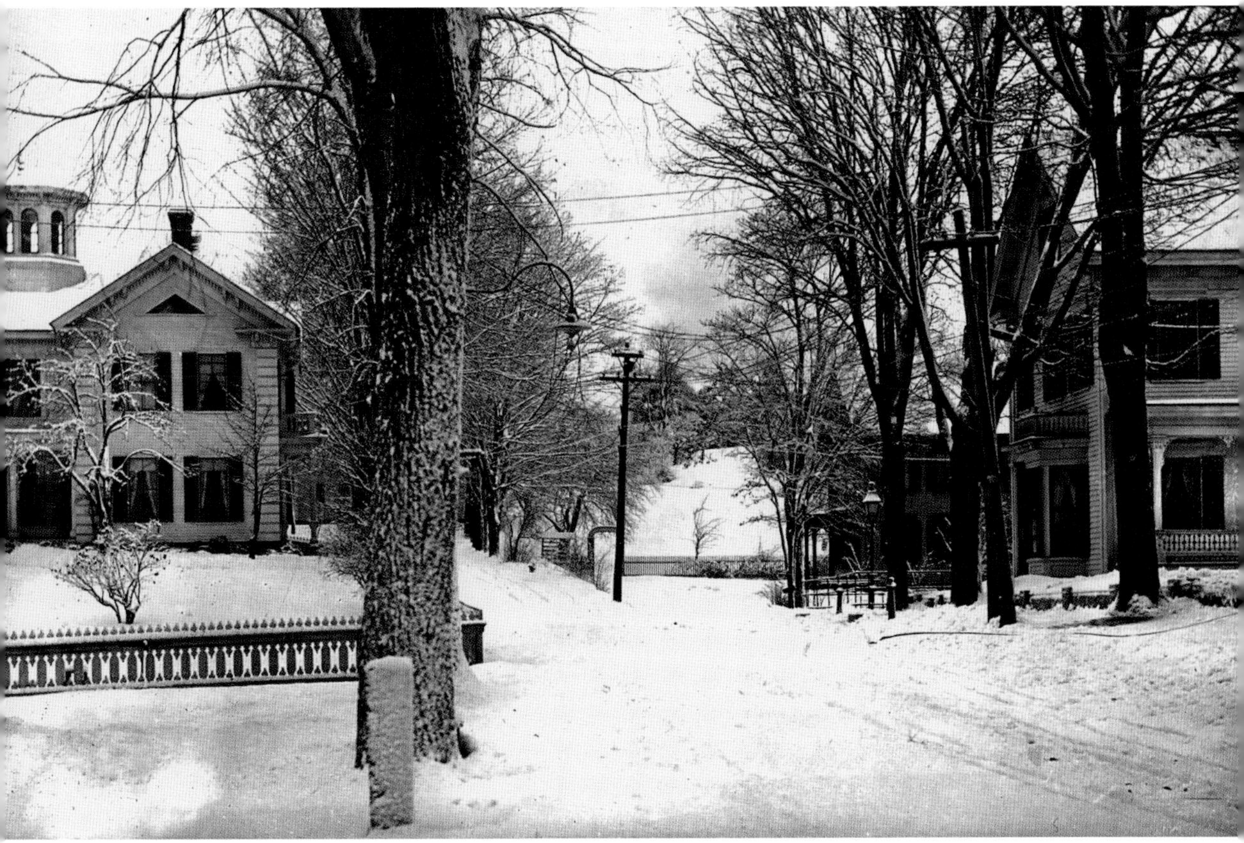

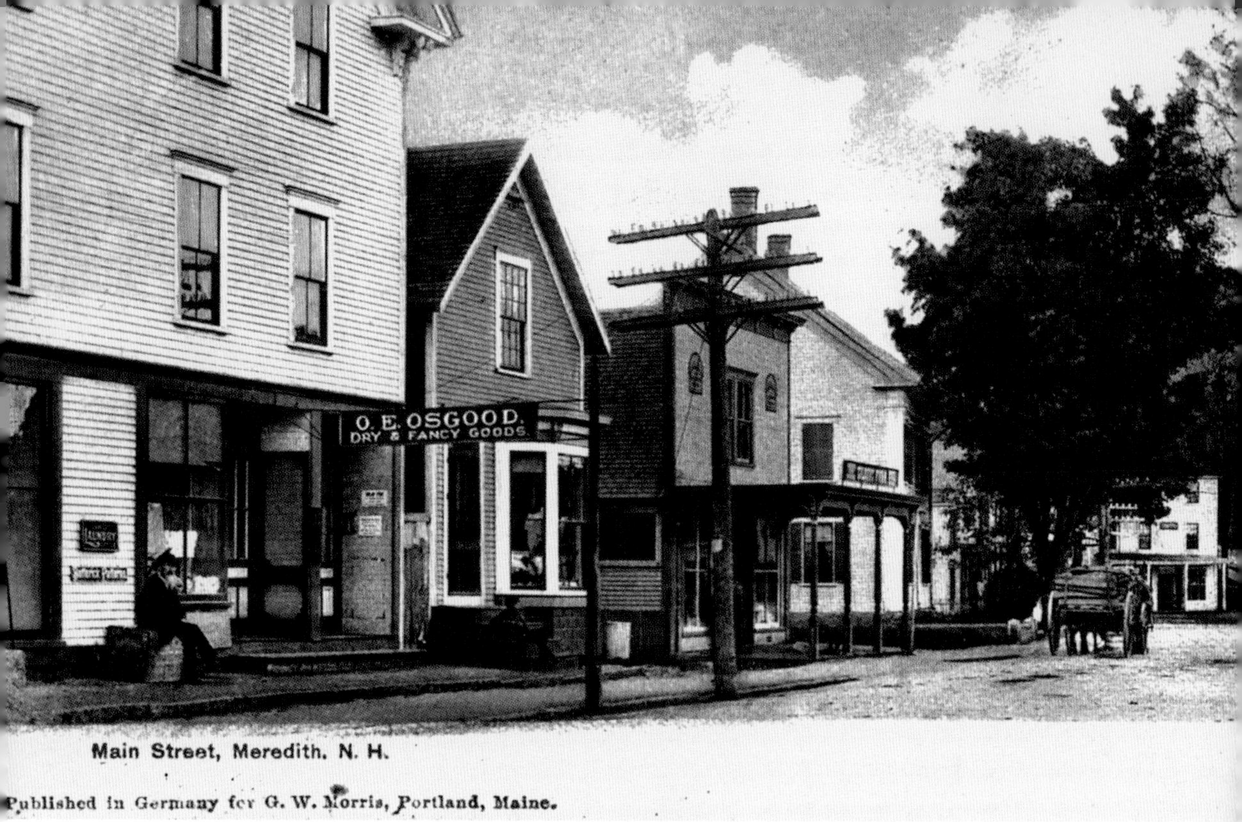

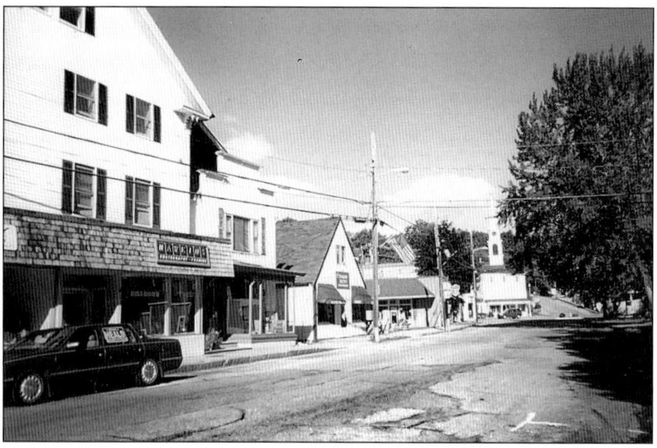

Main Street is pictured in this *c.* 1880s view looking east. Included in the photograph is O. E. Osgood's dry goods store (far left), located in the old town hall. Farther down on the left are Gilbert Pynn's tin shop, the Randall garage, and the Moses home (at the end of the street). In the distance (on the right) is the Ladd building, located in Post Office Square. In the present-day view are, from left to right, Hawkins Photography, Hunter's Needlework, and the Italian Bistro. In the brick building (known as the Latchkey Building) are the Free Range Boutique and Ruel's Barber Shop. Next to the Latchkey Building, on the corner of Water and Main Streets, are Waukewan Antiques and Phu Jee Chinese Cuisine.

The Meredith Diner is pictured in 1930. It was Herbert Pond who brought the diner to Meredith from Worcester, Massachusetts, but soon after he sold out to Temple Lynds, who in turn sold it to Everett Chase. One year later, the establishment was taken over by his brother Carl Chase. It was then moved to the driveway off the Bickford Rust property, as seen in this photograph. On May 20, 1936, the Meredith Diner caught fire at 2:00 P.M. In front of the diner was the Sinclair gasoline station. Today this site is the well-landscaped lawn of Emery and Garrett Groundwater.

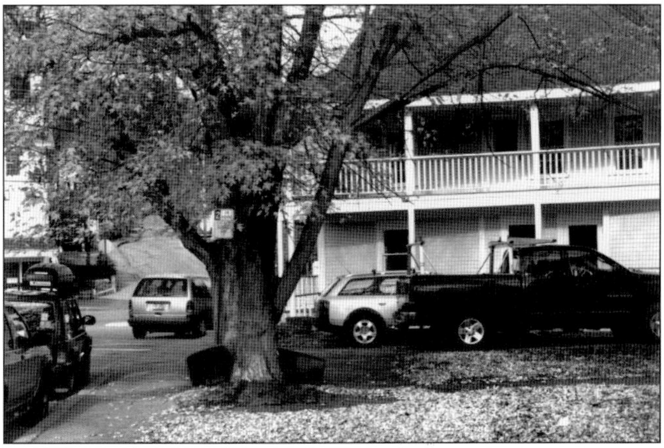

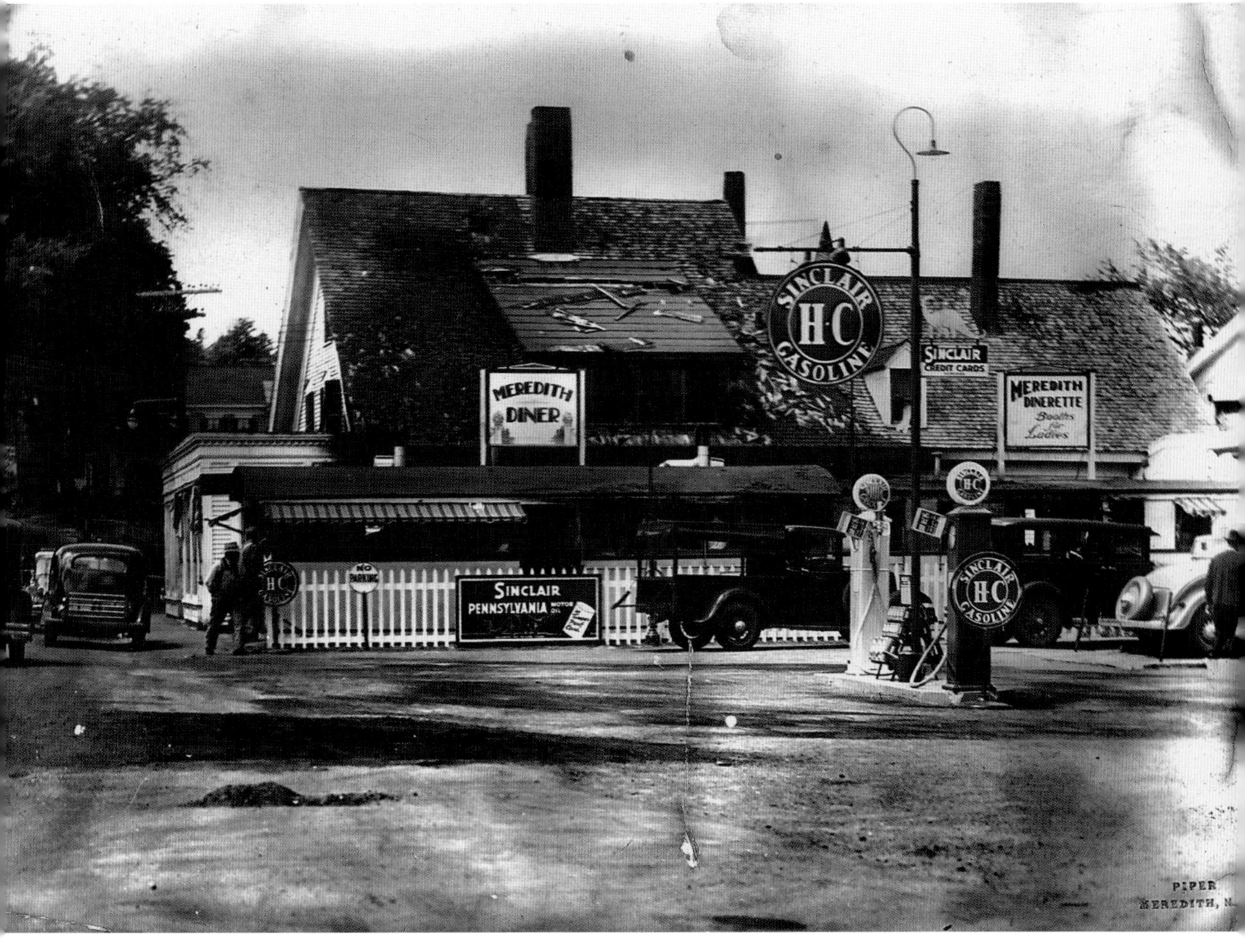

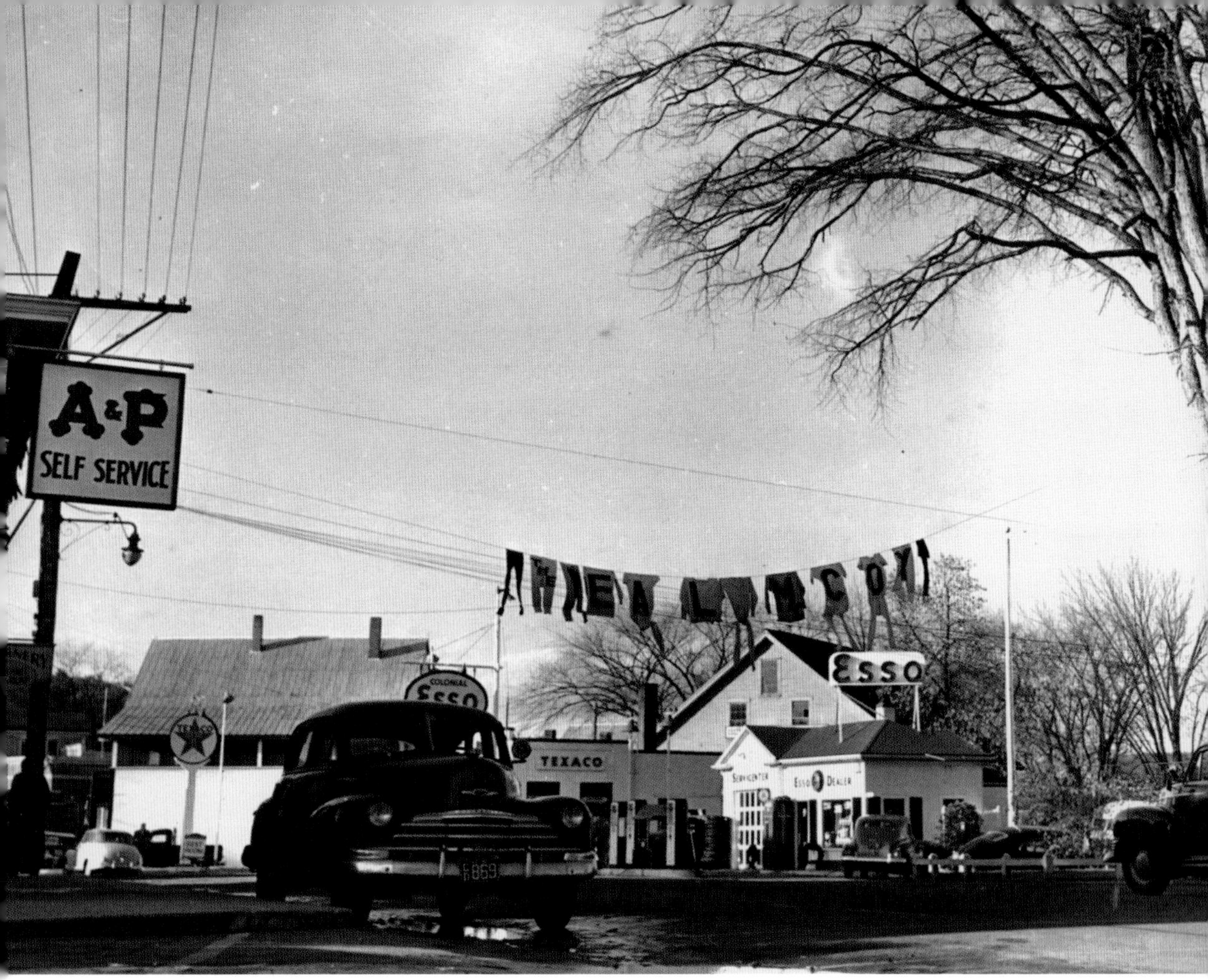

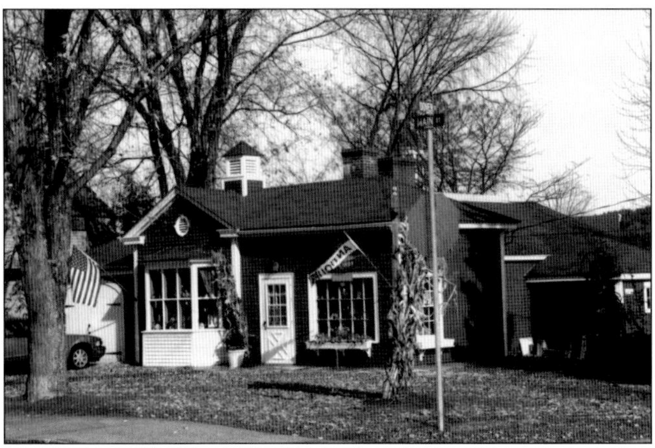

Sprague's Esso gas station (right of center) did business on Main Street from the 1940s to the 1960s. Brad Sprague also operated a bus service for charter and school transportation. Sprague was a very popular man in the community—he was a selectman, a county commissioner, and a friend to all. Today the site at the corner of Dover and Main Streets has been transformed to become the Alexandria Shop II, an antiques shop.

The Meredith Garage (Randall's Garage), seen to the left, was a landmark on Main Street in the early 1900s. The Moses house, on the right, later became the site of the Rust Building, which was occupied by Rust Electric, Harvey's Drug Store, Dr. Pottle (a dentist), and Gordon's Barber Shop. Today it is the site of Main Street Park, where many gather for social occasions. The building to the left is the present location of the Italian Bistro.

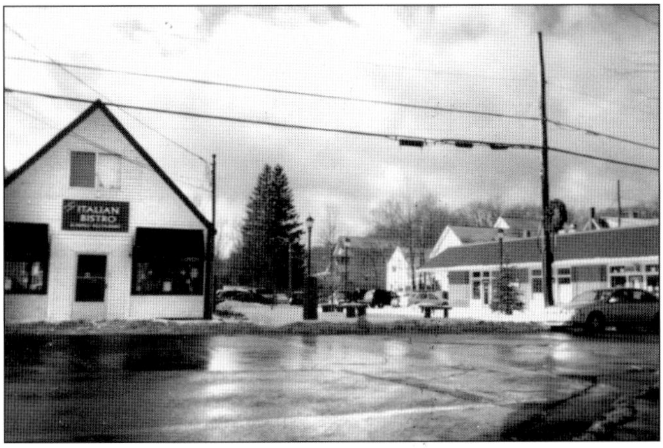

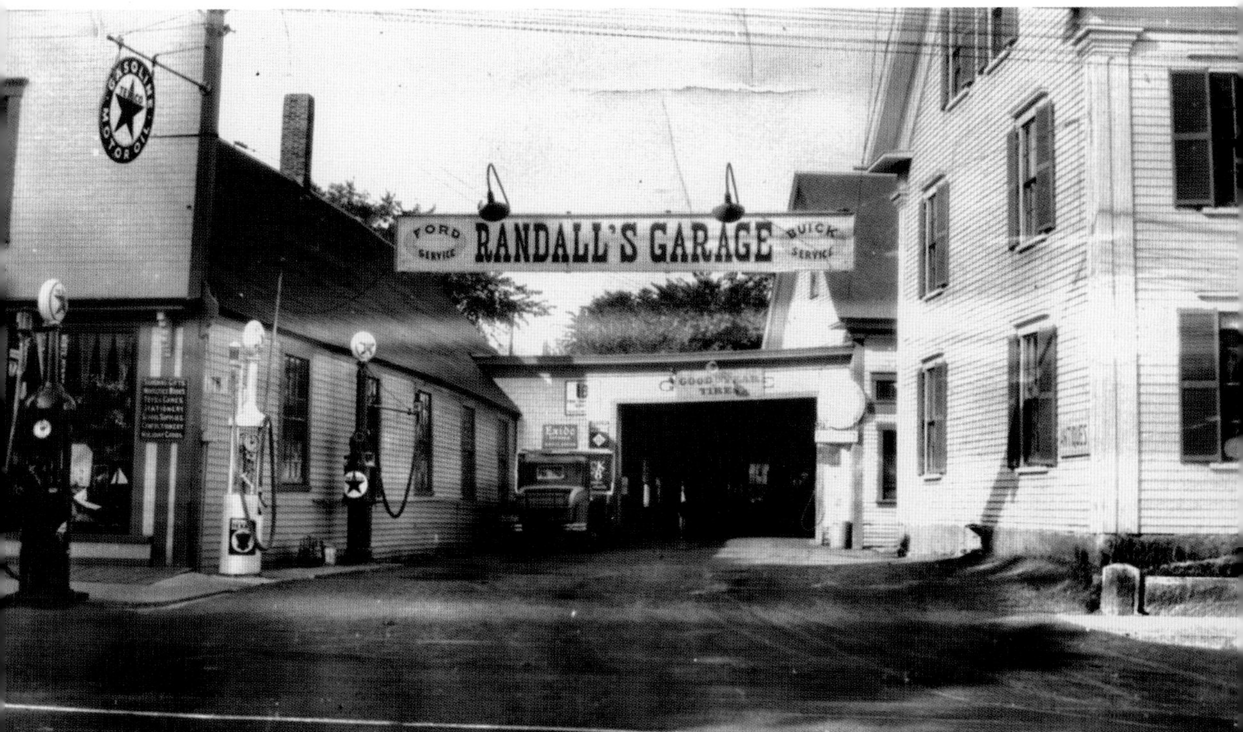

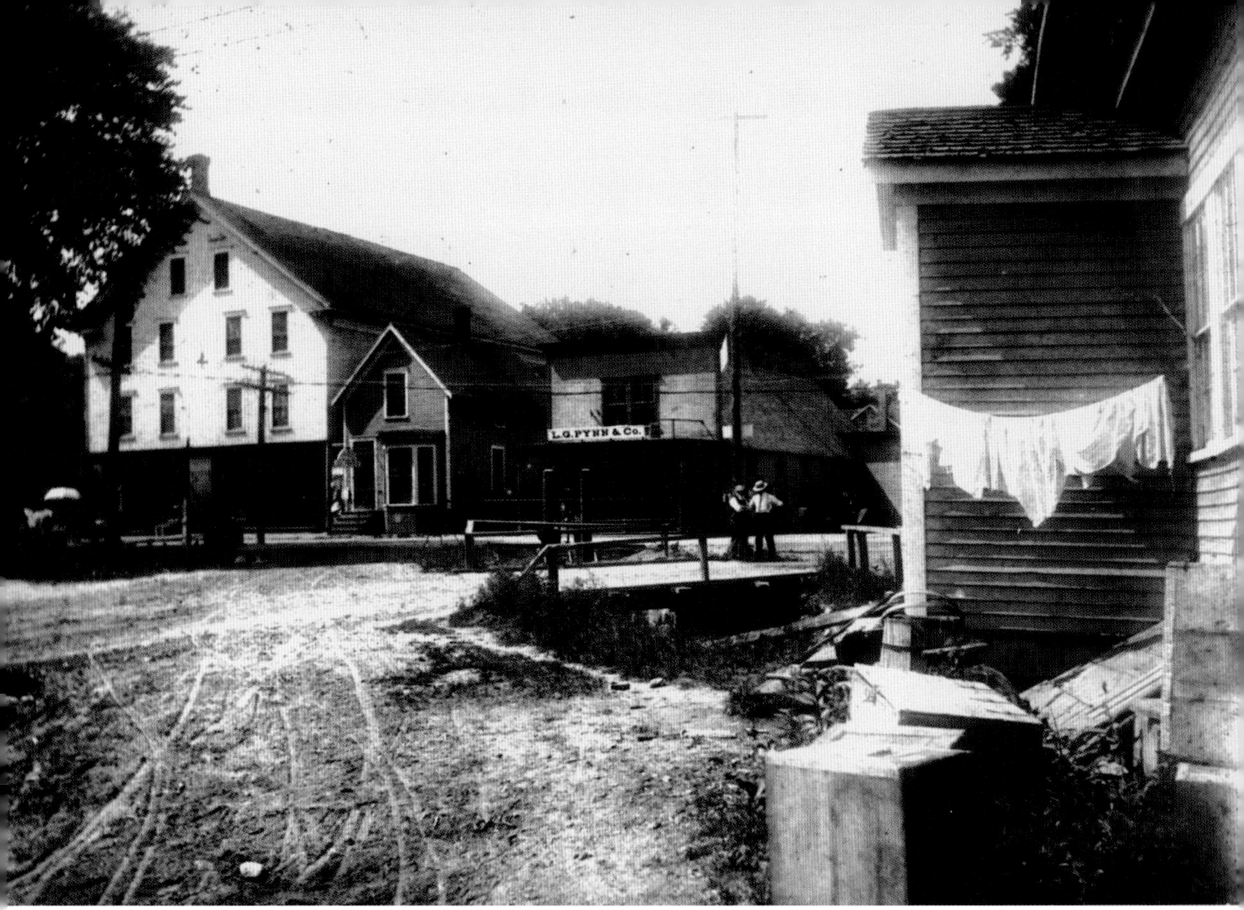

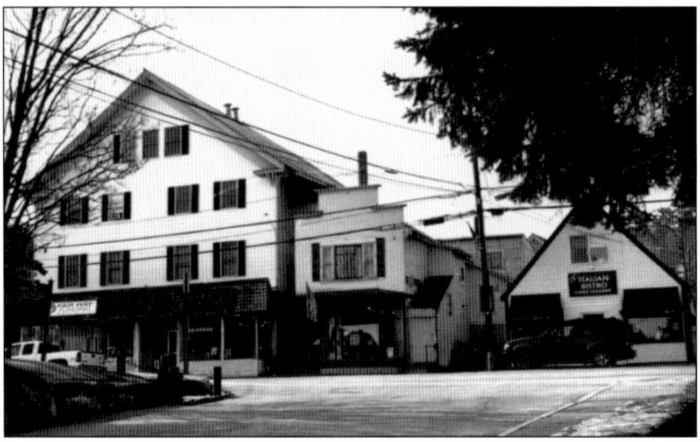

Seen from Dover Street are, from left to right, three Main Street stores: the building that housed the town hall on its second floor; Cram's Bakery and Quick Lunch; and L. G. Pynn and Company (later a variety store). Today Fair Way Funding and Hawkins Photography are located on the street level of the old town hall building. Nearby are Hunter's Needlework and the Italian Bistro. The building and laundry on the right was replaced with Sprague's Esso gas station.

Construction is being done on Main and Dover Streets in this early-1900s view. Today most of these buildings have been replaced by a town park and new retail businesses. The white building on the left is known as the Livingston Apartments. A new building has been erected on the corner of Main and Dover Streets in front of the apartment building. The new structure houses a retail business known as Fermentation Station.

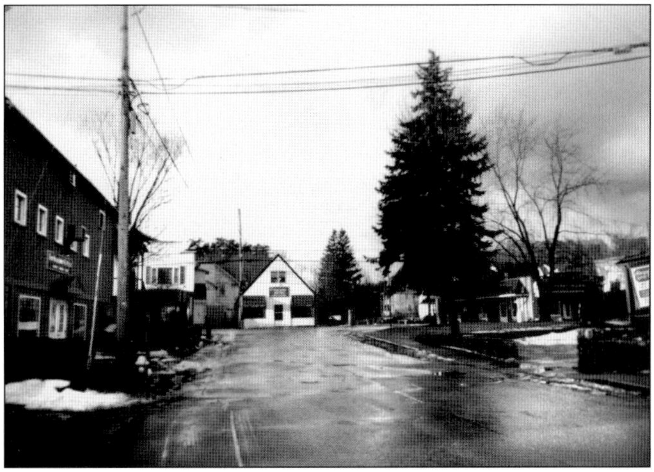

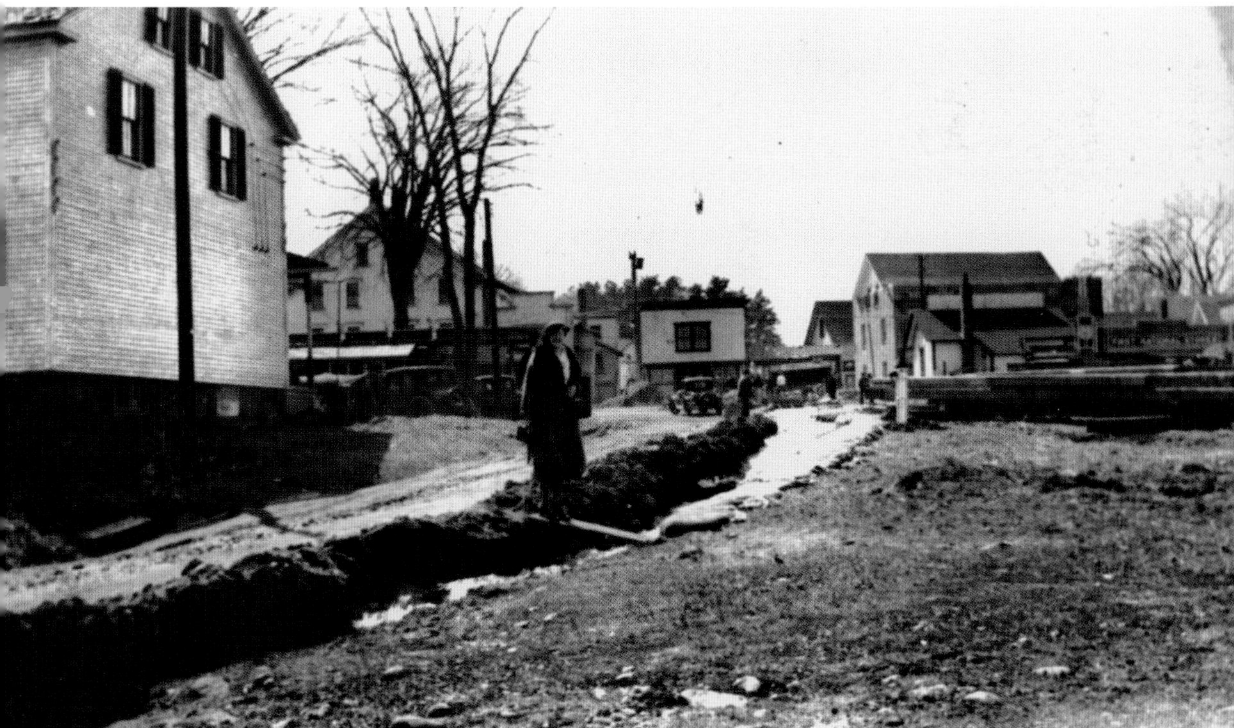

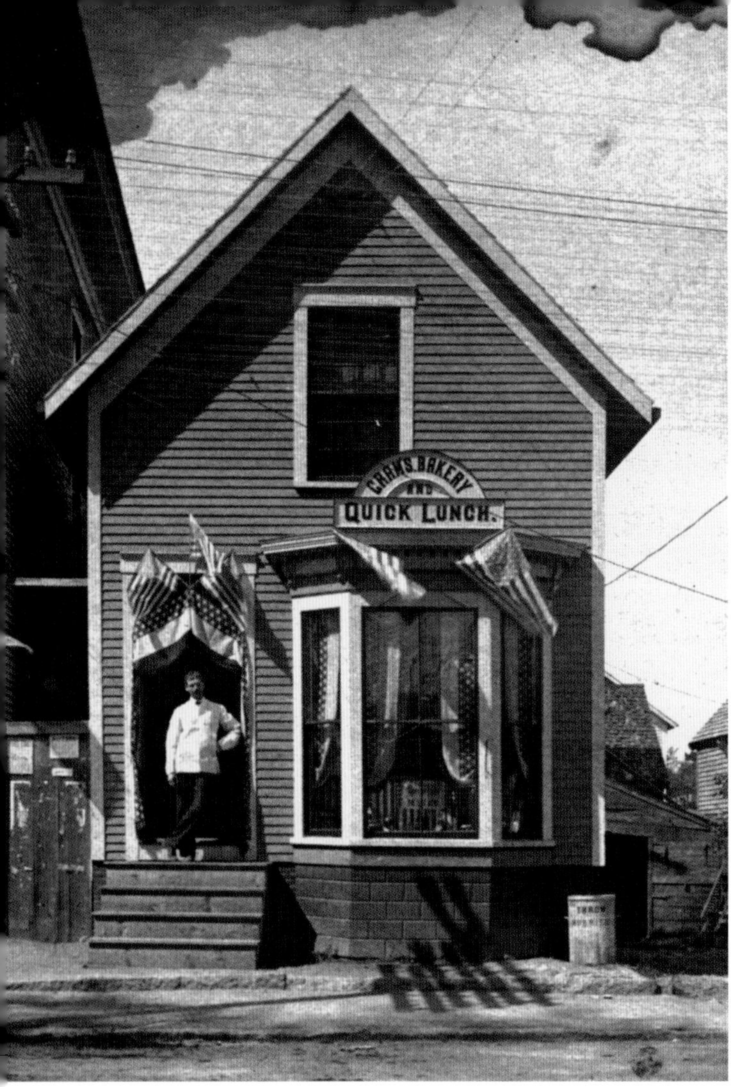

Cram's Bakery and Quick Lunch later became Jessie Allen's barbershop. Allen, a prominent member of the town, had one of the most extensive Civil War collections in the area. Today Hunter's Needlework occupies the property.

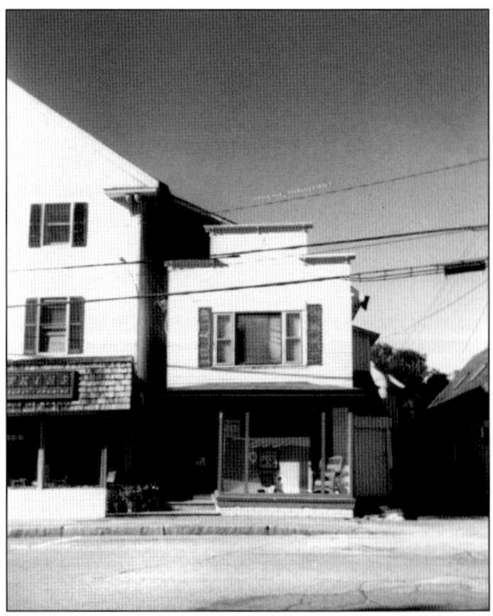

The Meredith Canal, pictured on November 6, 1903, provided the waterpower for the Sam Hodgson hosiery mill (operational between 1876 and 1889), at Corporation Square (the Mill Falls Marketplace). The canal passes directly under the Italian Bistro and Main Street, and eventually empties into Lake Winnipesaukee.

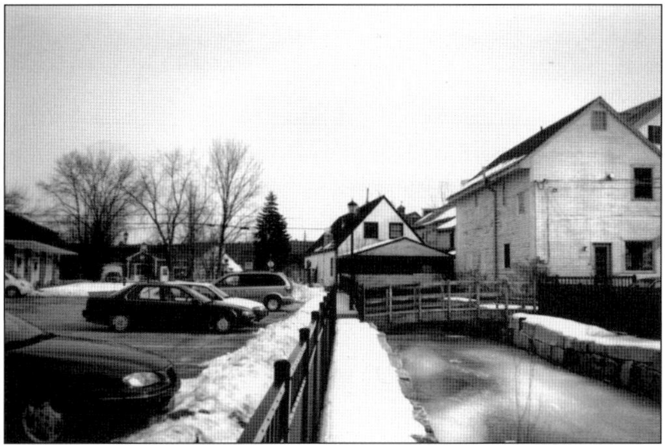

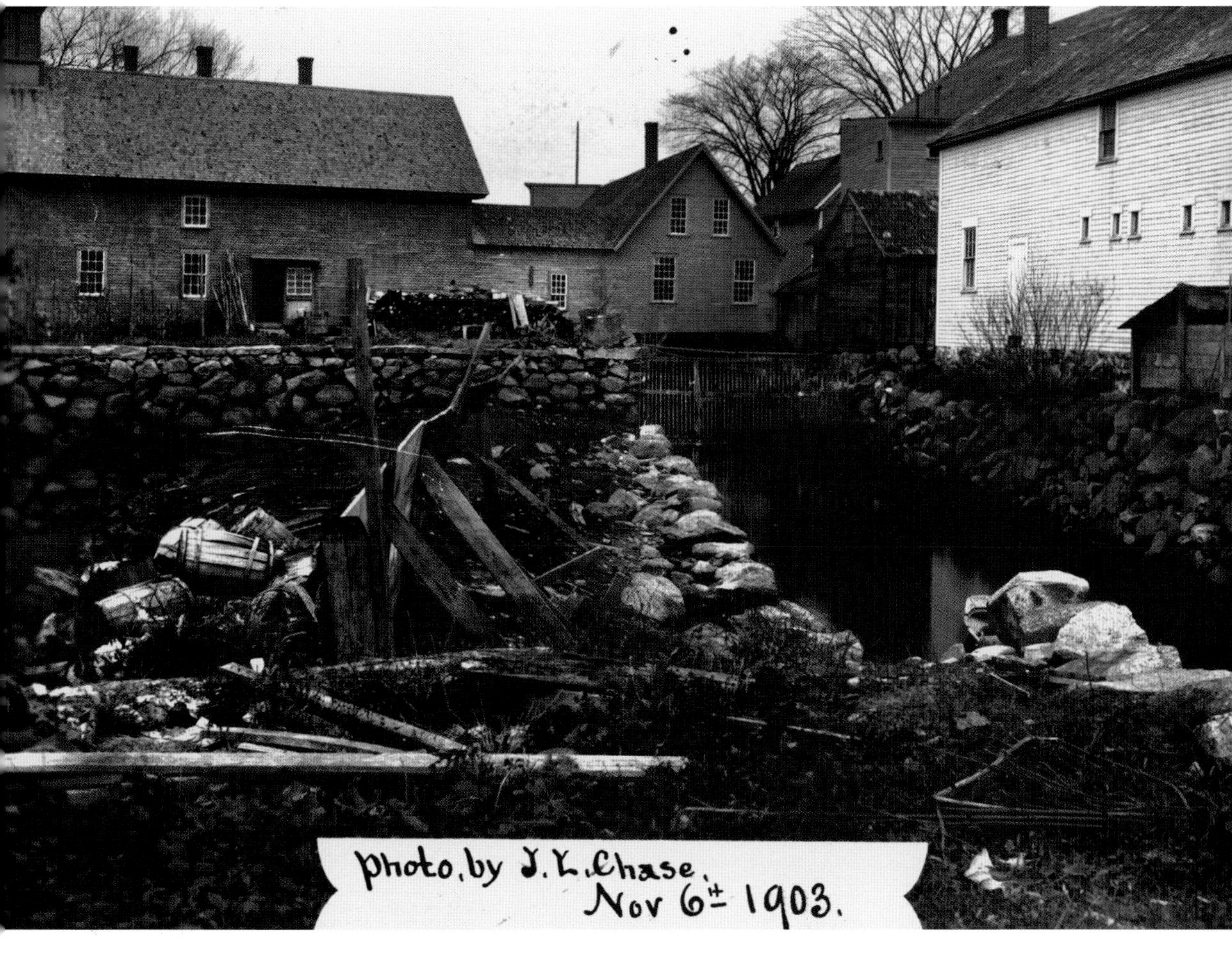

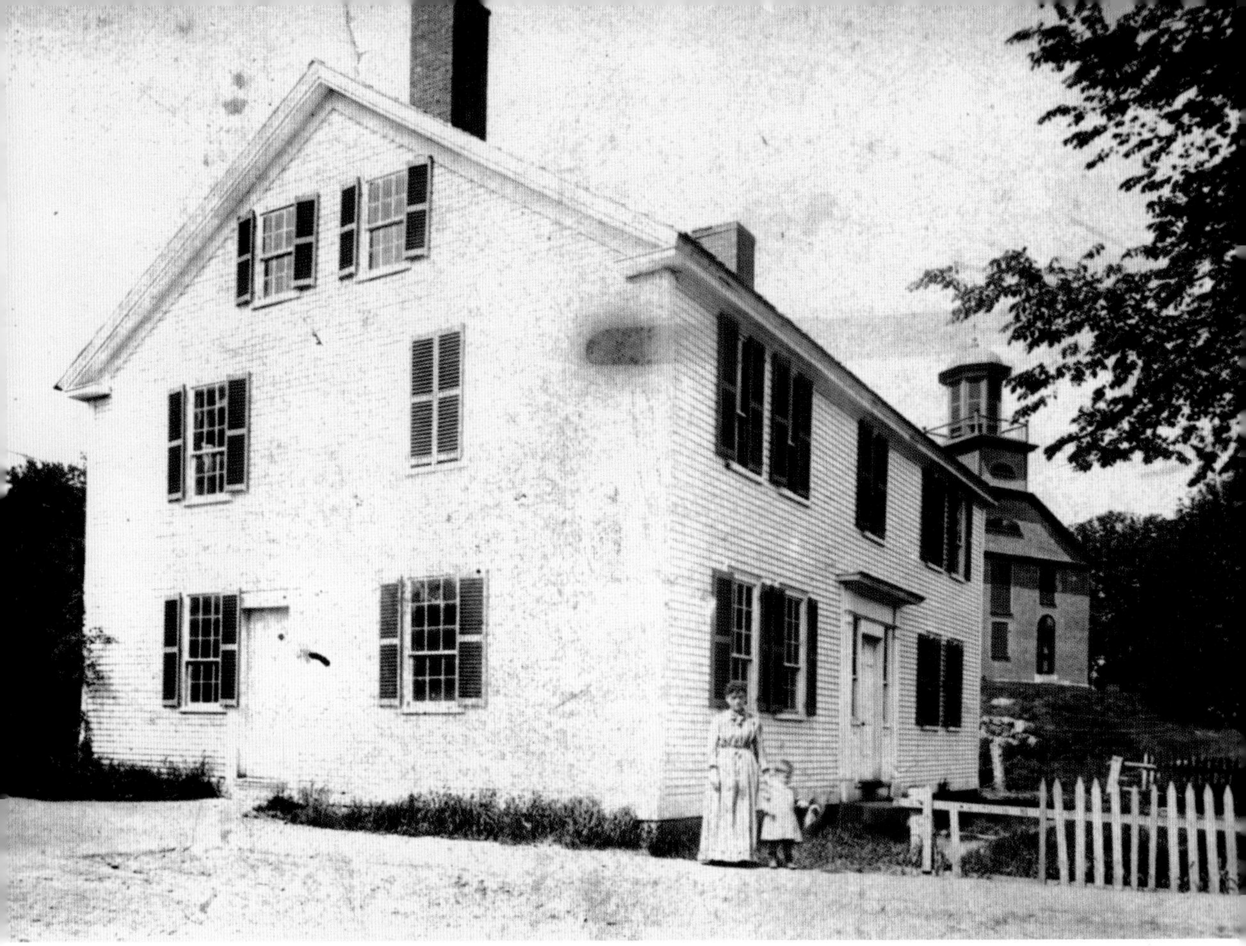

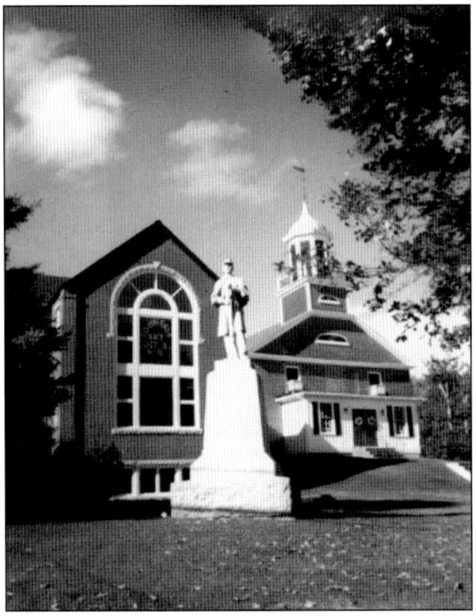

This Old Meredith House stood near the site of the present Baptist church. The structure was moved to Corporation Square, and is now home to the Livingston Apartments. The landmark building is still in use behind the post office. Today this area is the front lawn of the Baptist church. The Civil War monument on the property is dedicated to Maj. E. E. Beede and the 12th New Hampshire Volunteer Regiment.

The Philbrick house was located on High Street, across from the Baptist church. Pictured *c.* 1890 are Ralph C. Philbrick (with lead steers); Arthur E. Philbrick (with back steers); Alfred Perkins (on back seat); and Grandma Philbrick and Mrs. Warren (sitting in sleigh). Today the site has become the front lawn of the public library and the Baptist church, on Main Street.

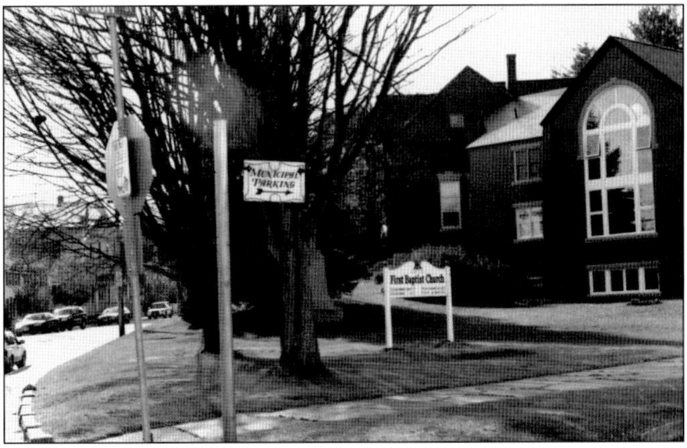

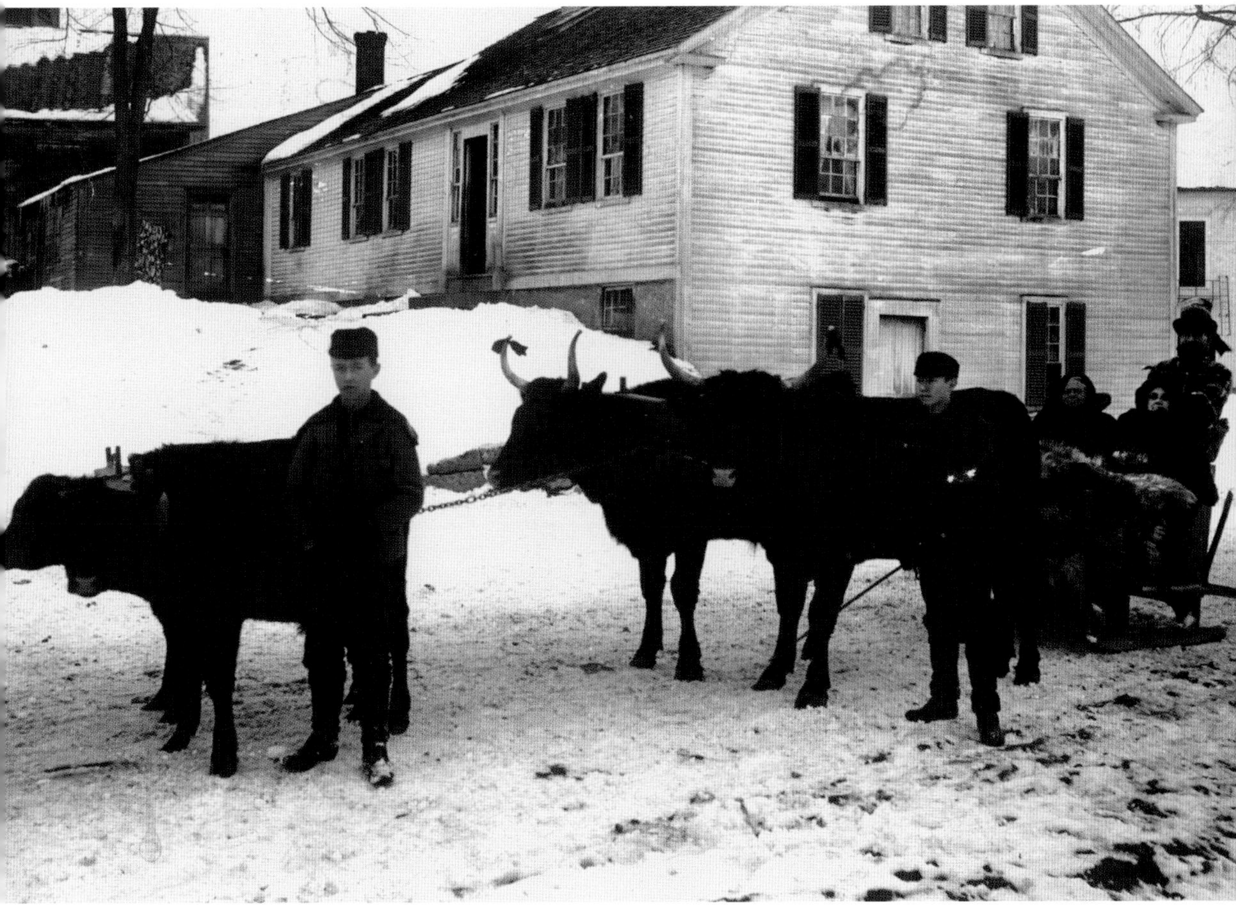

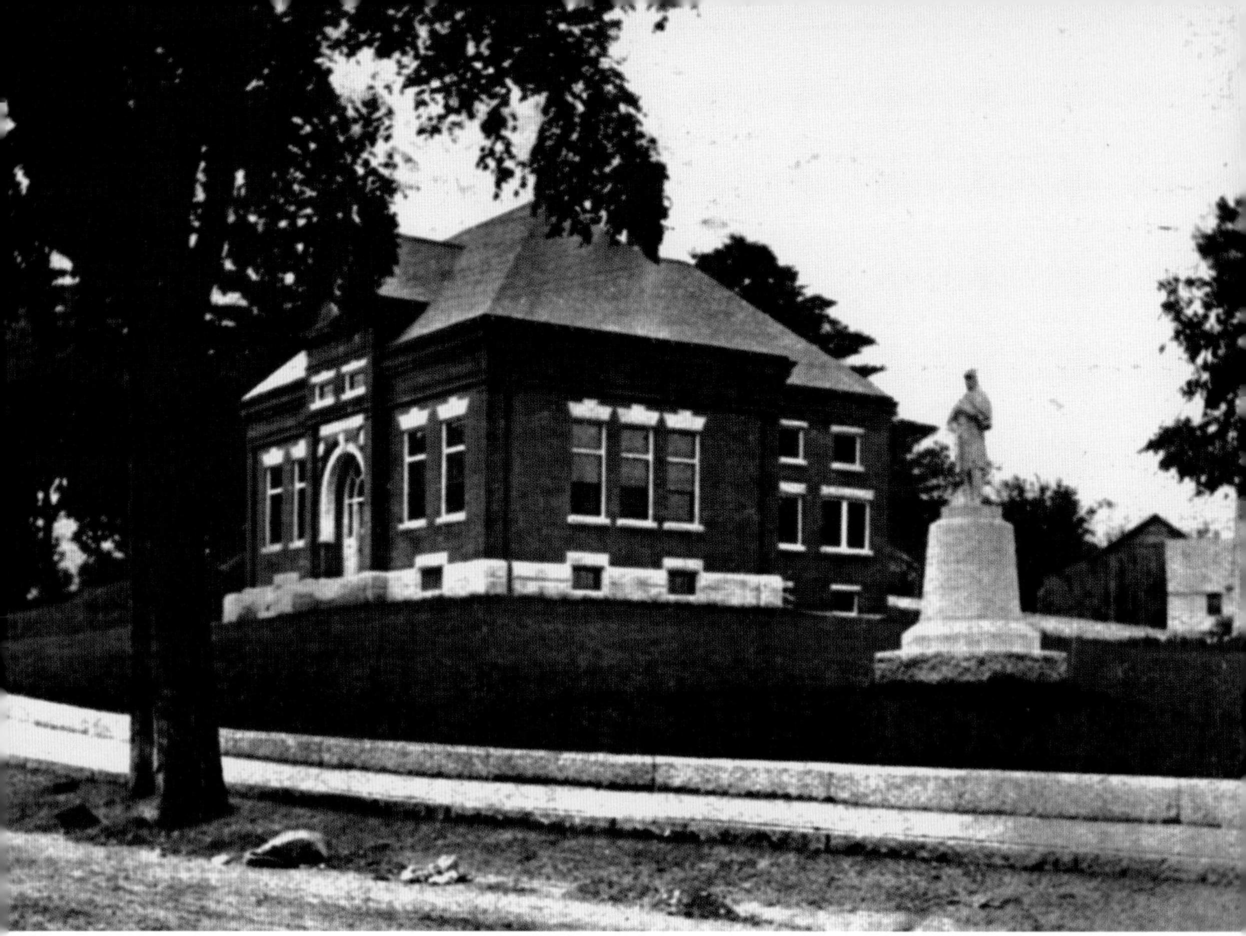

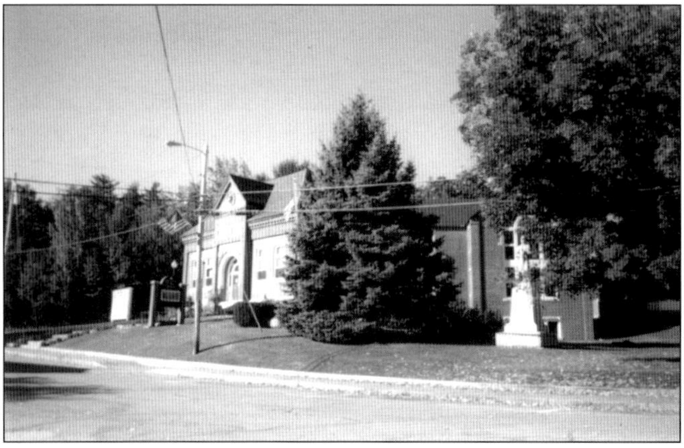

The Meredith Public Library is pictured in 1909. In 1882, the Meredith Public Library was founded by George F. Sanborn. He offered a room next to the newspaper office to launch the library, and he served as the town's first librarian. During its early years, the library moved to several temporary locations around the village until 1901, when Benjamin M. Smith donated his memorial library building. Smith's original $10,000 library, with its brick facade and slate roof, was placed on the National Register of Historic Places in 1985. The recent photograph shows an addition that was completed in 1988. It employs the same materials as the original building, and its two-story, arched-gable window echoes the main entry arch.

The post office was moved from the Ladd Block into a new brick building on Main Street, in the center of the village, in 1935. Today the post office appears unchanged, except for the POW-MIA flag now displayed and the absence of early-vintage automobiles in front of the building.

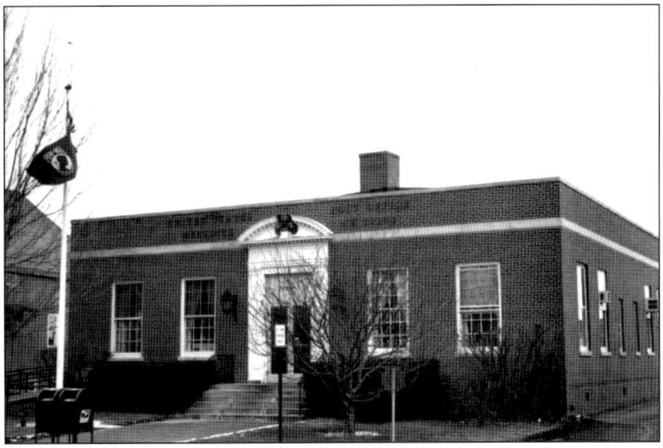

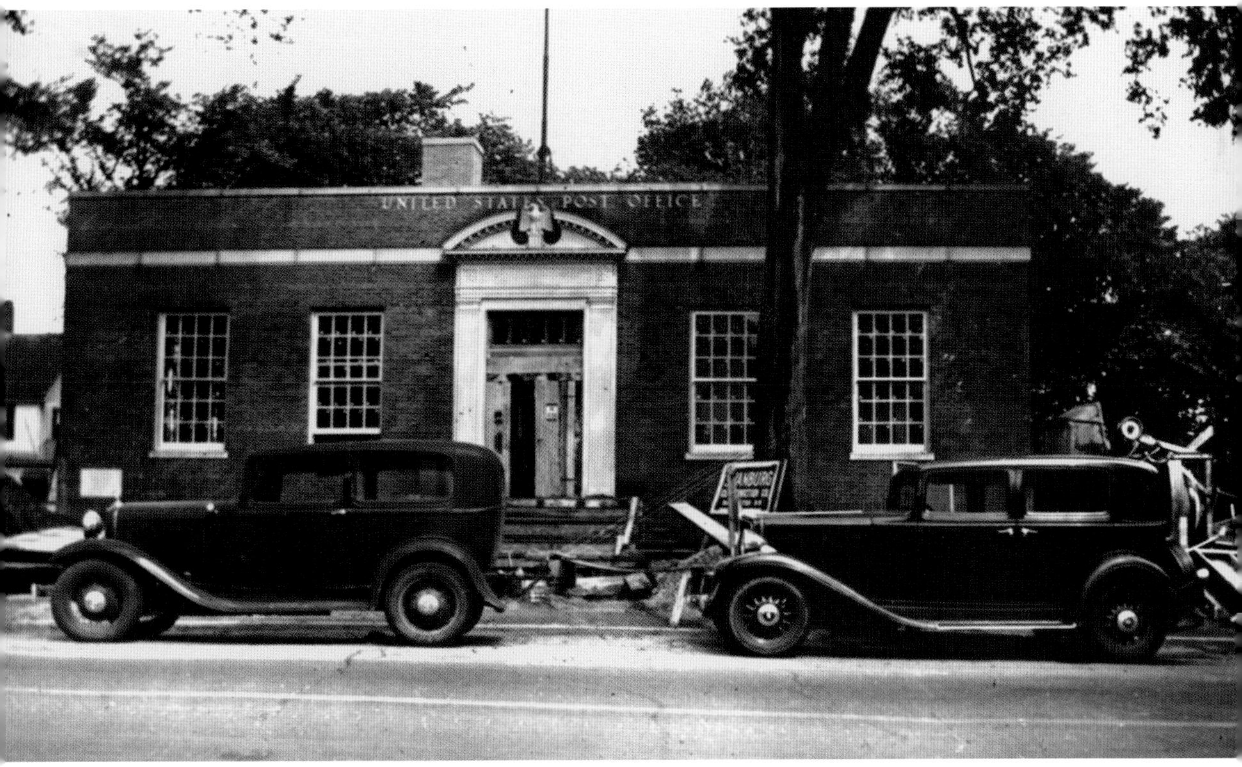

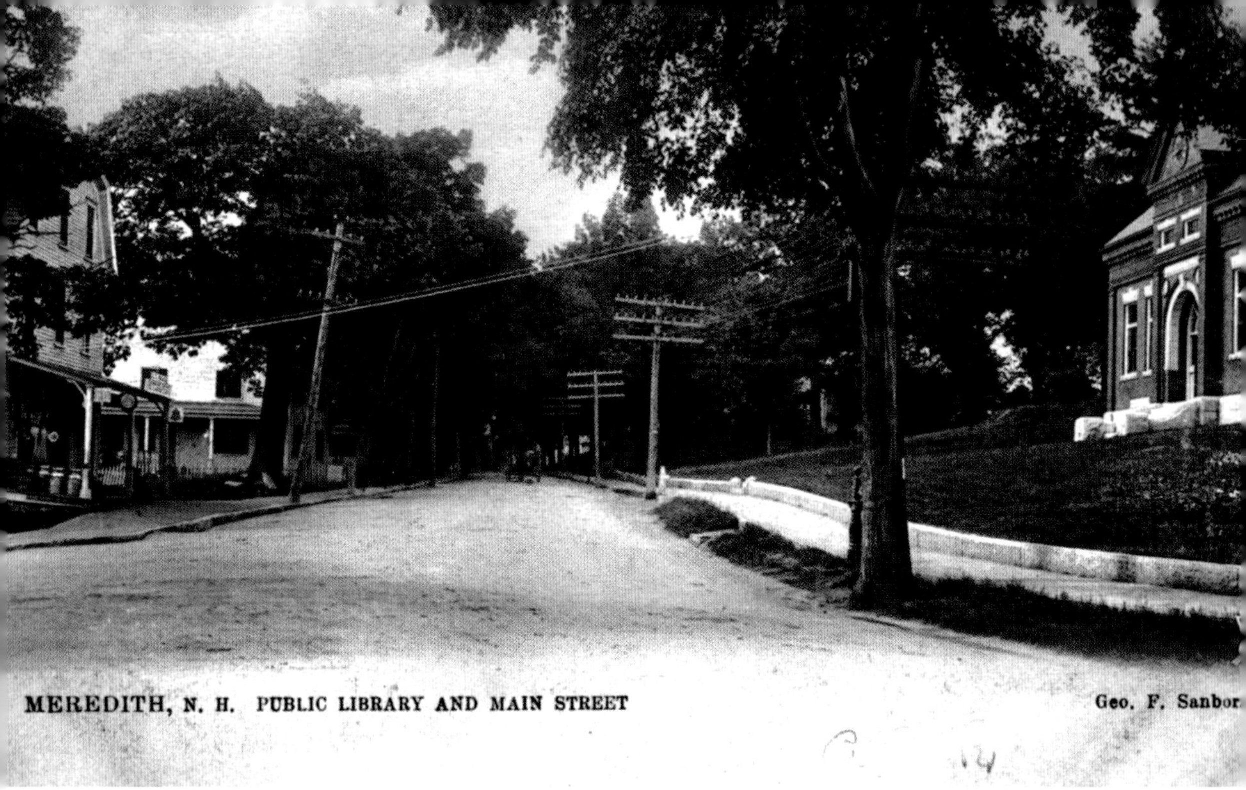

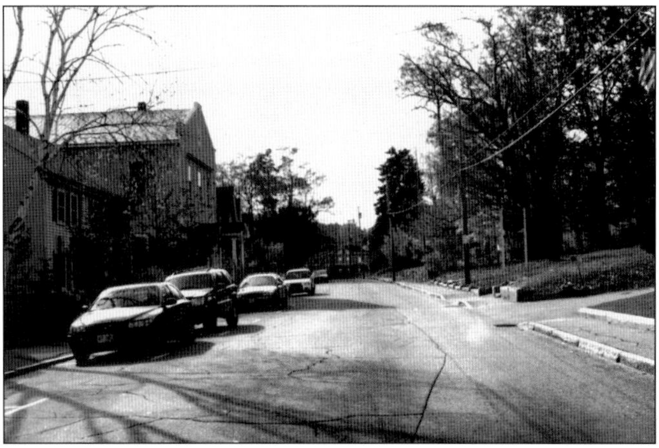

This view (looking south on Main Street from the junction of Lake and Main) shows the town library on the right, and the Adrian Williams Texaco station and the old Masonic hall on the left. The Masonic hall still stands, but it is no longer used by the Freemasons. The Texaco building is still there, but it no longer serves as a gas station.

Lang Street, once called Winnipesaukee Street, was named for Joseph Whidden Lang. Pictured in the earlier view (looking south on Lang Street) is the Meredith Village Freewill Baptist Church (about halfway down the street at the right). In the late 1800s, the first Meredith Meetinghouse was moved to Lang Street from its original location opposite the town pound on the Parade Road. Rev. Hosea Quimby was the first pastor. The old meetinghouse was used by the Freewill Baptists and later as a gymnasium for Meredith High School. The property has remained vacant since the building was torn down in the early 1980s.

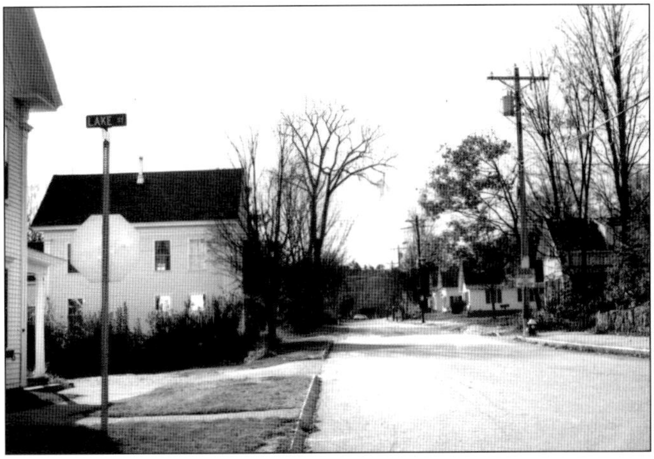

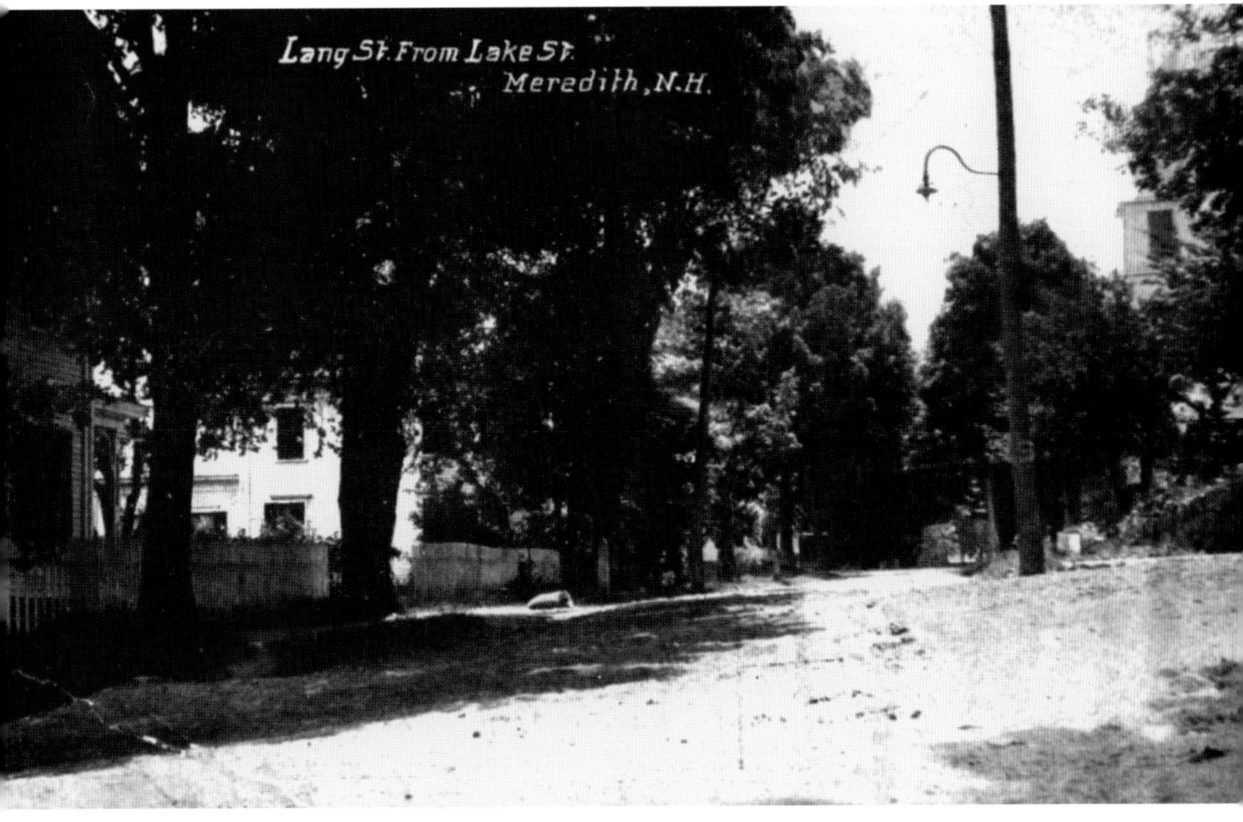

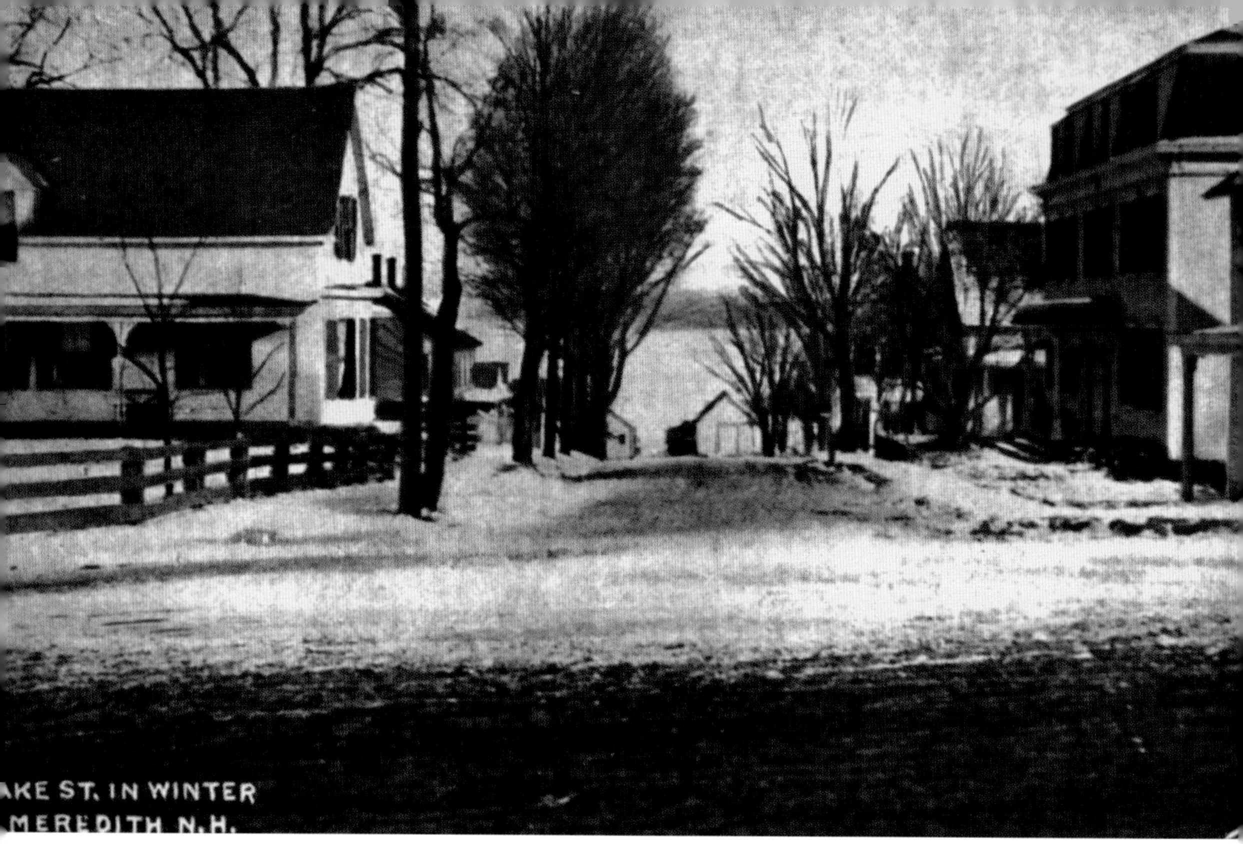

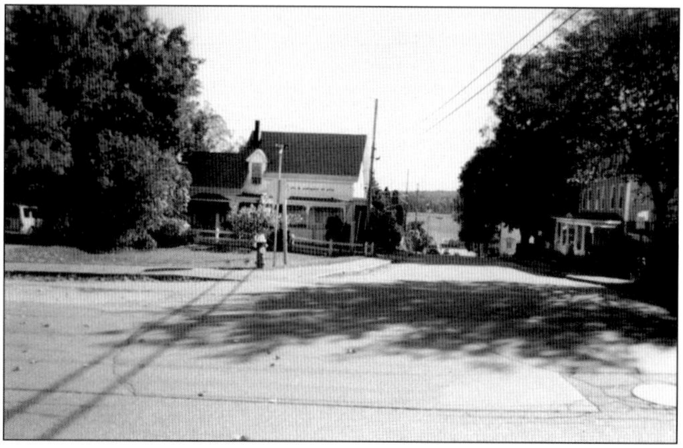

Lake Street is pictured during winter in the early 1900s. We are looking east to Meredith Bay and the town docks (at the foot of the hill). Little has changed over the years; the buildings are still there, but a new road (Route 3) was built in 1948 to direct the traffic on the shore of the bay and to relieve the growing congestion on Main Street in the village business district.

Main Street is pictured in a view looking north. During the early 1900s, this road was well lined with shade trees—a perfect entrance to the business section of the village. This winter scene depicts the solitude of the village and its stately homes. The public library is on the left, and the Elm Hotel is at the end of the road. The library still stands, but the Elm Hotel has been replaced by the post office. Some of the shade trees on the right have disappeared.

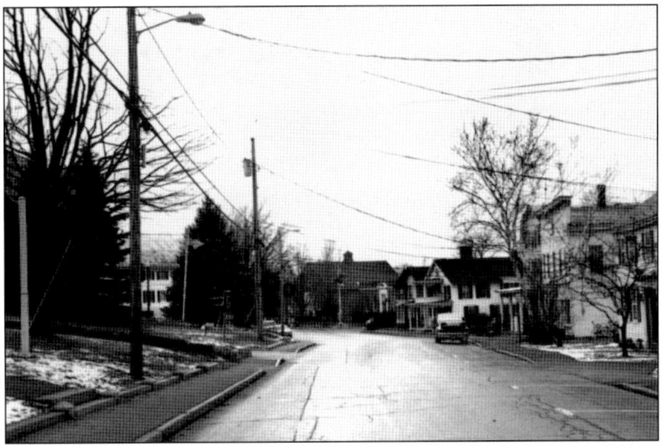

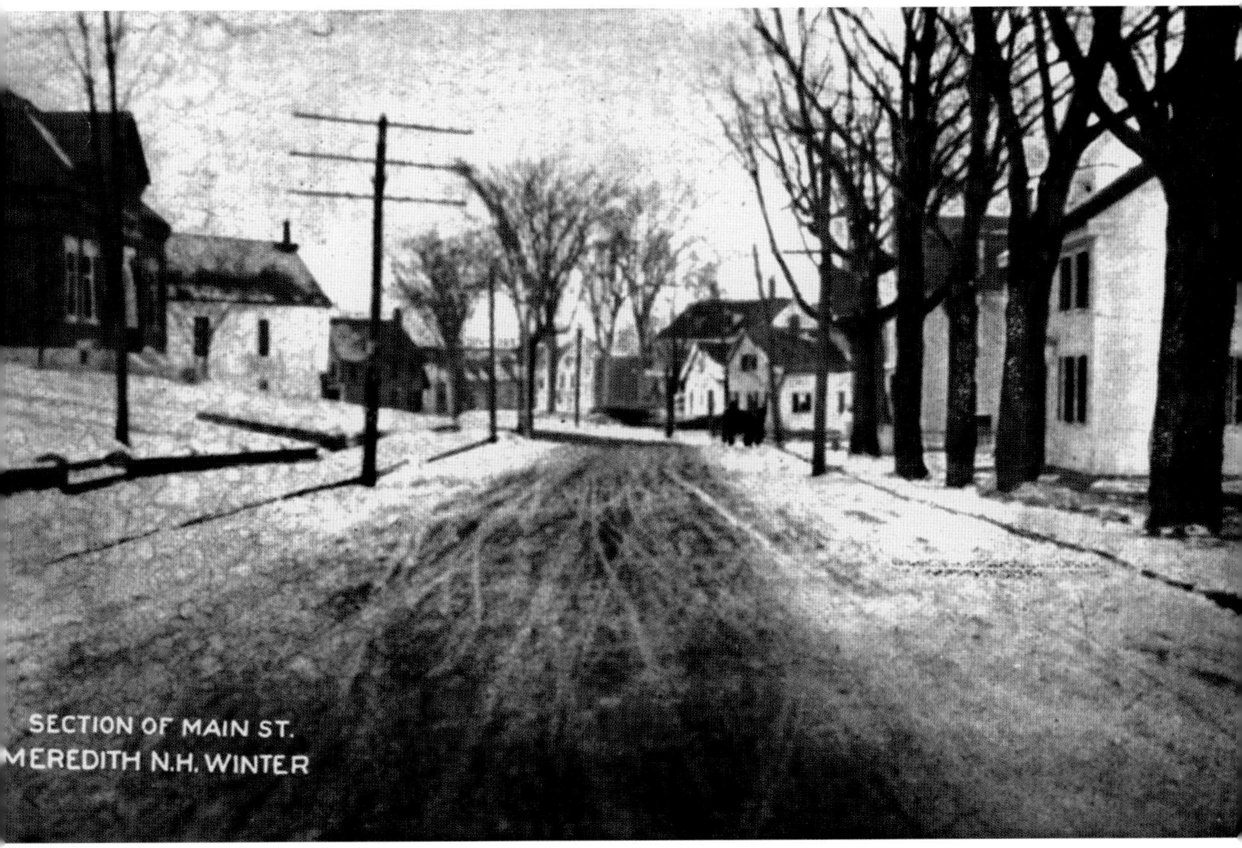

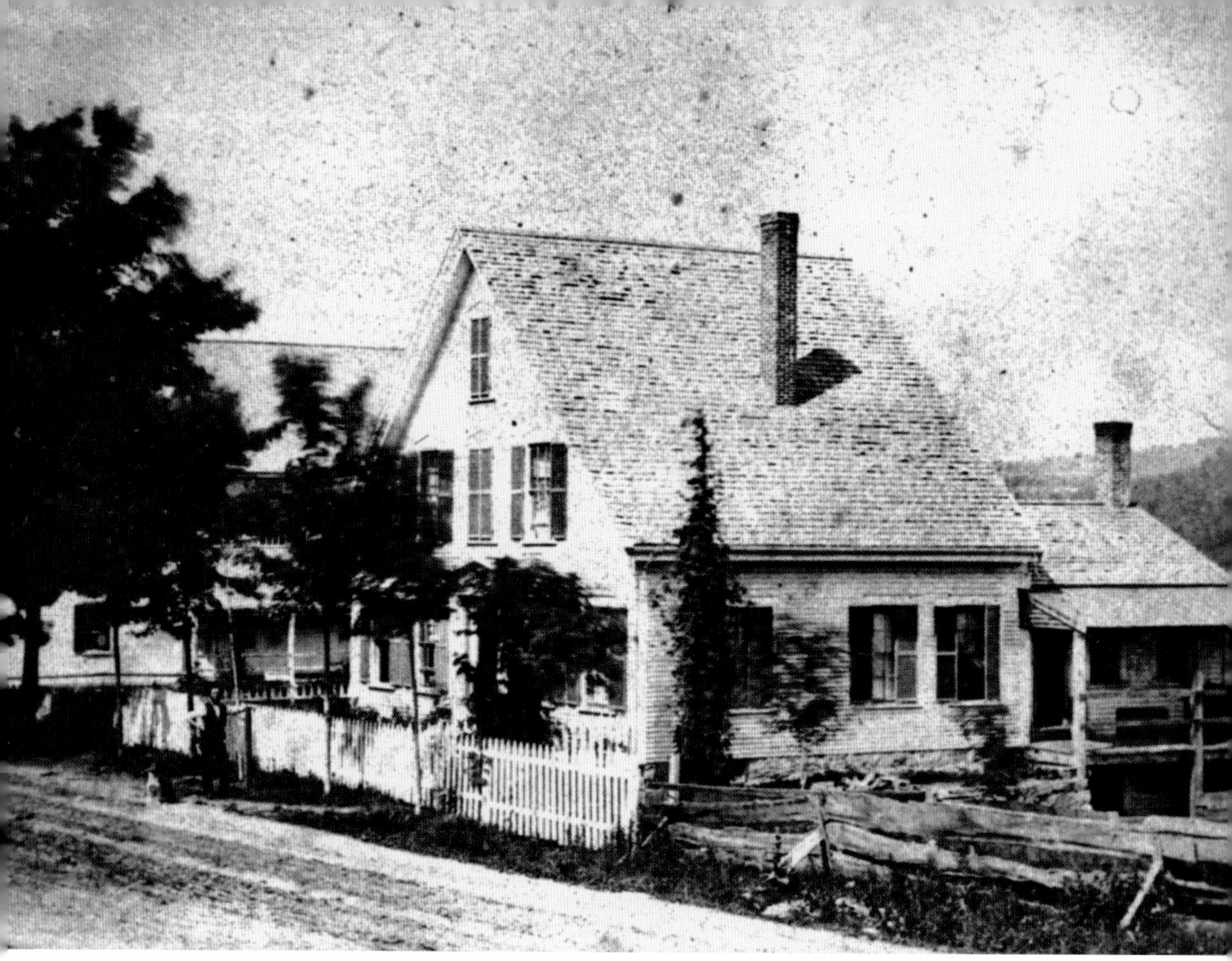

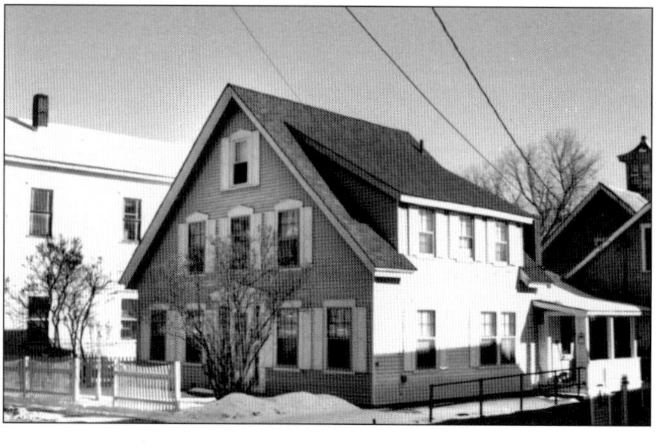

This fine old home is located at 106 Main Street, directly across the street from the old Meredith High School (Humiston Building) and the public library. For many years, this was the home of Ellsworth and Doris Cotton, prominent citizens in the town. This building is a fine example of the many private homes in the village proper.

The Boston & Maine depot is shown in the late 1800s. When the railroad came to Meredith in 1848, it changed the complexion of the town forever. Over the rails came the coal to power the steam engines, such as those at what was once the Meredith Linen Mills. Traveling salesmen and tourists alike would disembark at the Meredith station and board at one of the many fine hotels. This passenger and freight station, located on South Main Street, was moved in the mid-1900s, and the lot became a parking area for the Wickes Lumber Company.

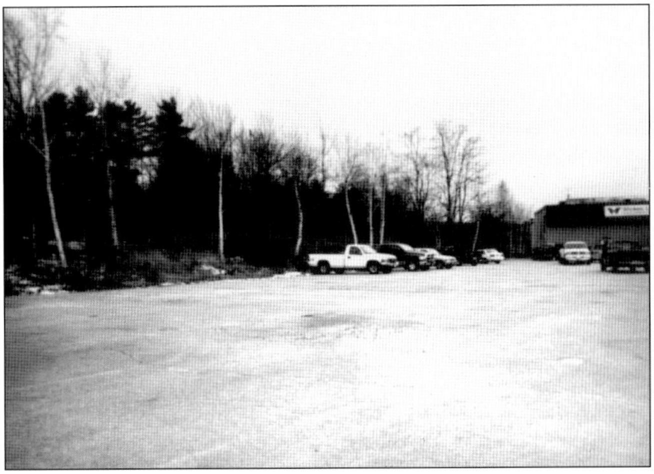

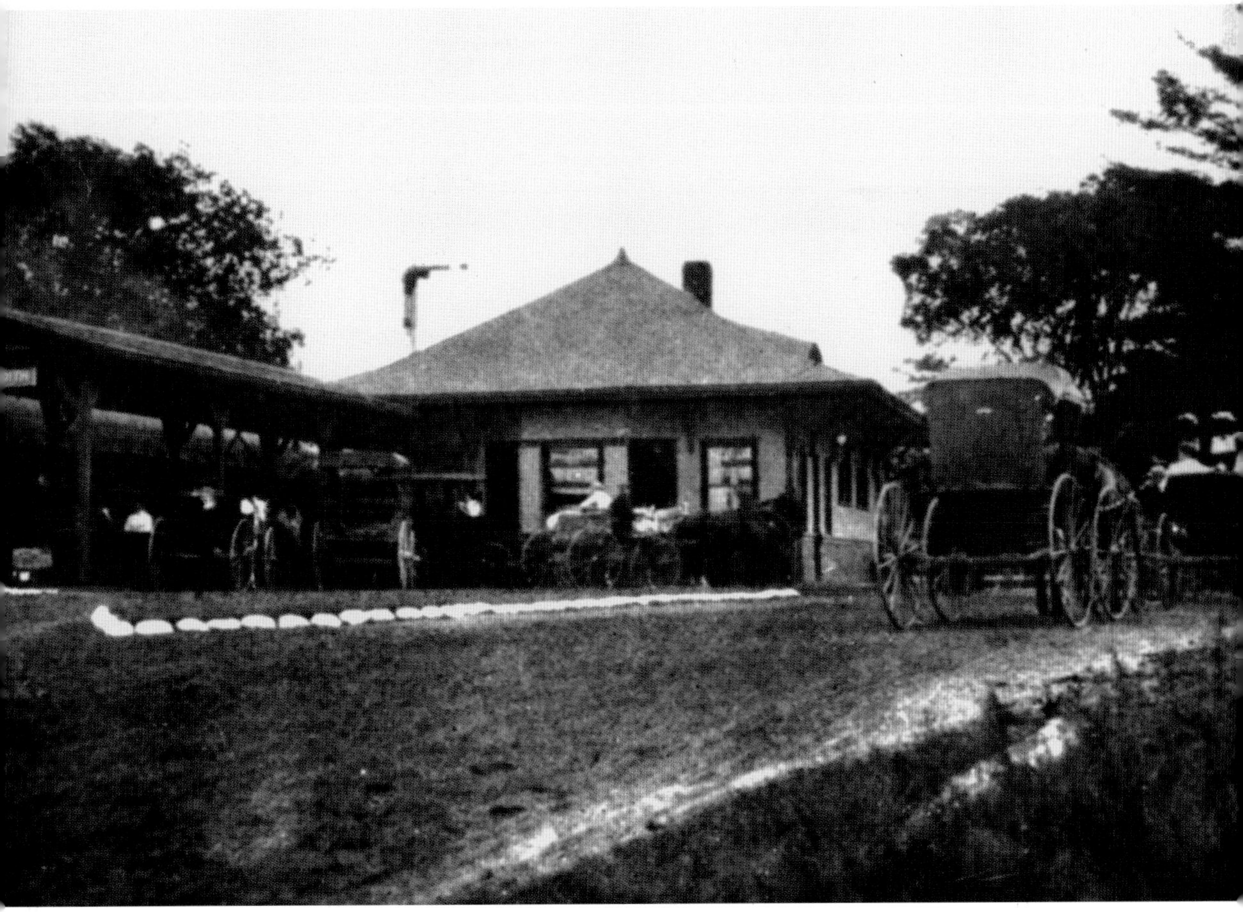

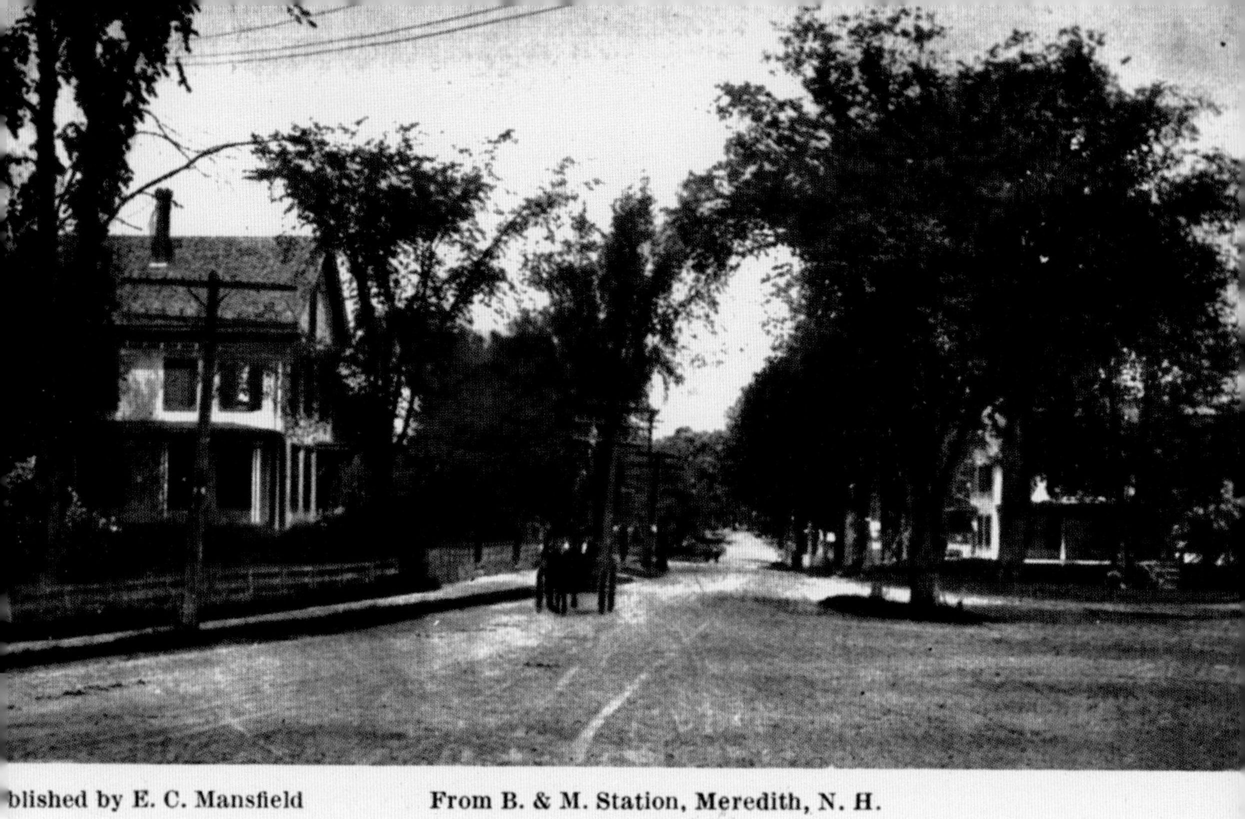

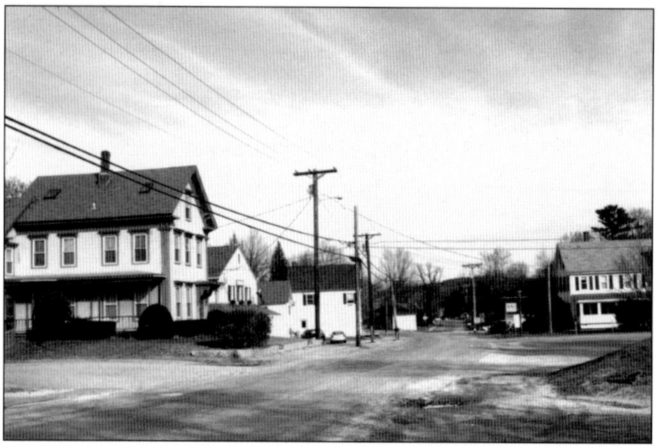

South Main Street is seen from the Boston & Maine station. Like many other Lakes Region towns, Meredith has become a popular year-round resort destination. Visitors arrived first by train, and in later years, by automobile. Two primary routes to the White Mountains intersected in the village, a fact that encouraged the village business district to develop into a regional trading center, a function it continues to serve today. After the state relocated the highways around the village to follow the lakeshore in 1948, the lake frontage was set aside for the town's use, opening up former industrial land to the public for strolling and picnics. Today many of the shade trees that once stood here have disappeared, but the two buildings on the left and right still remain, with few changes.

The Webster House, located on Towle Hill (on the Center Harbor road), is pictured in 1907. Under the management of L. E. Hawkins, the Webster House was a popular boardinghouse that had capacity for 25 guests. This house was the original site of the Towle House, later known as the Mountain View House.

Chapter 3

Churches, Schools, and Hotels

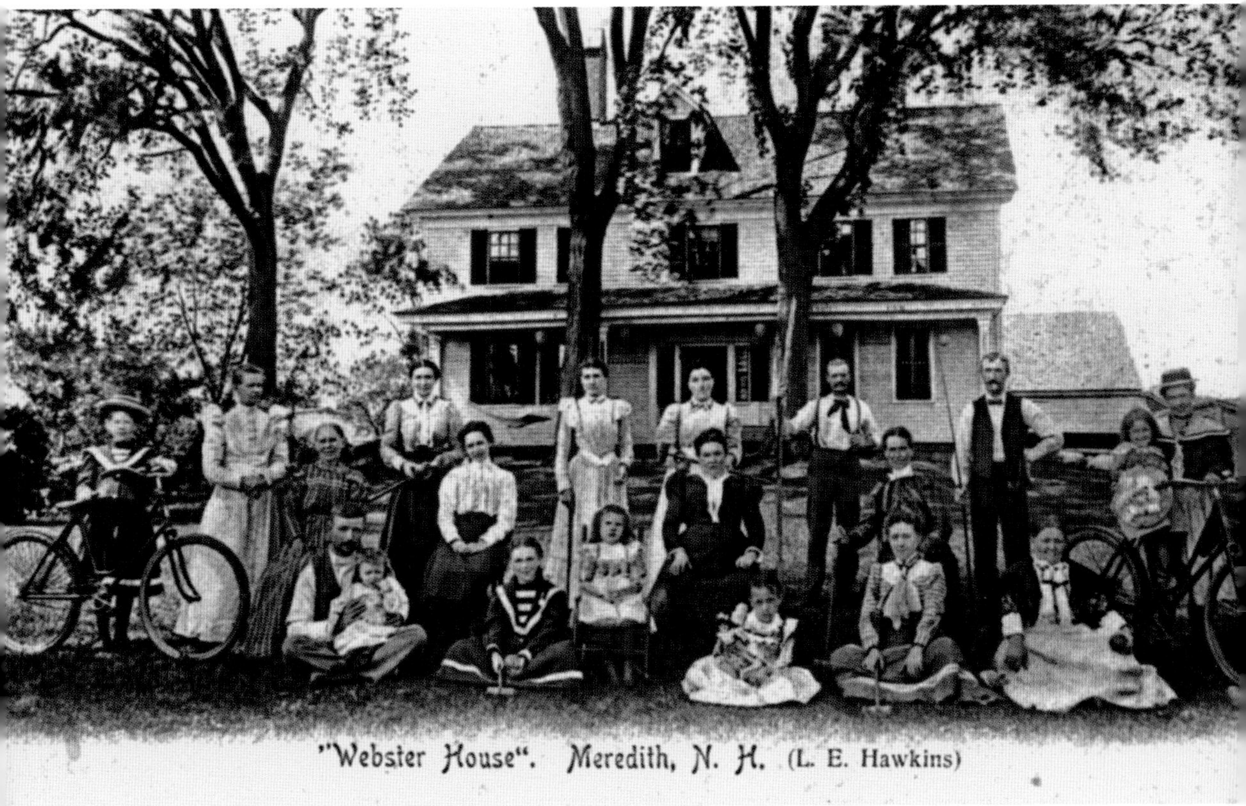

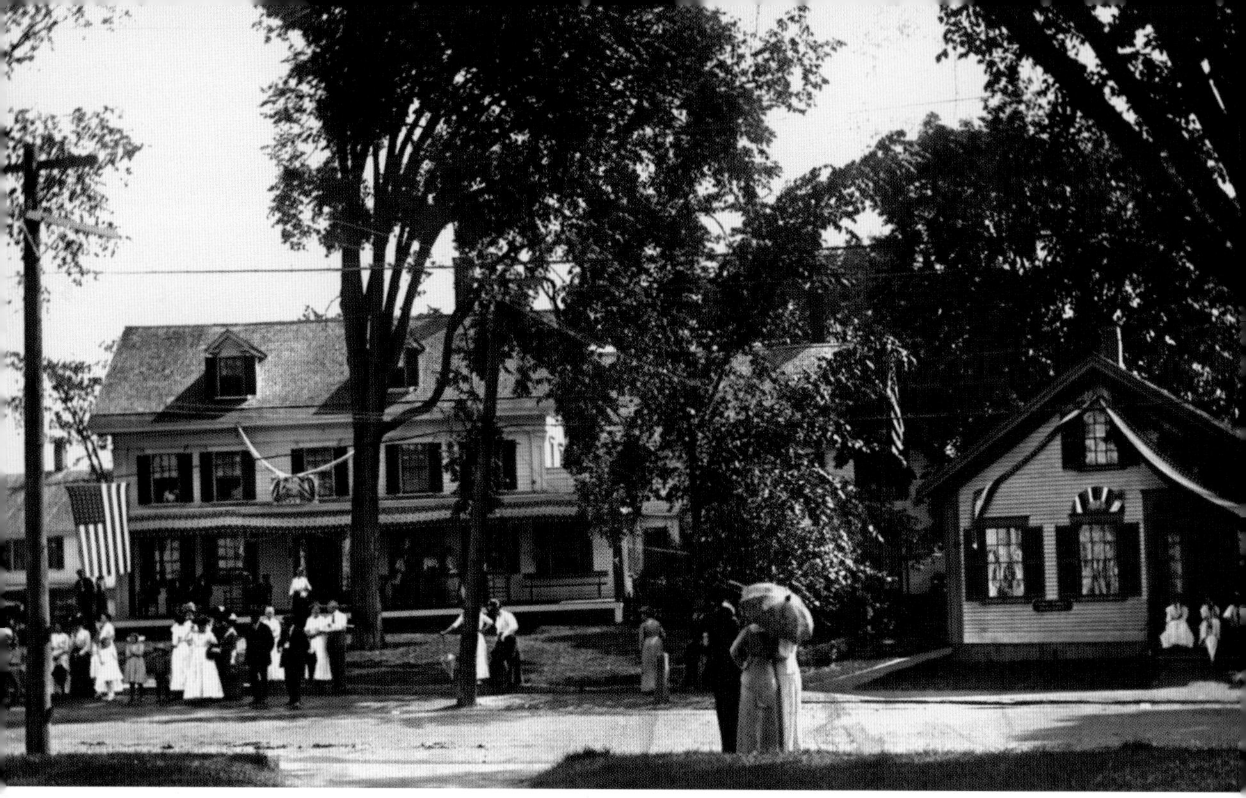

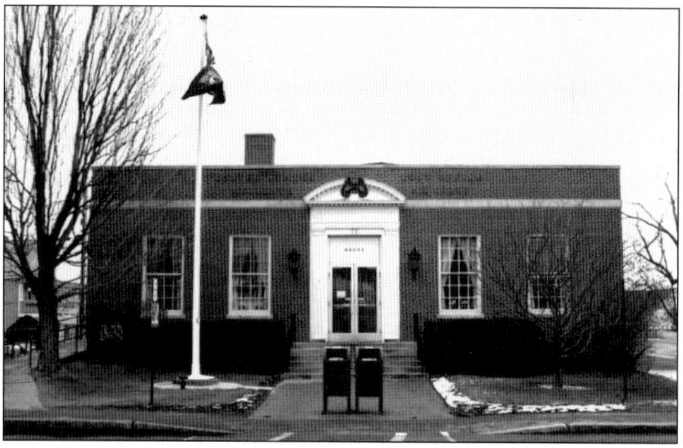

In the early 1900s, the Elm Hotel (located on the site of the current post office) was a popular resting place that housed as many as 50 guests. The proprietor was A. H. Shaw. The hotel was the center of many social activities, such as wedding receptions, conventions, and the like. The Emery Funeral Home (right) was replaced by the present-day Wood Shop. A new building was constructed to the left of the post office during the 1970s to house a retail business known as Fermentation Station and offices on the second floor.

The Maples, located on Highland Street, was a popular lodging place for visitors to the Lakes Region. In 1907, Ellen and Aaron Clough were the proprietors of this establishment, which accommodated 20 guests. From 1974 to 1978, Wayne and Wendy Chase operated the boardinghouse under the name Meredith Manor. Today it is a private home.

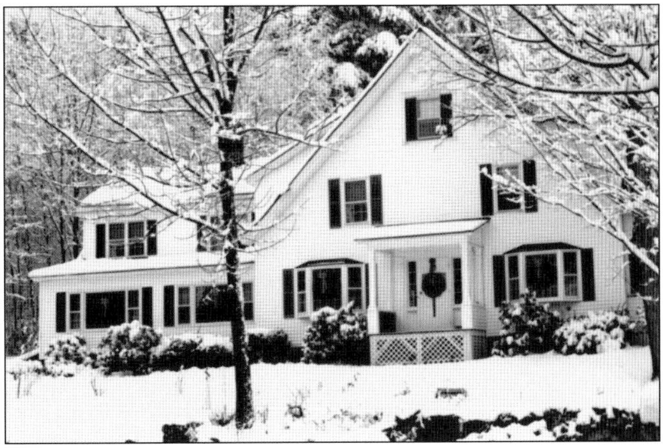

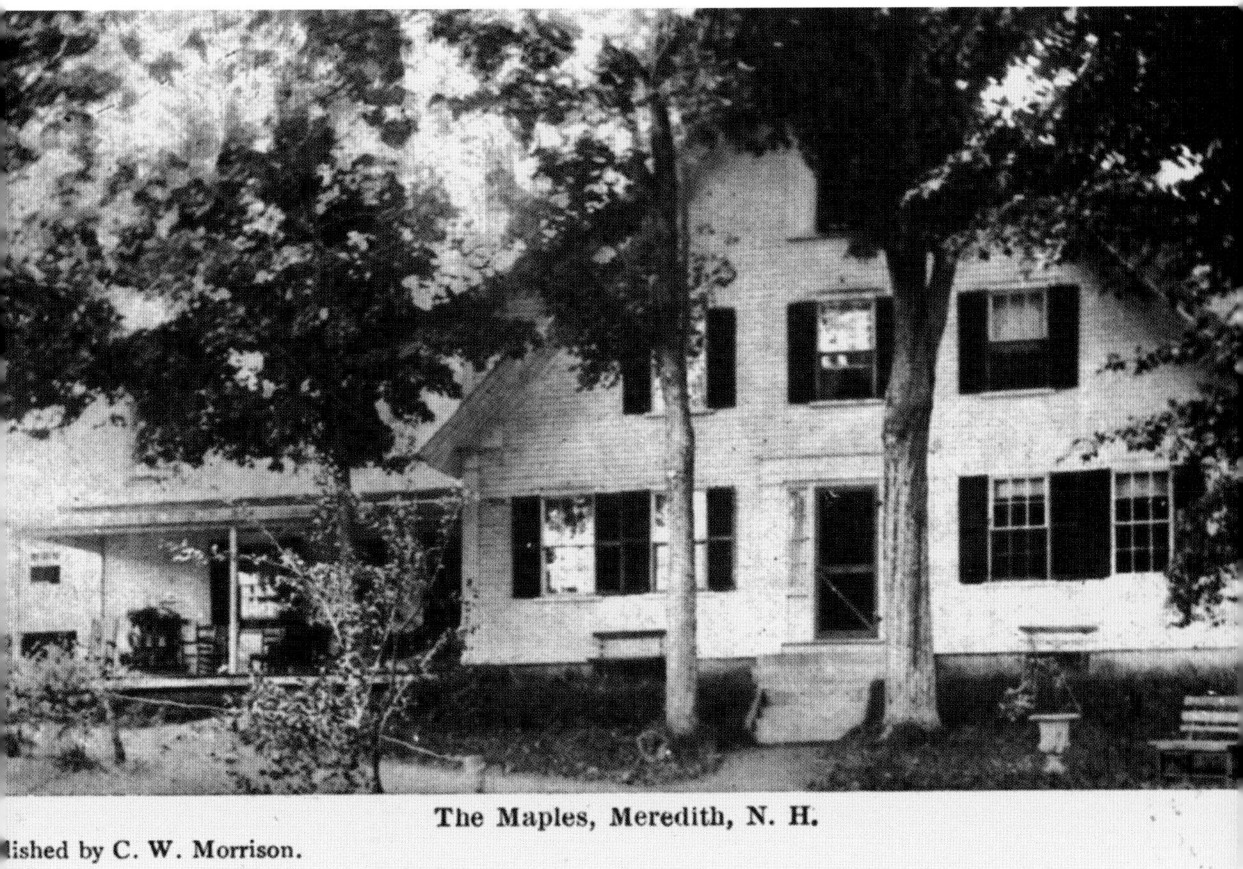

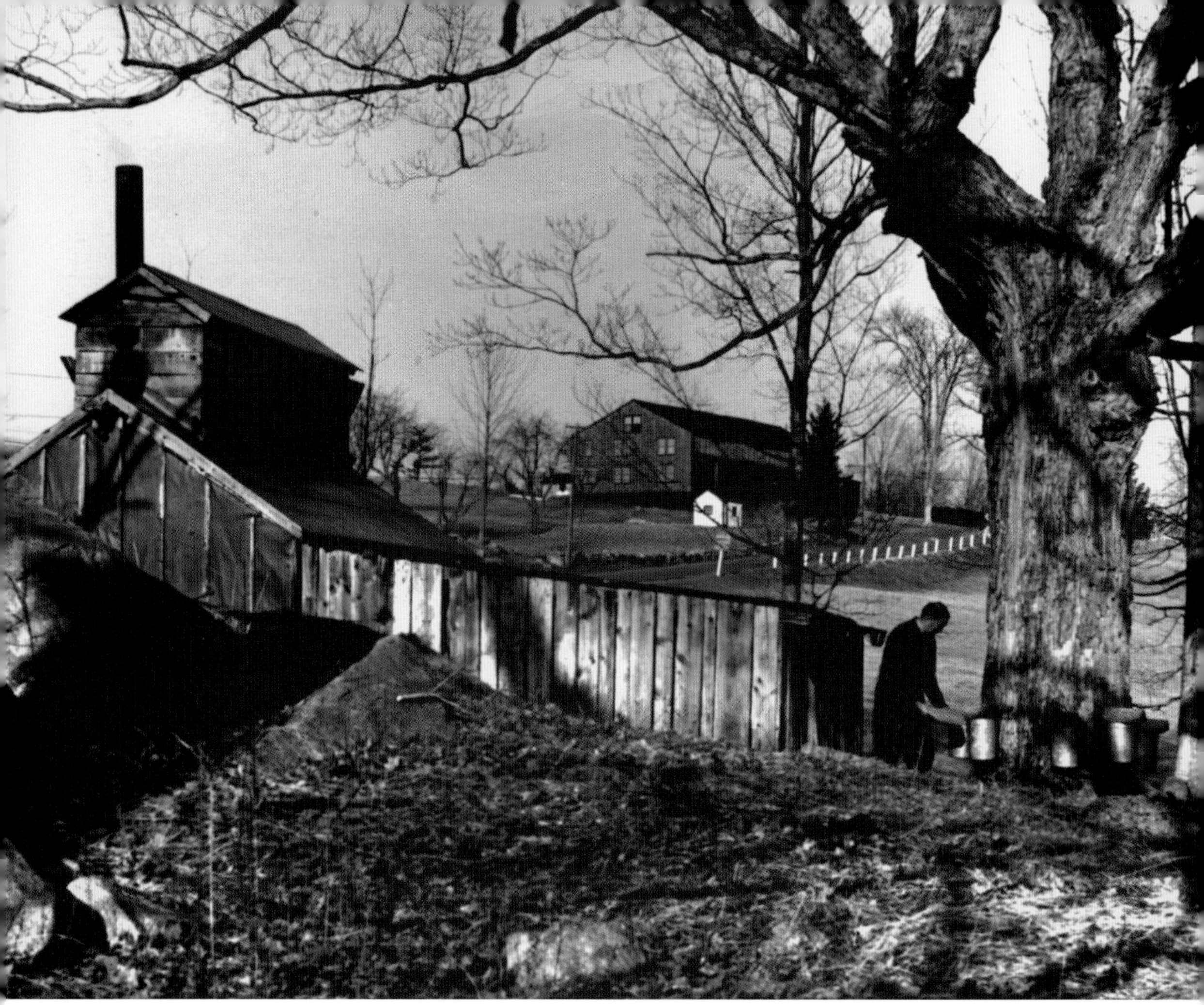

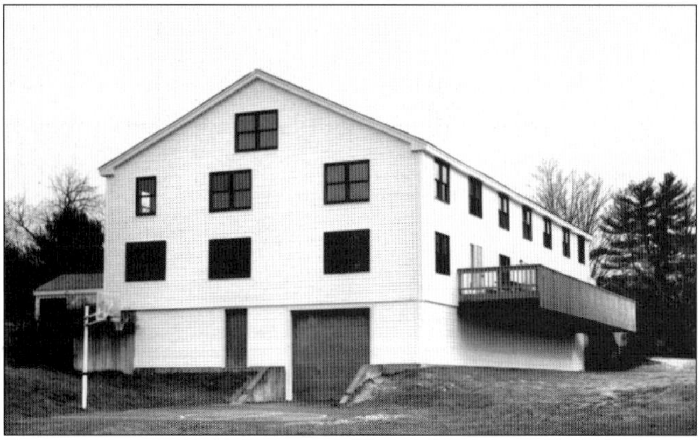

Wicwas Lake Farm Lodge, pictured in the early 1900s, was built and operated by Joseph F. Smith. Located in the foothills of the White Mountains, the farm overlooks beautiful Lake Wicwas. The lodge is 96 feet long and 42 feet wide. A screened piazza extended across the entire front and commanded a view of the lake and western mountains. Today this property is the site of a private school known as the Lakeland School.

During the 1940s and 1950s, St. Clair's Tourist Home (at 117 Main Street) was advertised as being clean, comfortable, and reasonable. The same advertisement continues: "Continuous hot and cold water and showers. Open the year round. No meals served. Rates on request. Mr. & Mrs. John St. Clair." Today this a private residence.

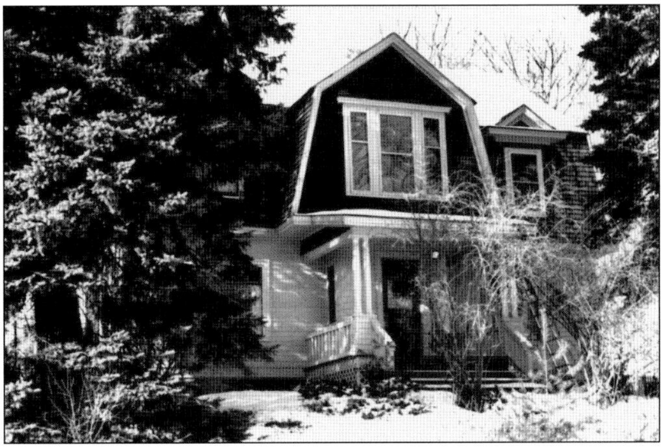

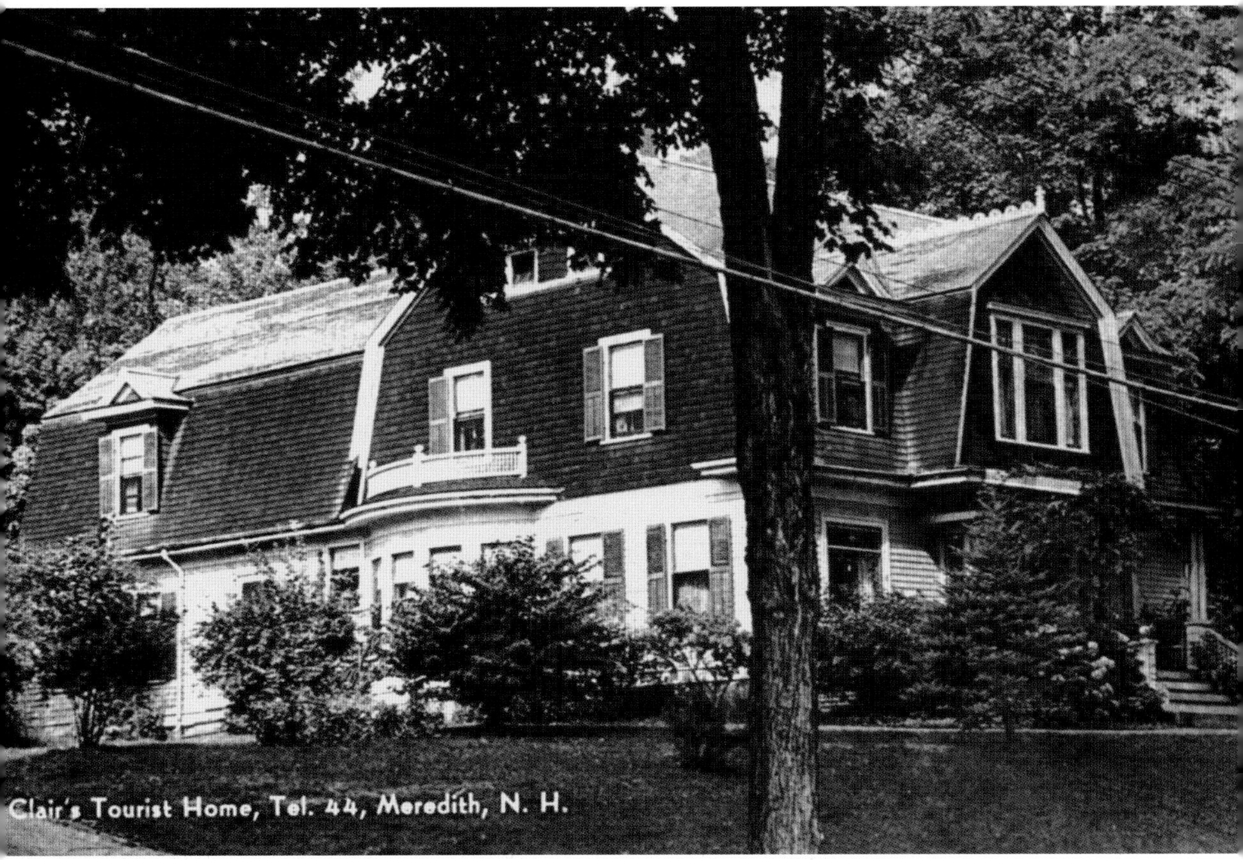

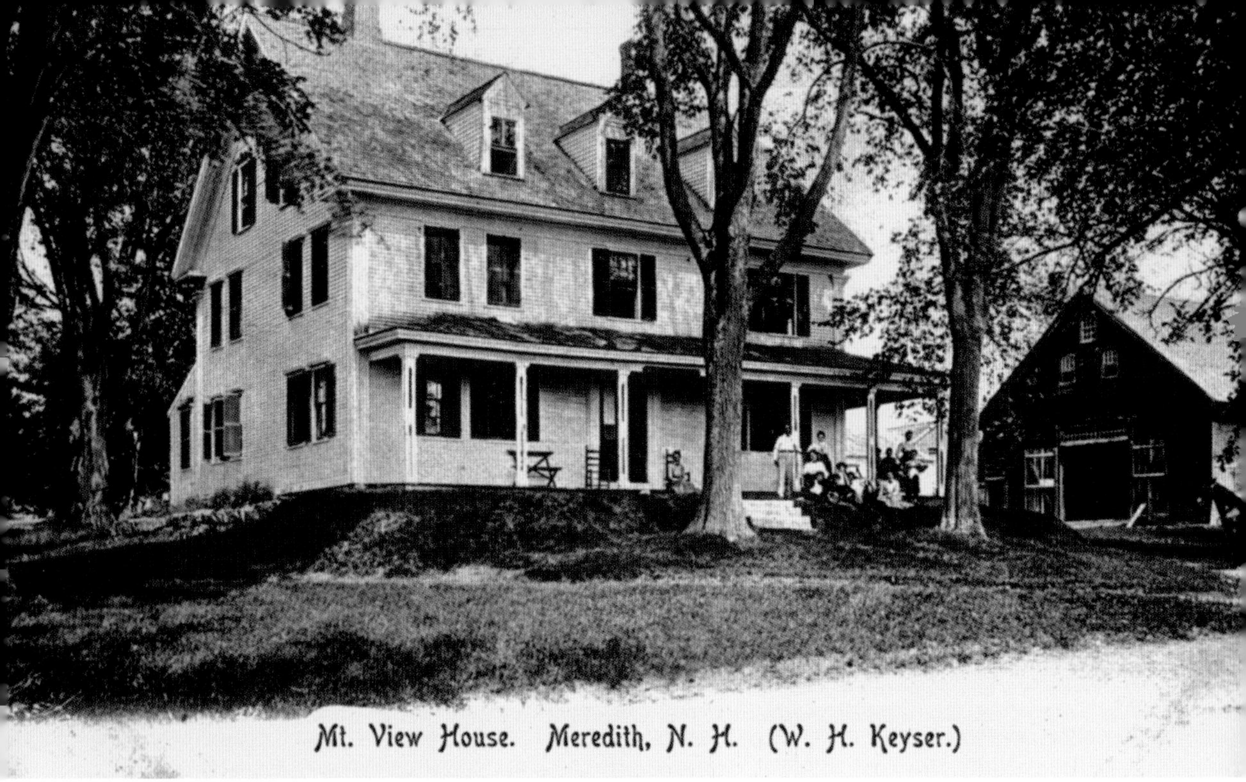

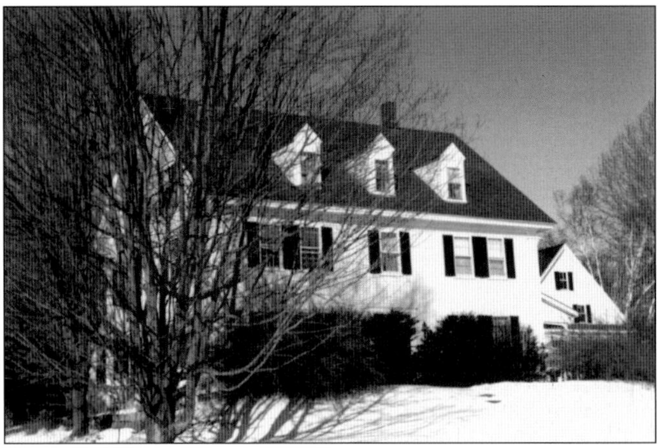

Mountain View House, also known as the Towle House, was built by John Towle. He and Charles Towle were the children of old Esquire Towle, who owned this large farmhouse, shaded by beautiful elms on the hill, near the junction of the old and new roads to Center Harbor (the old Center Harbor road and Route 25). During the early 1900s, this house was a boardinghouse known as the Webster House. In later years the property served as a guesthouse, a farm, and a gift shop. Today a it is a very fine private home.

Pictured here are the Inns at Mill Falls. The hosiery mill, which stood at what is now the intersection of Route 25 and Route 3, was destroyed by fire on December 28, 1889. A new mill was built, and a linen mill later occupied the property. That concern was subsequently replaced by an asbestos mill, which moved elsewhere in 1983. That year, Hampshire Hospitality Holdings bought the mill property. Many of the nonhistoric structures in the complex were razed, but the historic old mill was preserved. The mill was then reconstructed into a four-floor marketplace. Most of the original hand-hewn beams were saved and still exist in the building today. Two wings were constructed to accommodate a new restaurant. A half-ton copper cupola that had been atop a North Woodstock church was acquired and placed on the mill roof. A shopping plaza with three

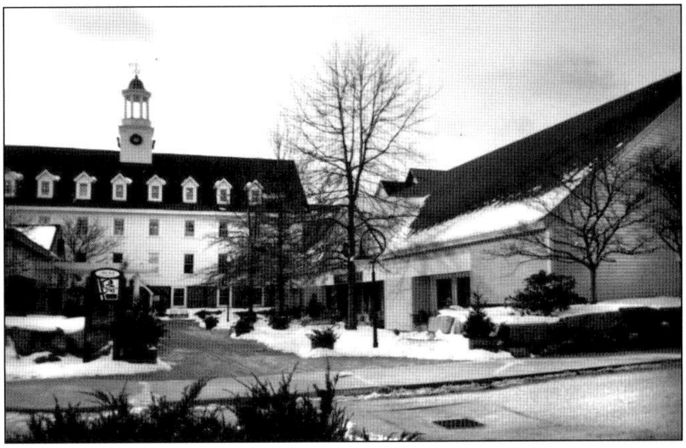

new retail buildings was created, and the magnificent 54-room Inns at Mill Falls was added to the central complex. The area was beautifully landscaped and the waterfall was exposed. The opening of the Mill Falls Marketplace was the end of the industrial chapter for Meredith, but just the beginning of a new era for the town.

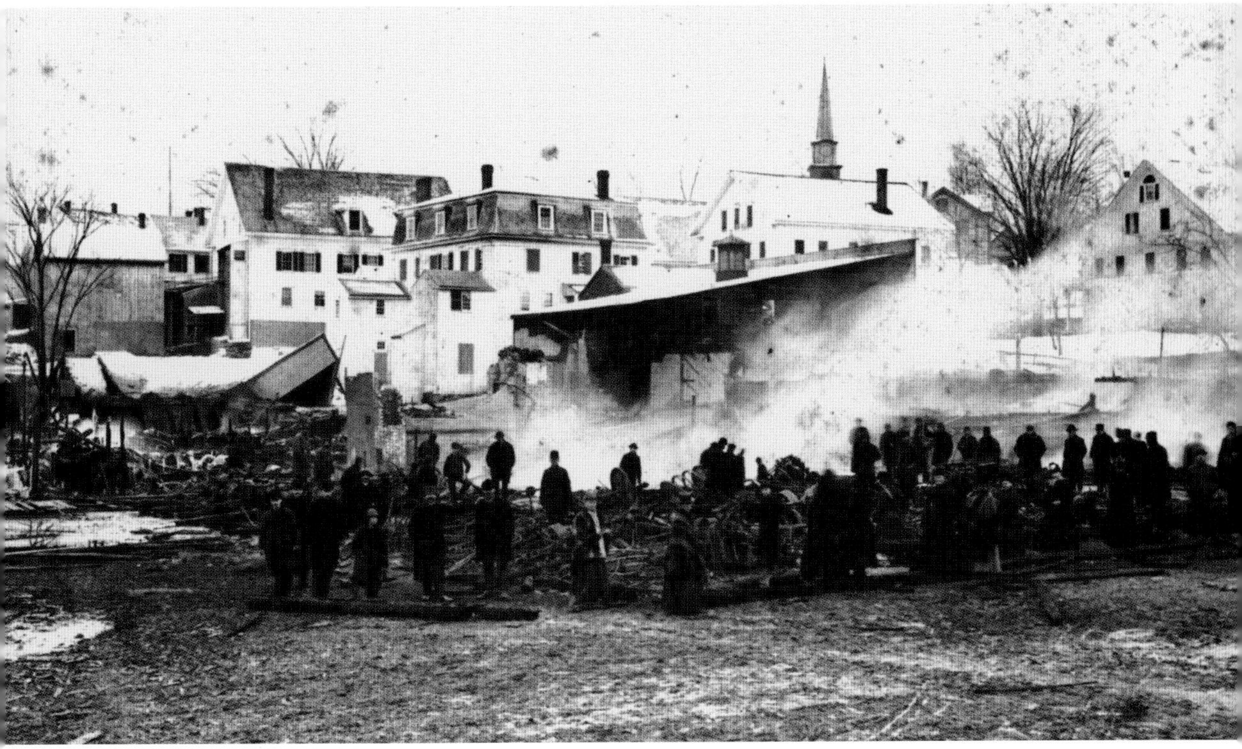

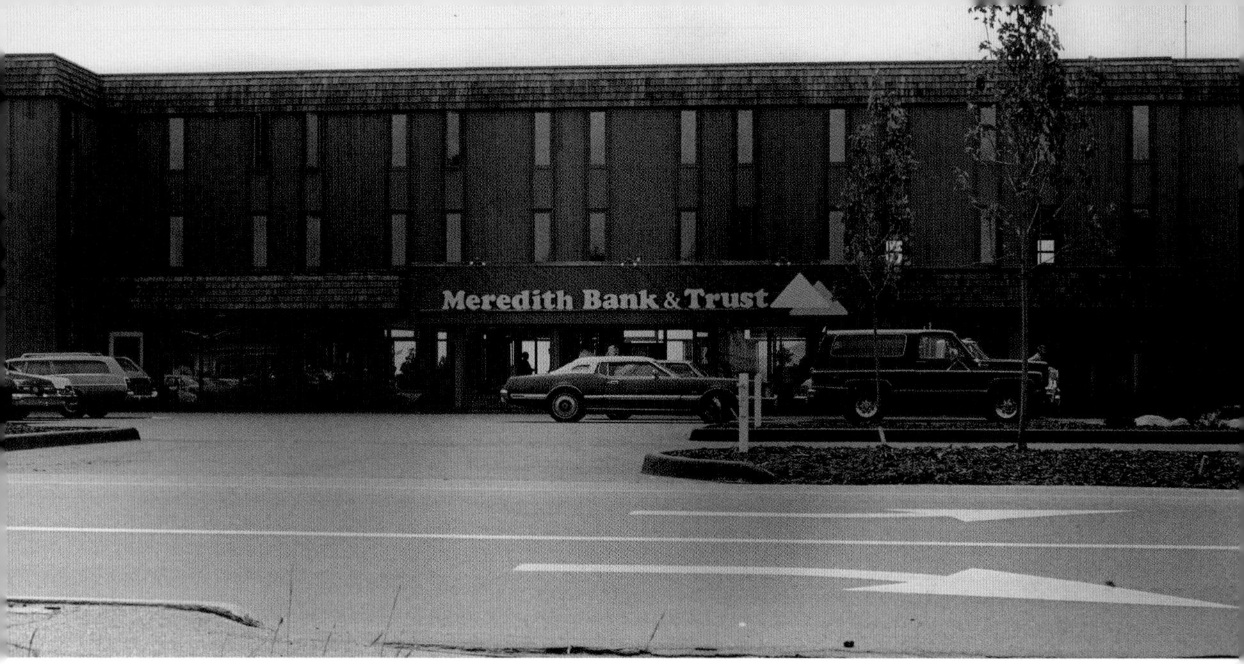

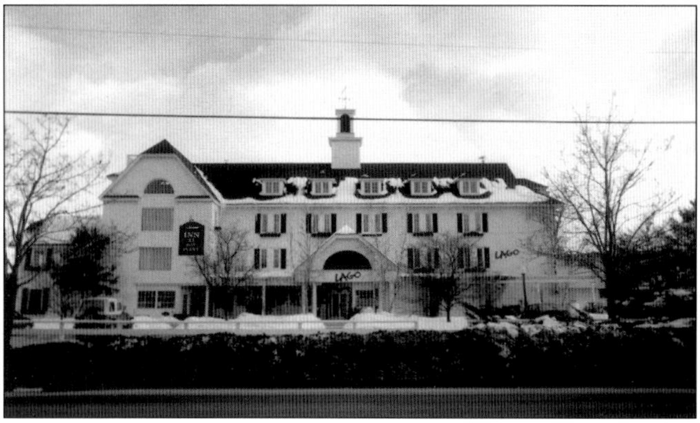

In 1968, Miles Israel and Nelson Piper purchased this lakeside property and constructed a three-story, flat-roofed office building. In 1993, the building came up for sale. Although the structure itself was rather undistinguished, it dominated one of the most visible and most desirable locations in town. Hampshire Hospitality Holdings, owners of the Inns at Mill Falls and the Mill Falls Marketplace, purchased the site. After a total reconstruction, the Inn at Bay Point and the Boathouse Grill were opened here in May 1995. Much remains the same today, except the restaurant is now known as Lago.

Carl Chase and his family opened a new restaurant in 1950 on Route 3, directly across from the town docks. In 1968, Chase transformed this property into the Country Towne House, a restaurant that remained in the Chase family until 1994, when it was sold to Hampshire Hospitality Holdings. A new inn was built and became part of the Inns at Mill Falls complex. It is now known as Chase House at Mill Falls. An added attraction in the Chase House is the Camp, a fine family restaurant.

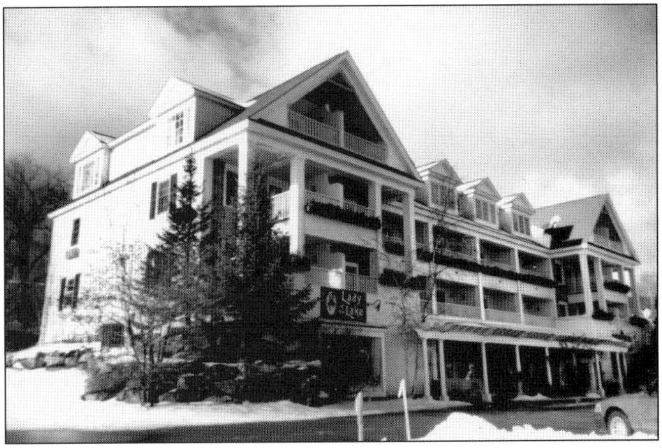

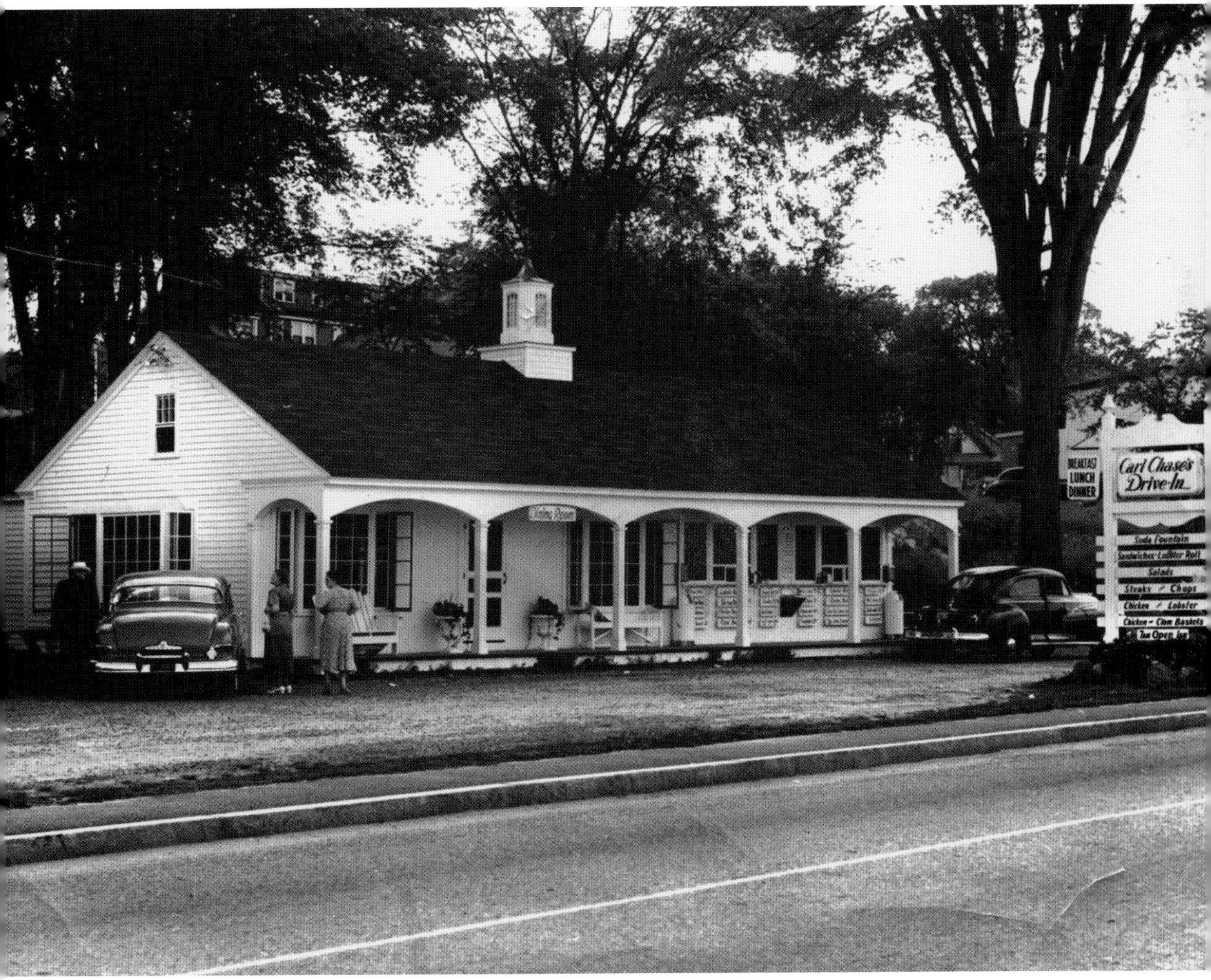

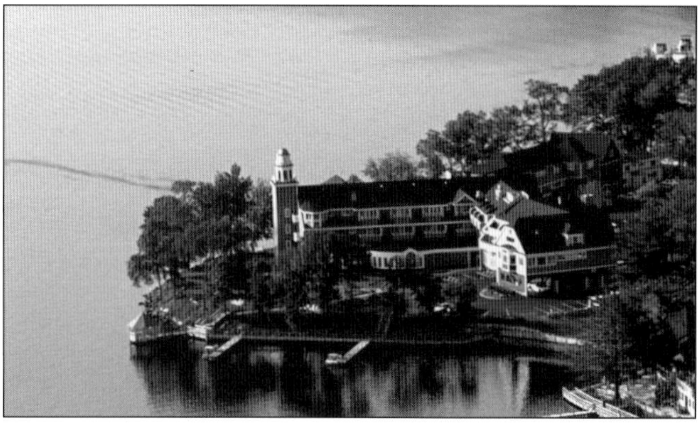

In 2003, after the St. Charles parish moved to a new facility, Hampshire Hospitality Holdings (HHH) acquired the old St. Charles church and land—one of the most desirable pieces of property on Lake Winnipesaukee. Rather than raze the church, HHH incorporated the structure into the design of Church Landing, constructed in the great shingled camp style of the 1880s. In May 2004, Church Landing opened its doors to the public. In addition to the spectacular new inn, Church Landing includes some 1,000 feet of new public walkway on the waterfront. This creates about three-quarters of a mile of adjoining public walkway along Lake Winnipesaukee, connecting Church Landing with the Town Docks (a restaurant), the Christmas Loft, two town parks, and the existing walkway system that extends past the Inn at Bay Point.

Located at the foot of the Center Harbor road (Route 25), the St. Charles Catholic Church and the Trinity Episcopal Church were both organized around 1900. The first church was known as the Chapel of the Holy Sepulchre, and was located on the Center Harbor road where Trinity Episcopal Church now stands. The Trinity Episcopal congregation moved into the former chapel after the Catholic parish moved to the lakeside location in the village. Today Rev. Robin Thomas Doller guides this small but active parish.

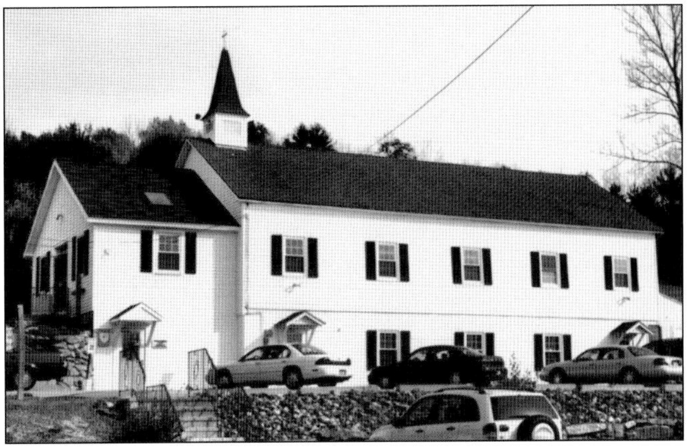

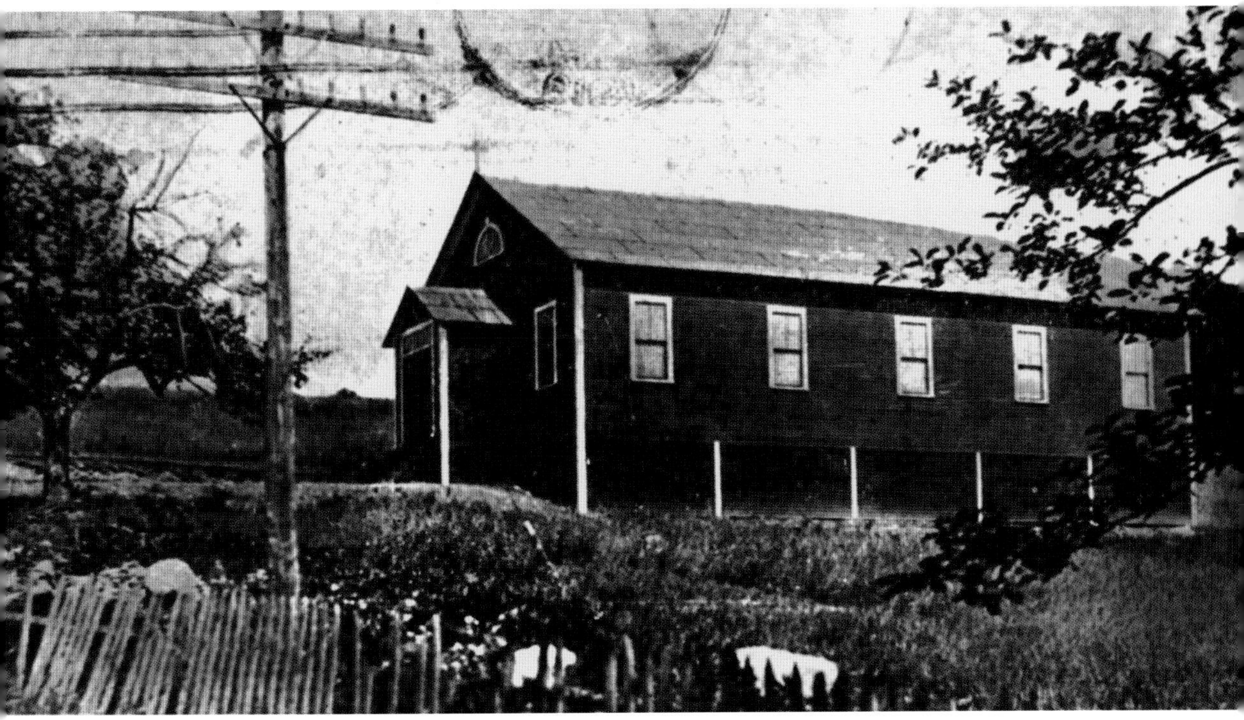

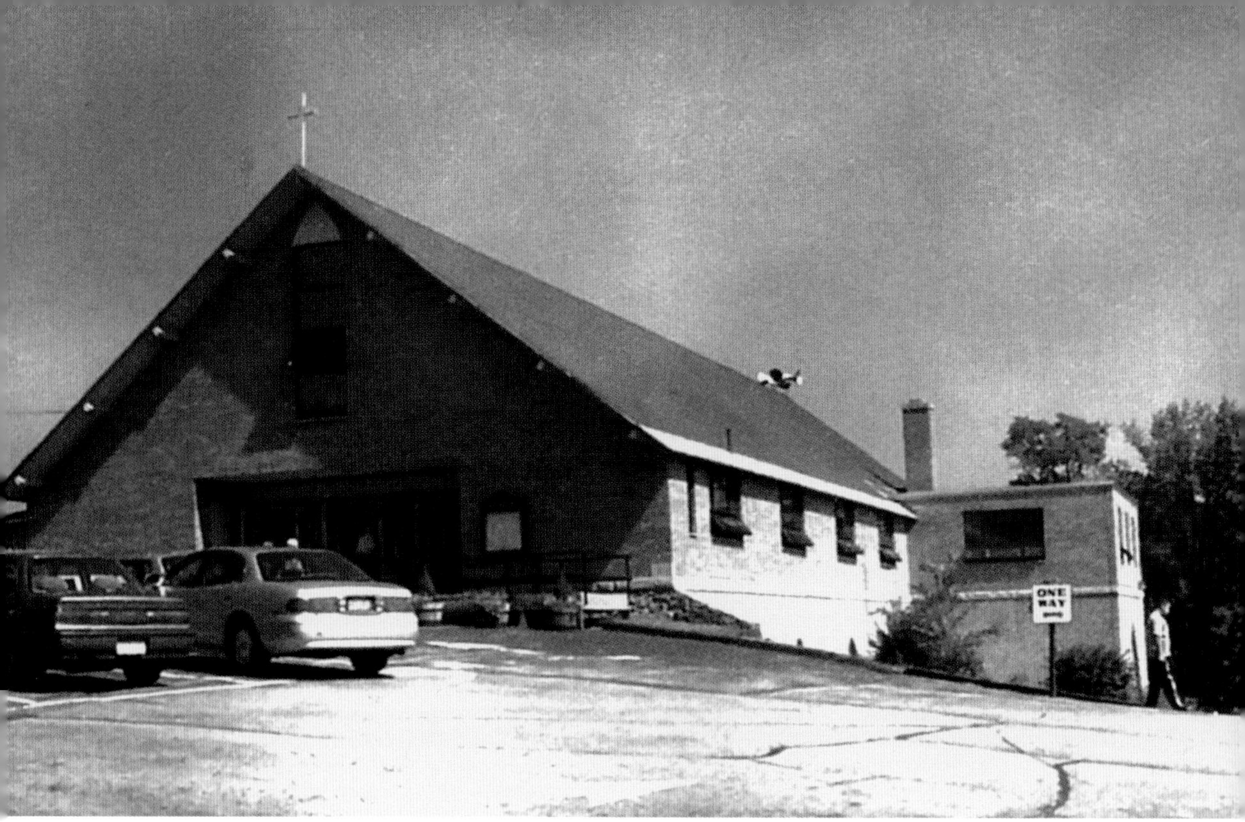

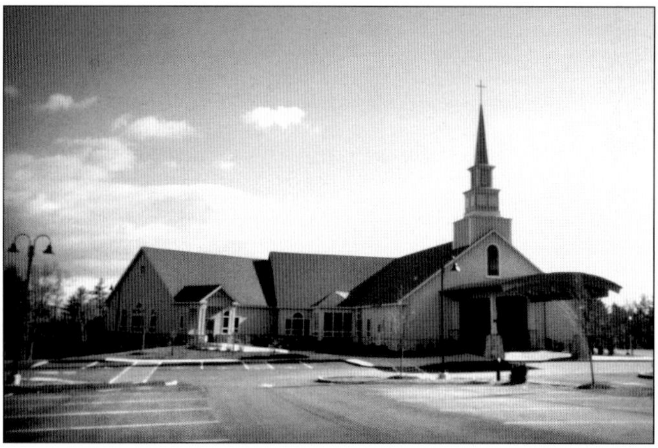

Pictured is St. Charles Catholic Church, on Meredith Bay. After leaving the Chapel of the Holy Sepulchre in the mid-1900s, the St. Charles congregation relocated to a house of worship in the village, on Route 3, across the highway from the Meredith Fire Station. In 2003, the church sold its property to Hampshire Hospitality Holdings, and the parish transferred to a new building on the Meredith–Center Harbor town line, on Route 25. Today, St. Charles Borromeo Catholic Church, with Rev. Richard B. Thompson as pastor, is a very active parish.

Seen here is the Meredith Center Baptist Church. The church was organized in 1810 by 15 devout worshipers. Under the leadership of Rev. Stephen Pitman and Rev. David Knowlton, it was called the Second Freewell Baptist Church of Meredith. The present church edifice was erected in 1831, and with Rev. Gordon Avery, the church continues to guide the faithful.

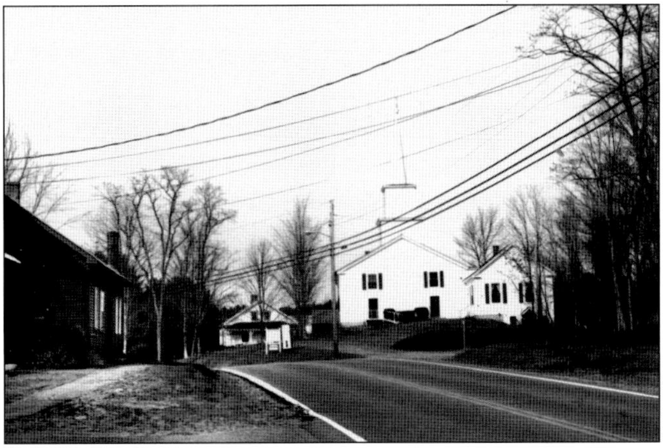

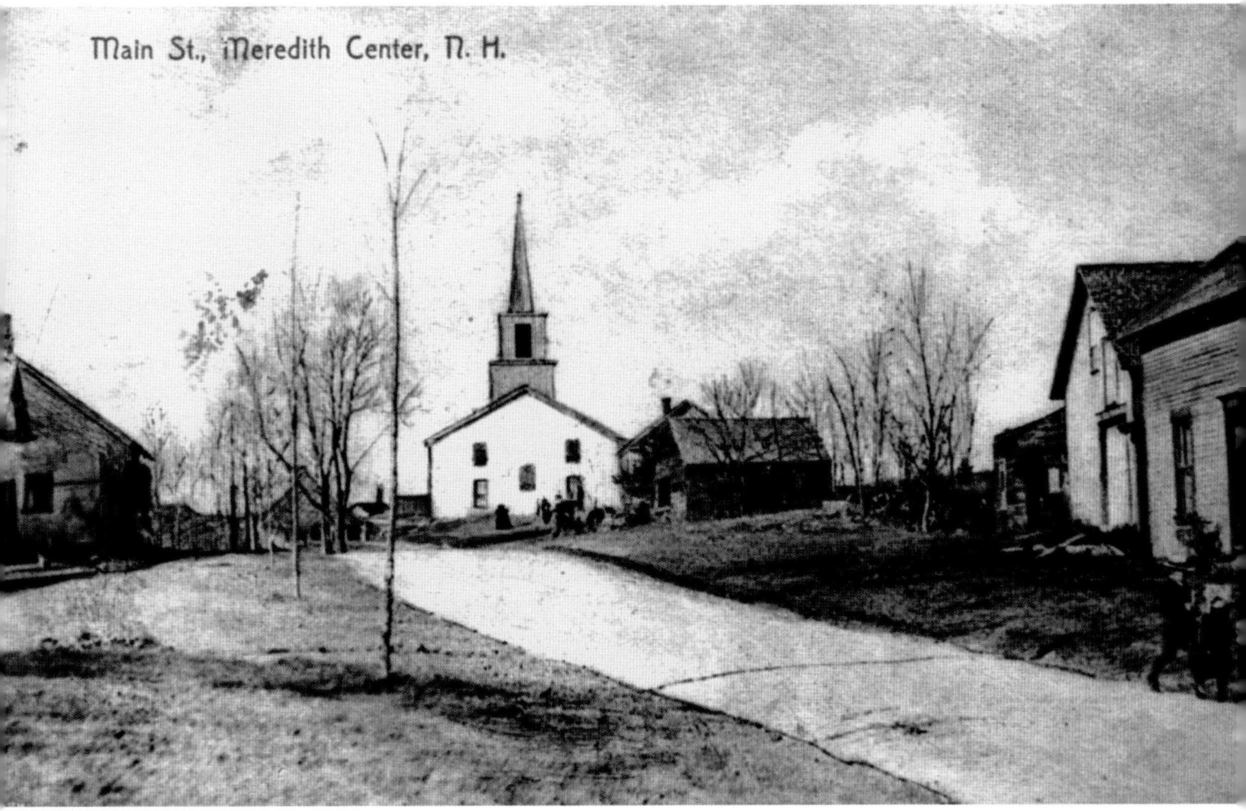

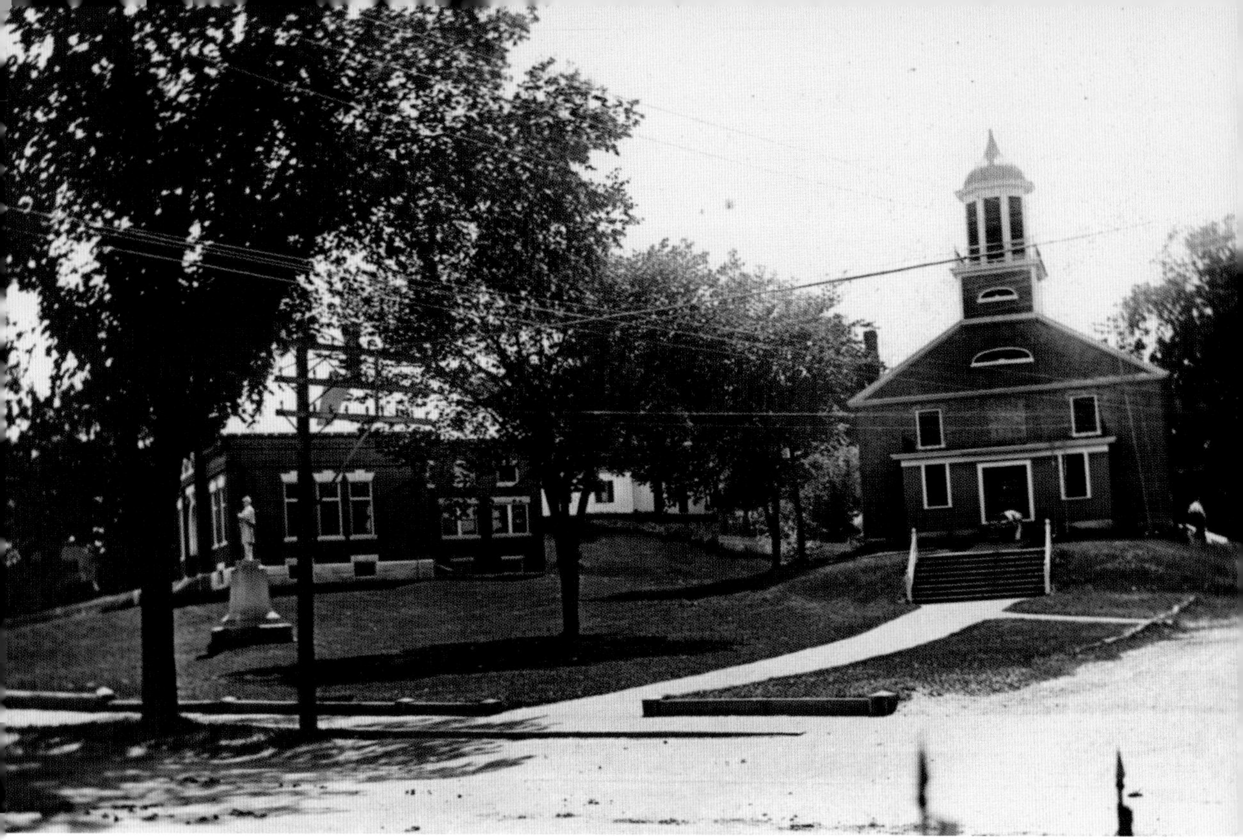

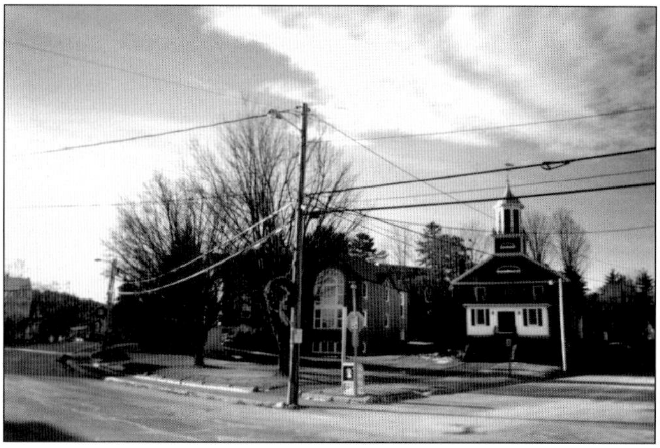

The Second Baptist Church Society is located in the center of the village on Main Street. The church was incorporated on December 14, 1797, and held services for a large and active parish until May 20, 1831. In 1834, it was decided that a meetinghouse of brick would be built "upon a rock" on a 40-by-50-foot parcel of land in the village. For several years, there was no settled pastor, until Rev. Samuel Cook was ordained; he remained to serve there until 1845. In 1860, the title Second Baptist Church was changed to Meredith Village Baptist Church. Today, a very active parish, under the leadership of Rev. Stephen Neill, continues the tradition of Christian worship. Over the years, very few changes have occurred. On the front lawn of the Baptist church and library stands the Maj. E. E. Beede monument, dedicated to the 12th New Hampshire Volunteer Regiment, which served during the Civil War.

Located on St. James Street is the Advent Christian Church. Prior to 1840, the church started in Meredith in a little building on Boardman Hill, on Meredith Neck. Later, when the attendance waned, meetings were held in the village in the old Grand Army of the Republic hall (in the Nutting Block) and in Ladd Hall. The current church is located on St. James Street. Today this beautiful edifice is known as the Meredith Calvary Bible Church (Advent Christian), and Rev. Roger Brown serves as pastor.

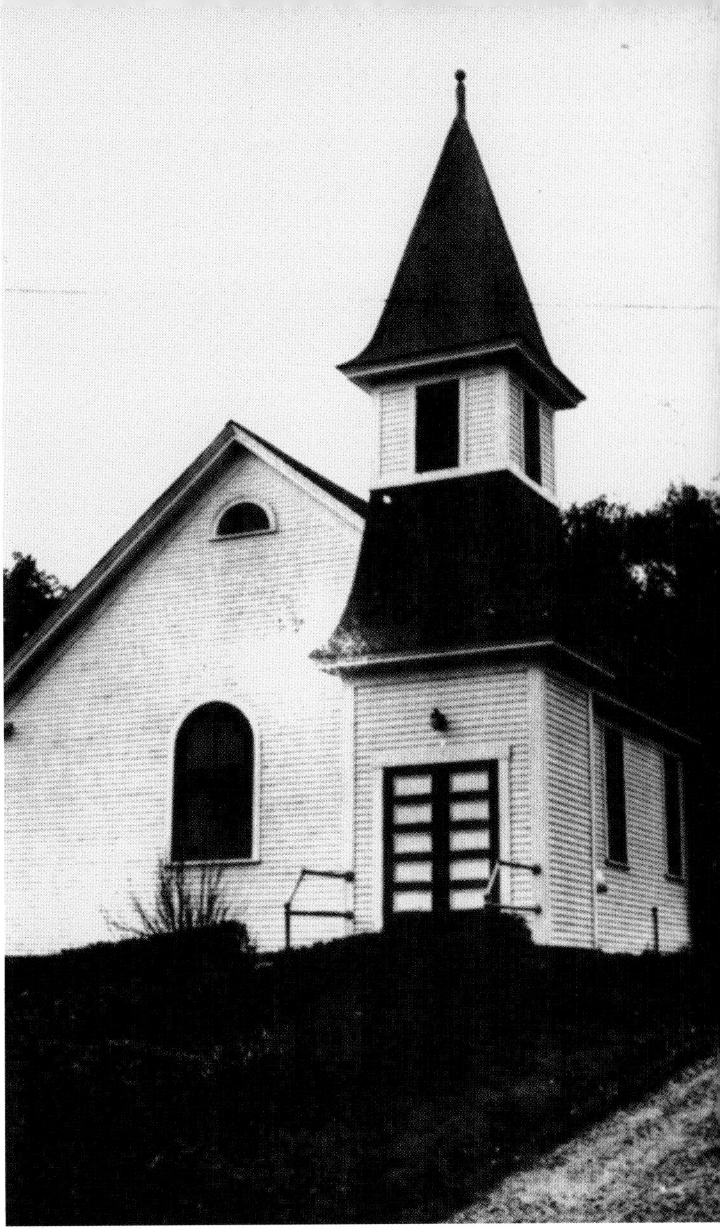

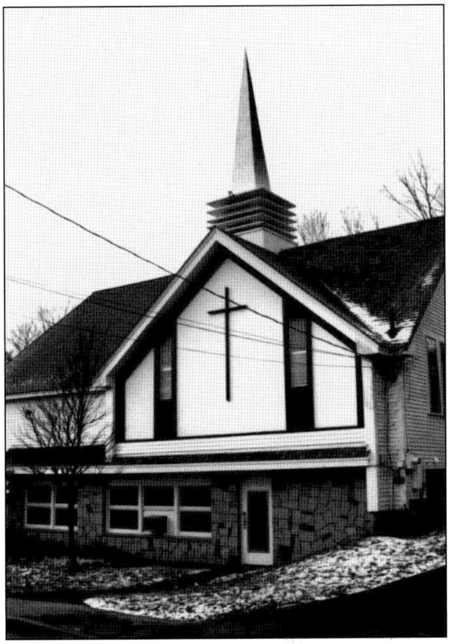

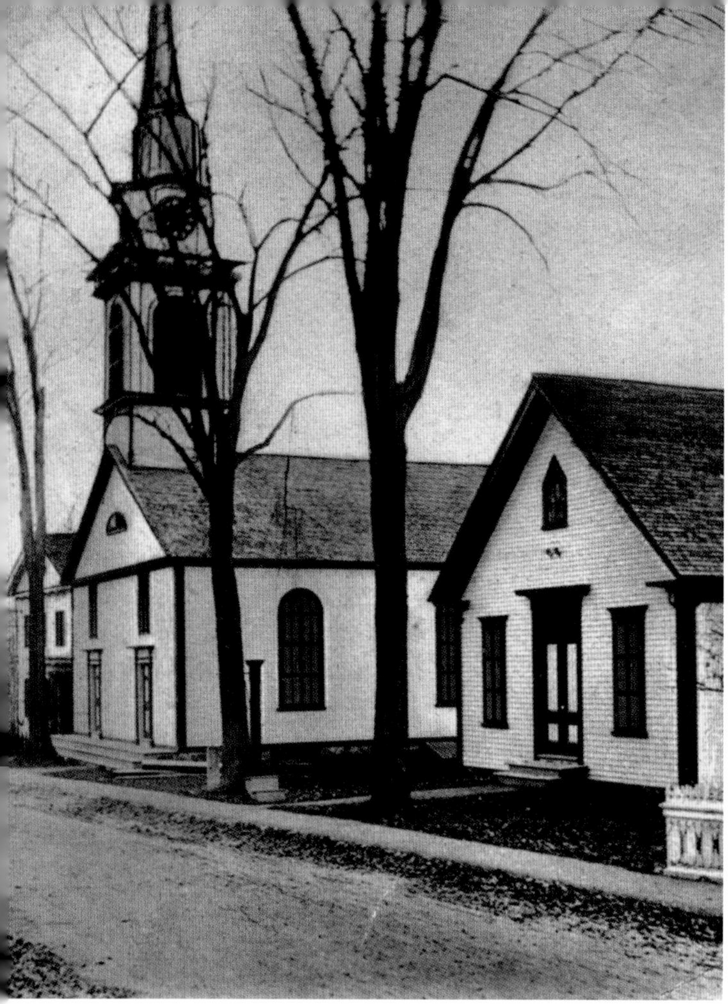

The Congregational church is located on Highland Street in the center of the village. The First Congregational Society in Meredith was incorporated by a special act of the legislature in 1817 and was authorized to transact all its legal business. The first meetinghouse was situated about a mile from Meredith Village on the Center Harbor road, near the Towle place. On April 20, 1831, the name First Congregational Church in Meredith was adopted, and Rev. Joseph Lane was installed as pastor. In 1833, a meetinghouse was erected near the Frank Clough home, just opposite Clough Park on Winnipesaukee Street. The church remained there until 1842, when it was moved to its present location on Highland Street. Today, this congregation (now known as United Church of Christ) has Rev. Dr. Russell Rowland as its pastor.

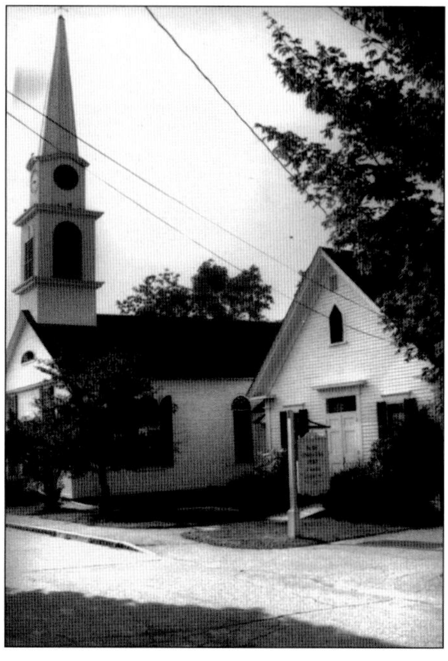

The Bear Island Church is pictured here. During the 1920s, a number of island residents wanted to have a place of worship on the island. Rt. Rev. Edward Melville Parker (bishop of the Episcopal Diocese of New Hampshire) and Rev. Kenneth Ripley Forbes wanted a summer chapel to be constructed at the "highest point on Bear Island"—an observatory tower built in 1900 by Ellery C. Mansfield. The tower was repaired and enclosed. The sanctuary was built of local stone and was erected between May and July 1927. On July 31, 1927, the chapel was dedicated by Bishop Dallas in memory of Bishop Parker. The church was intended to be a religious center for the residents of Bear Island regardless of religious affiliation. The church is now used for nondenominational services during the summer months.

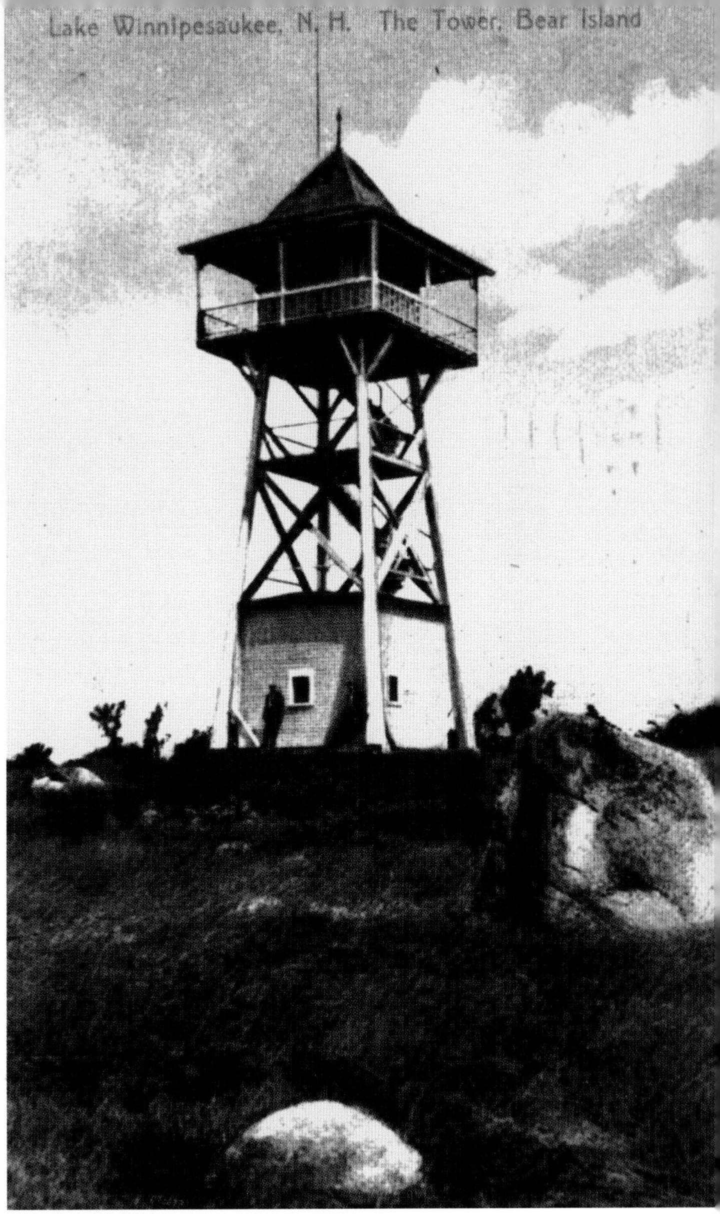

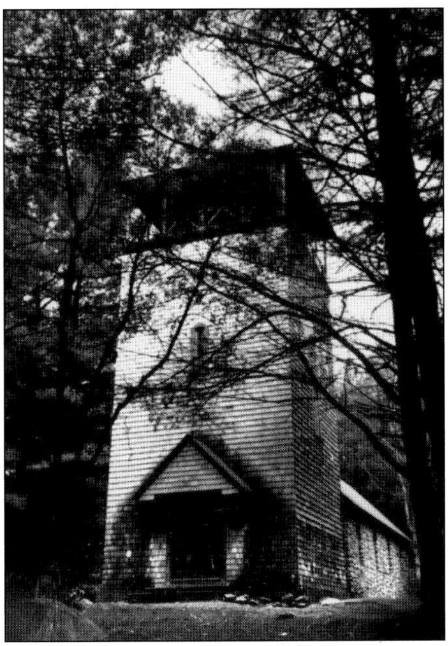

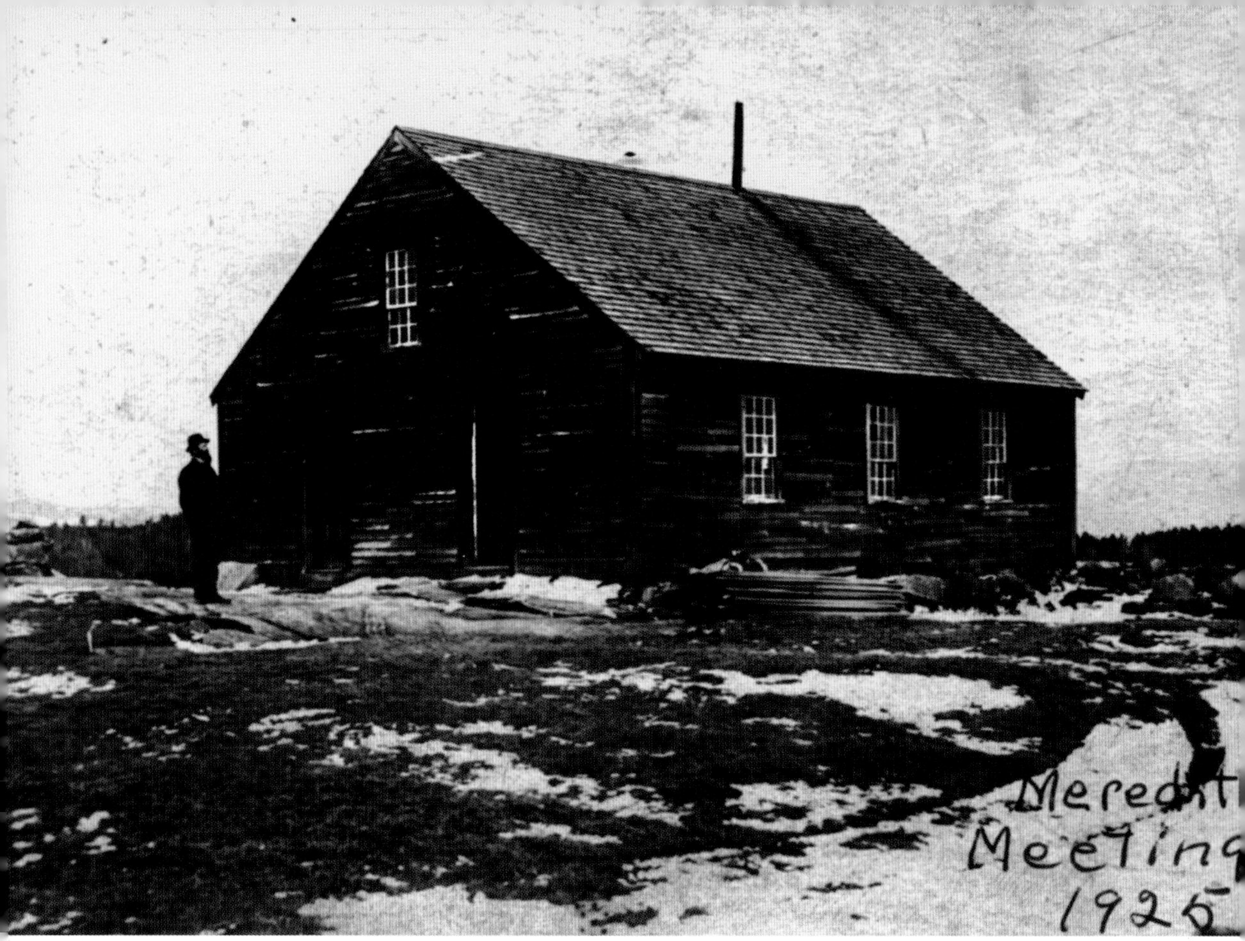

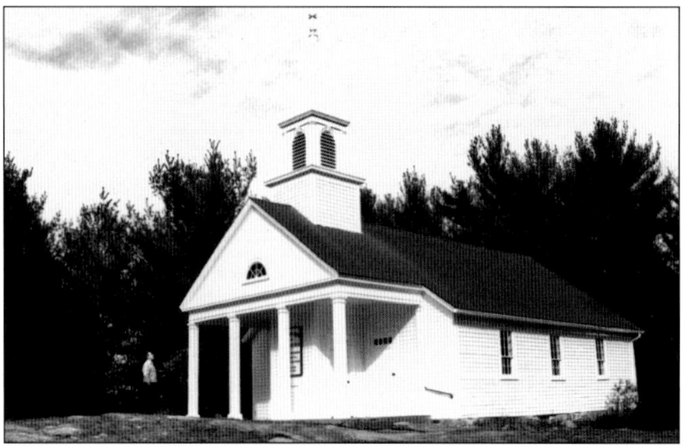

The Meredith Neck Meetinghouse was constructed in 1839 by Neck residents who wished to be separated from the Village Free Will Baptist congregation. As late as the second or third decade of the 20th century, the church was a center of religious worship and social activities for the community. At a cost of nearly $3,000, the building was given a portico, a steeple, and a coat of white paint in 1955. Except for an occasional marriage or funeral, the church is now used only in August, mainly for services. The bell that was recently hung in the steeple dates from the late 1800s and was originally used in the side-wheeler *Mount Washington*. The older picture shows John C. Young of Lakeport, and the present-day view shows the author standing in the same spot.

Pictured is Meredith High School, located on Main Street. Providing education for the children has been a challenge to the citizens of Meredith since the town's incorporation in 1768. The first schools were the one-room district schools. Around 1875, Ebenezer and Cassandra (Swasey) Stevens donated property for a new village school, which accommodated all the village public school grades. The schoolhouse was the center of local education until it was replaced in 1914 by a larger brick school that became known as Meredith High School, and then later became the Humiston Elementary School (named for John Humiston, a leading teacher in the town). Today, the Inter-Lakes School District administrative office is housed in this building. Meredith High School was active until 1958, when a new facility was built one mile north of the village on Route 25 East. Today, this new building is known as the Inter-Lakes Junior-Senior High School, which serves the towns of Meredith, Center Harbor, and Sandwich.

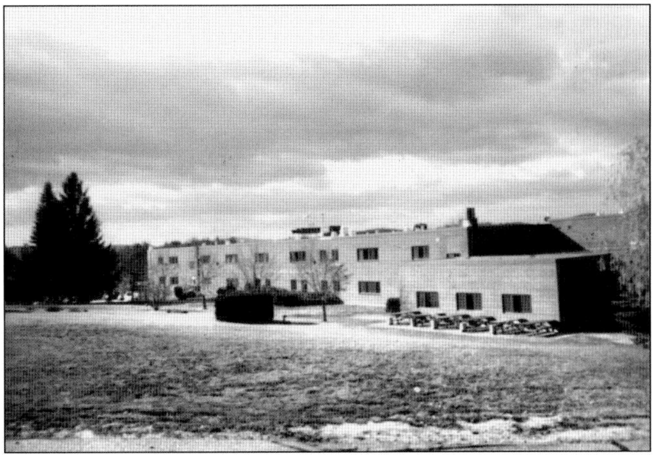

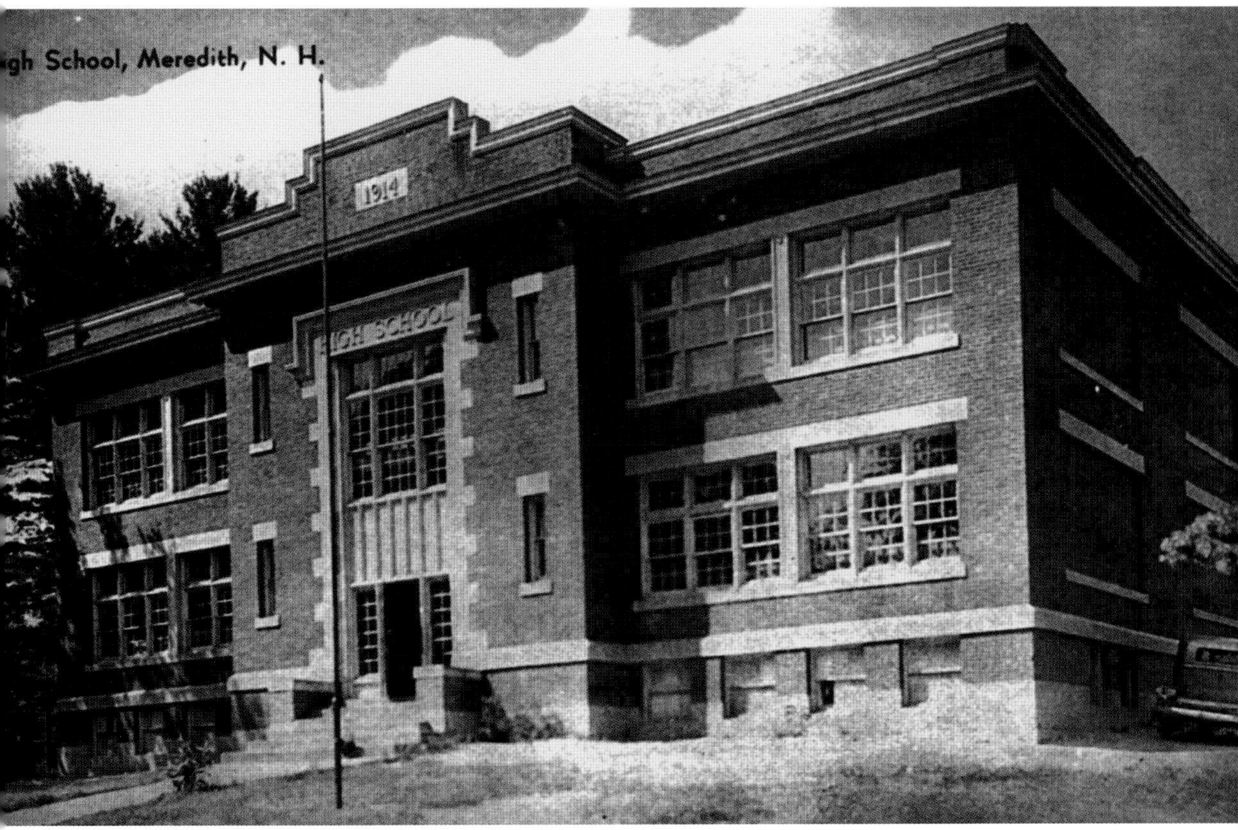

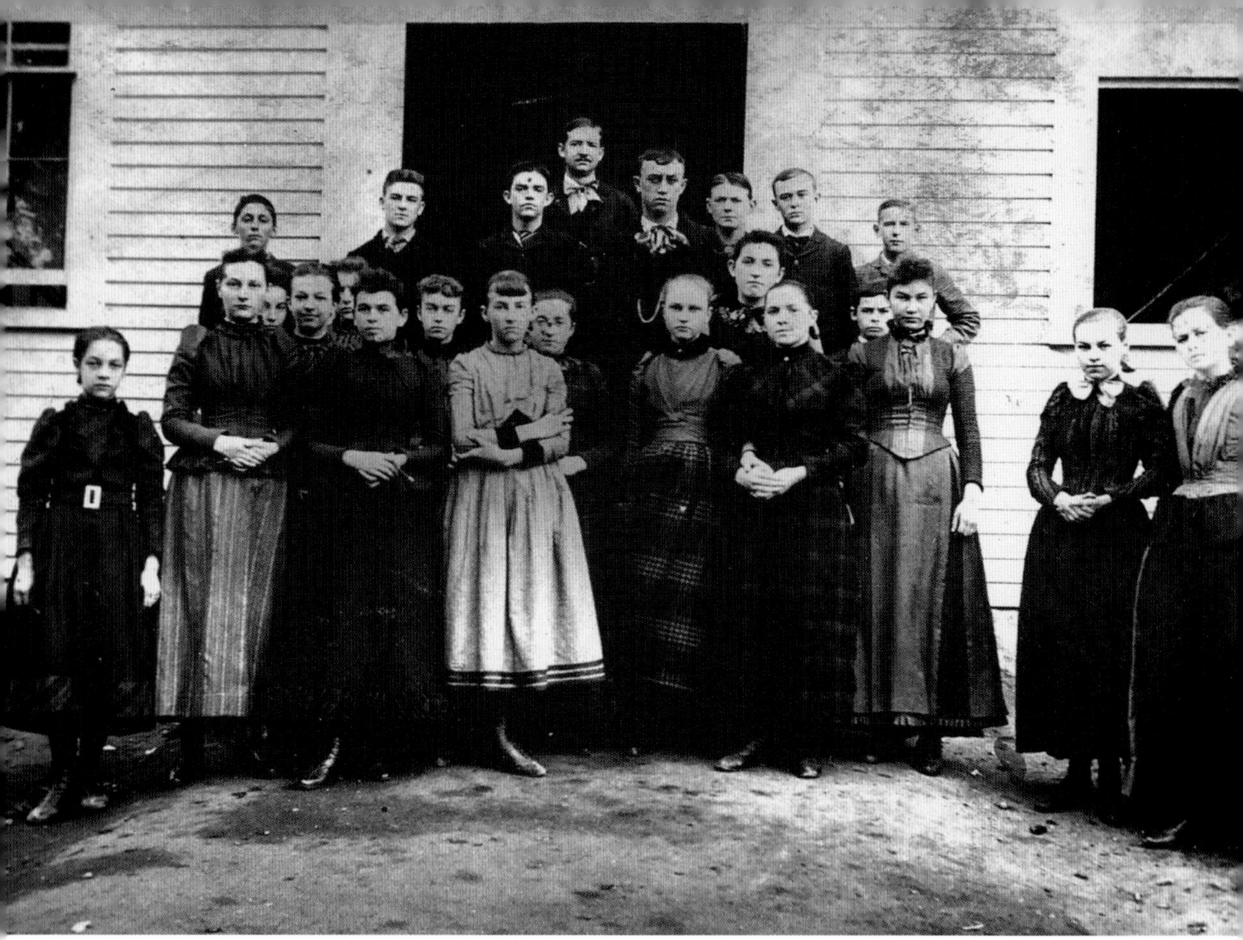

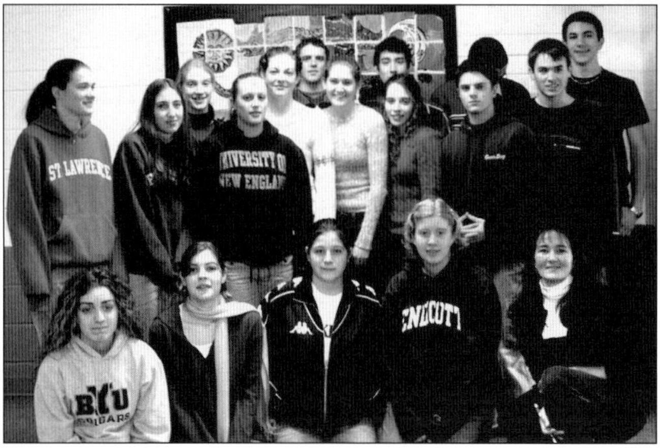

These students from the Meredith High School class of 1891 include Ada Burleigh, Carl Mansfield, Almon Hayer, Joseph Clark, Bessie Clough, and Florence Green. The present-day photograph shows a group of honor students from the Inter-Lakes Junior-Senior High School class of 2003–2004 and their teacher. From left to right are the following: (first row) Abby Billin, Cassie Hawkins, Elsie Benoit, Amanda Peaslee, and Mrs. O'Connell; (second row) Greta Olafsen, Sarah Stevens, Krystin Bowcutt, Allie Walton, Kaitlyn O'Neil, Kelsey Read, Kelsey O'Neil, Mark Bascom, Katelyn Michaud, Nick Connell, Kevin Krisak, Gary Lemay, and Paul Reese.

Shown is the Meredith High School baseball team of 1926. The team did quite well under the coaching of John Humiston. The players of the Inter-Lakes varsity baseball team of 2004 were dedicated and committed to their game. Derek Horne, Thomas Harrison, Josh Gentes, and Jeff Trent showed great leadership during their four years with the team.

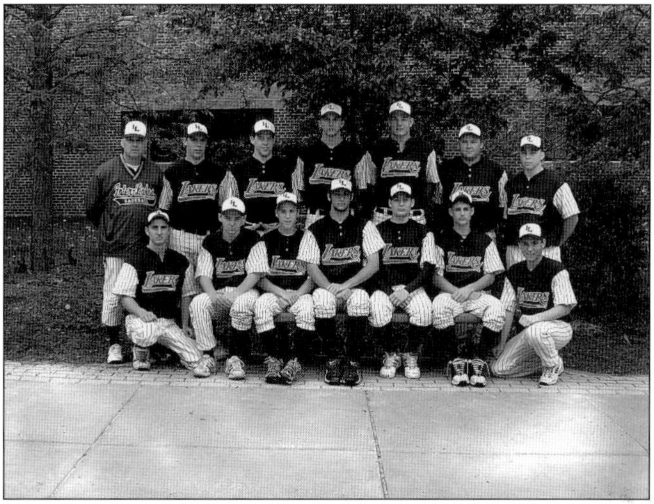

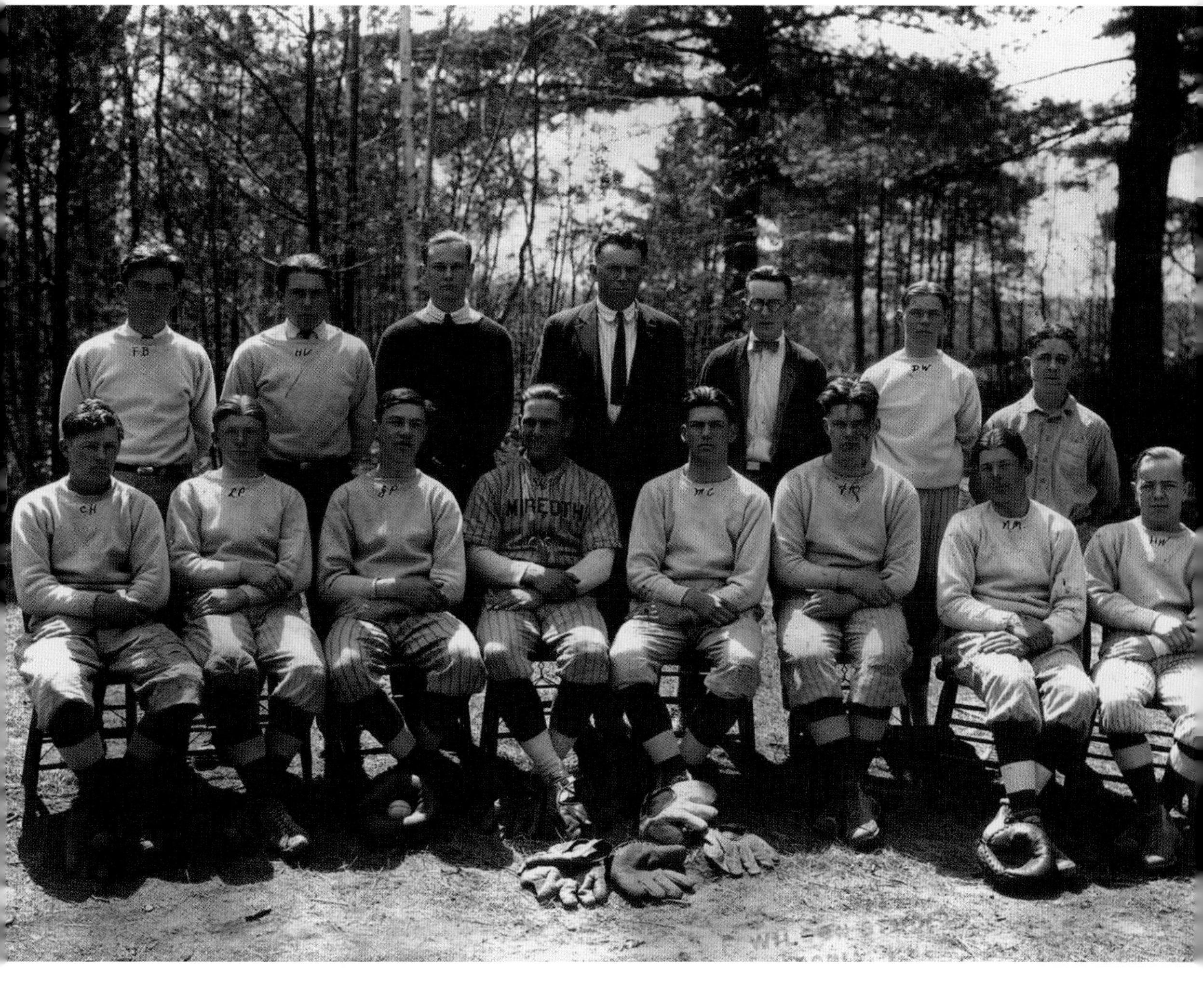

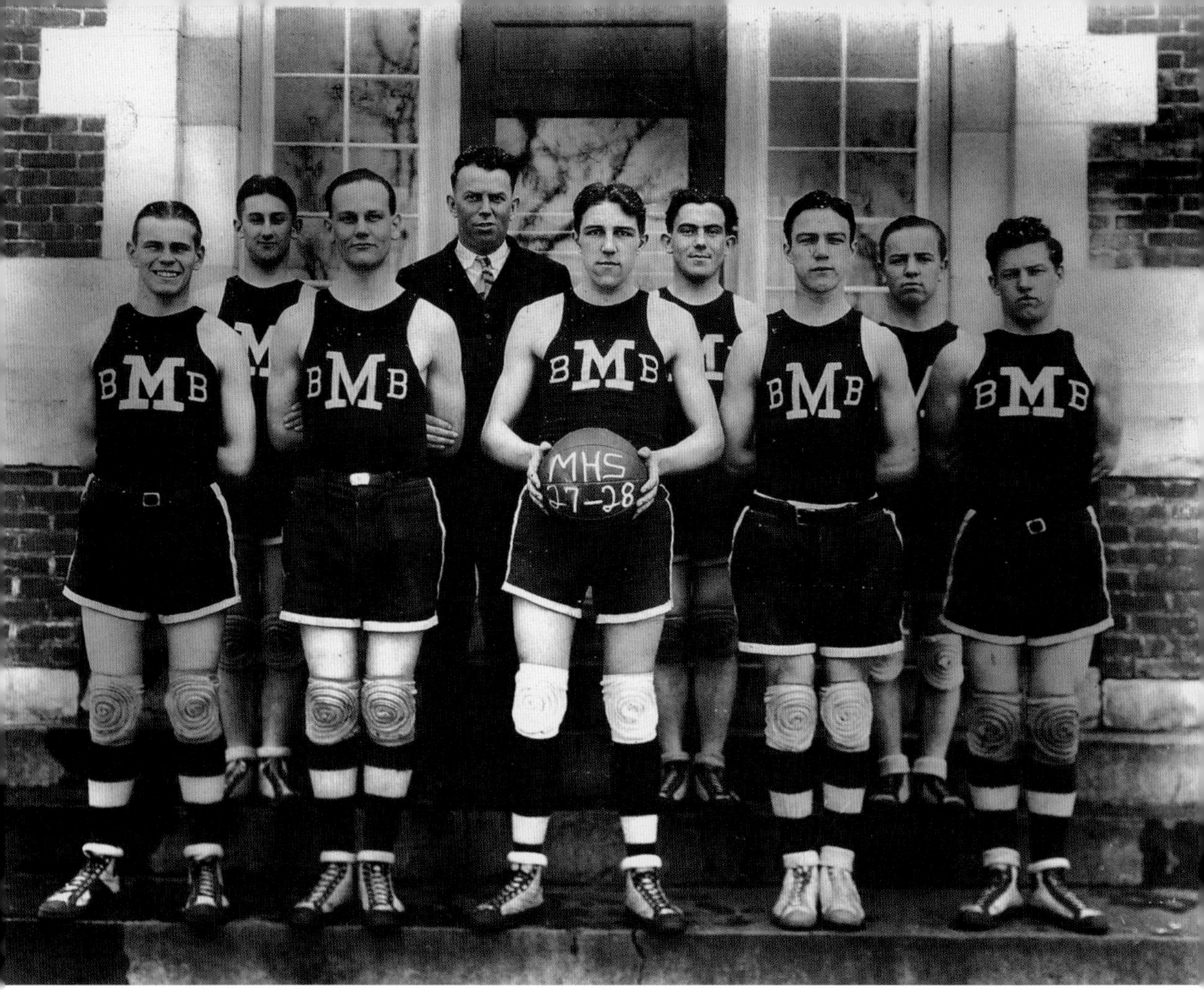

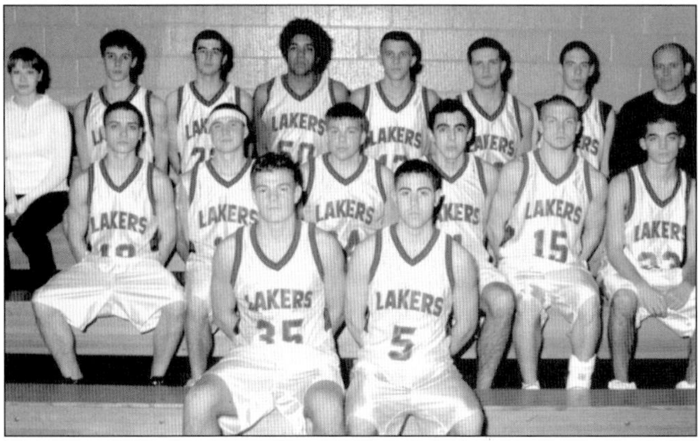

Pictured is the Meredith High School basketball team of the 1927–1928 school year. The team had a good season under the leadership of their coach, John Humiston. The Inter-Lakes varsity basketball team of 2003–2004, the defending state champions, had another victorious year. The team finished with a record of 19 wins and 2 losses. Seniors Jeff Carpenter, Calvin Akers, Jaimon Hancock, Tim Prescott, Chris Welch, Wes Thomas, and Jason Haines led the Lakers squad that year.

The Meredith Fire Department is pictured in the 1880s. Before 1895, a two-story wooden building in Corporate Square (now the back parking lot for the Inns at Mill Falls) was used as the town's first fire station. The department was established with the following proclamation: "Luke Fernald, Joseph Dodge, David Corliss, Jr., Nathaniel G. Corliss and John Busiel have given notice that we and our associates have formed ourselves into a company, to be known by the name of the First Fire Engine Company of Meredith village." The state legislature approved the formation of the department on July 1, 1831. In the early 1950s, the new fire station on Route 3 was built to accommodate the growing needs of the community.

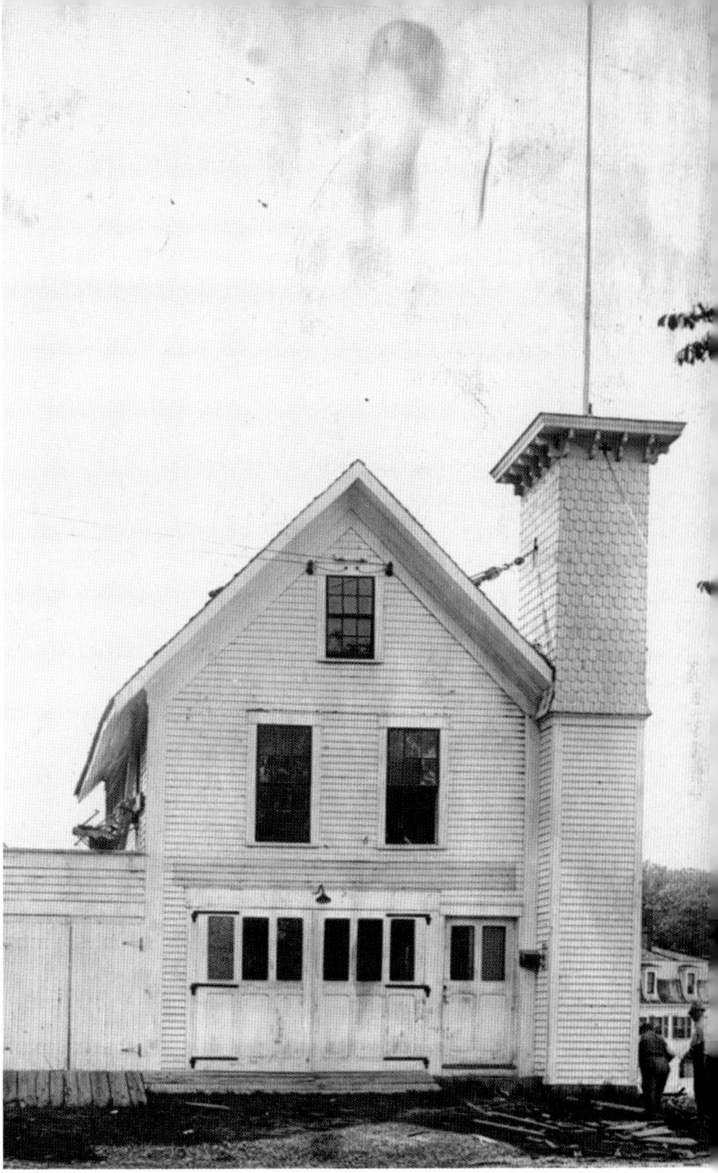

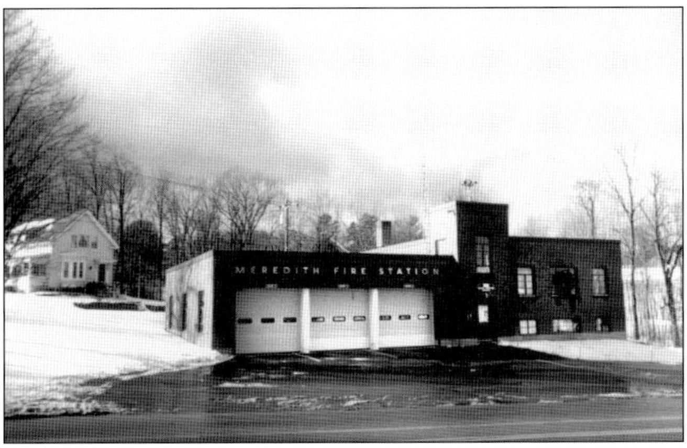

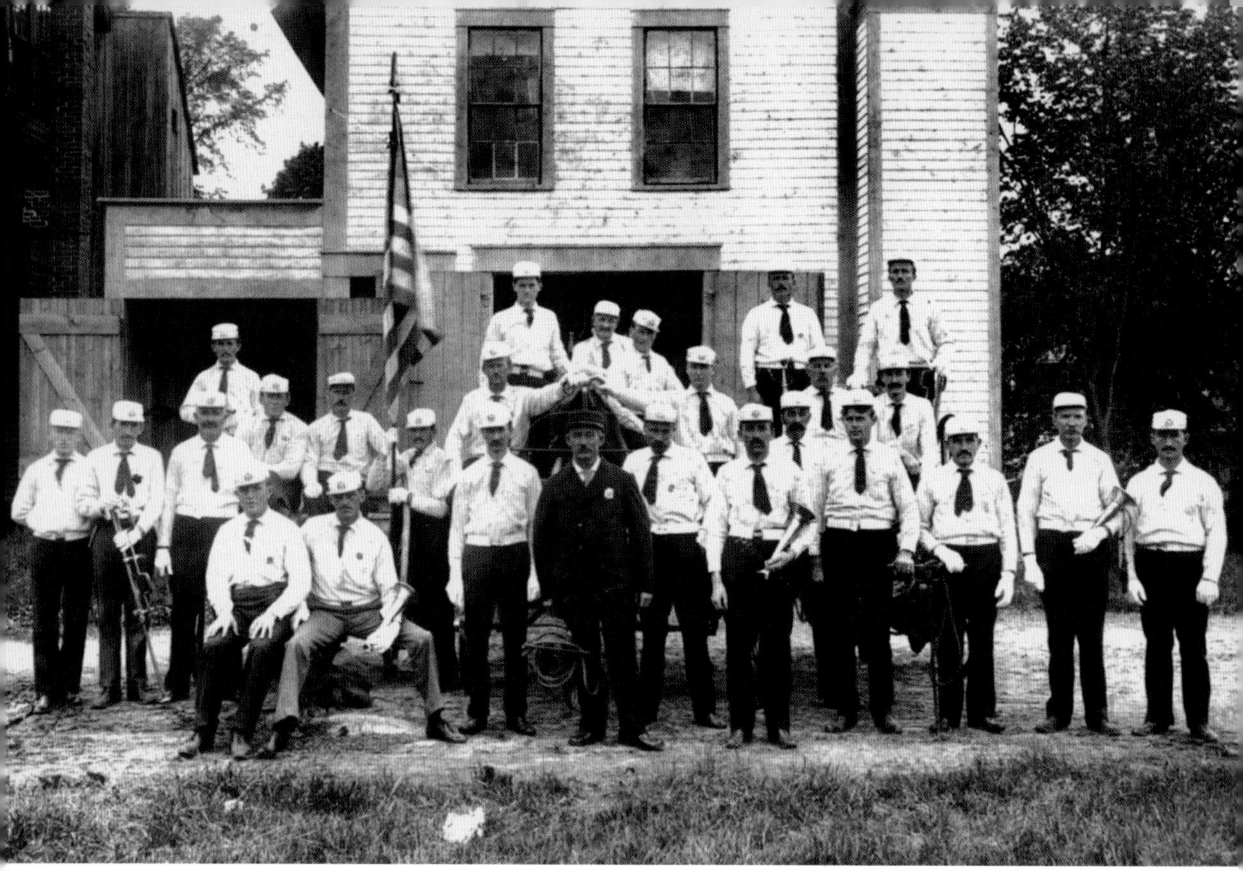

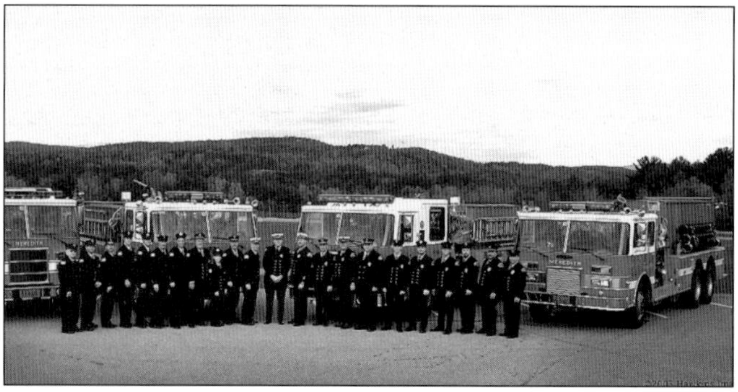

Since the origin of the Meredith Fire Department in 1895, the force has steadily developed throughout the years. In the early picture, the man at front center is Himes Jones, fire chief from 1895 to 1906. The man holding a speaking tube is Harry Dow, deputy chief. Dow served as chief from 1906 to 1907. The members of the present-day fire department are, from left to right, James Rushton, Chris Plancon, Andrew Daigneau, Garrett Palm, Jason Cornelissen, Norman McGuigan, Donald Smith, Harold Currier, Sandra Ambrose, Harold Denison Jr., Thomas Joslin, Charles Palm, Andre Kloetz, Carl Smith, Steven Bennett, David Parker, Kris Kloetz, Nick Durand, Tom Range, William Taggett, Jay Haines, and Bev Lapham. These dedicated men and women risk their lives protecting the life and property of the citizens of Meredith and the Lakes Region.

This 1880s photograph shows workmen in front of the shook and lumber company, with Meredith Bay in the background. This business was important to the community, as it afforded employment for many people. The industry also provided a convenient market for much of the timber felled throughout the Lakes Region.

Chapter 4

Industry and Town Services

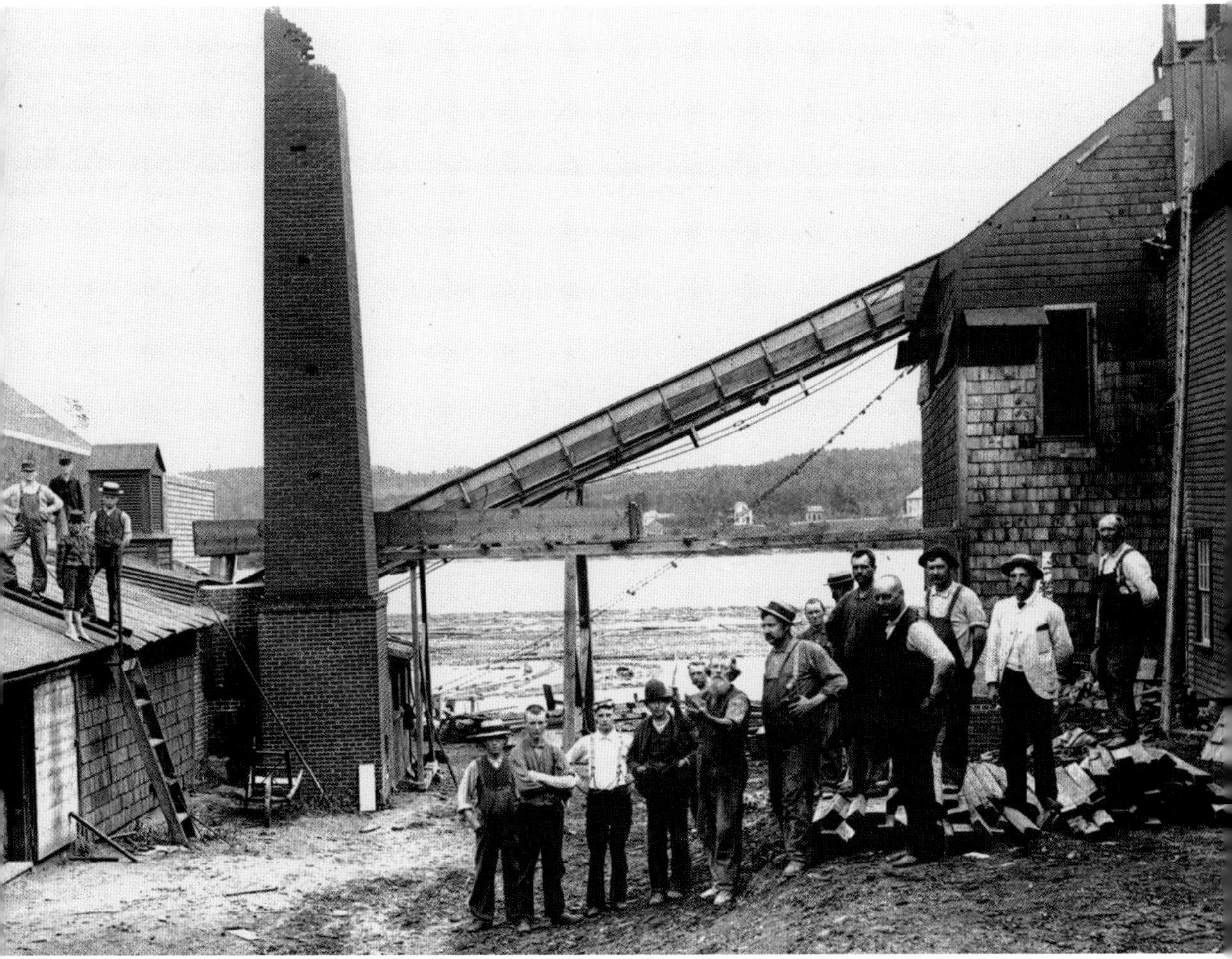

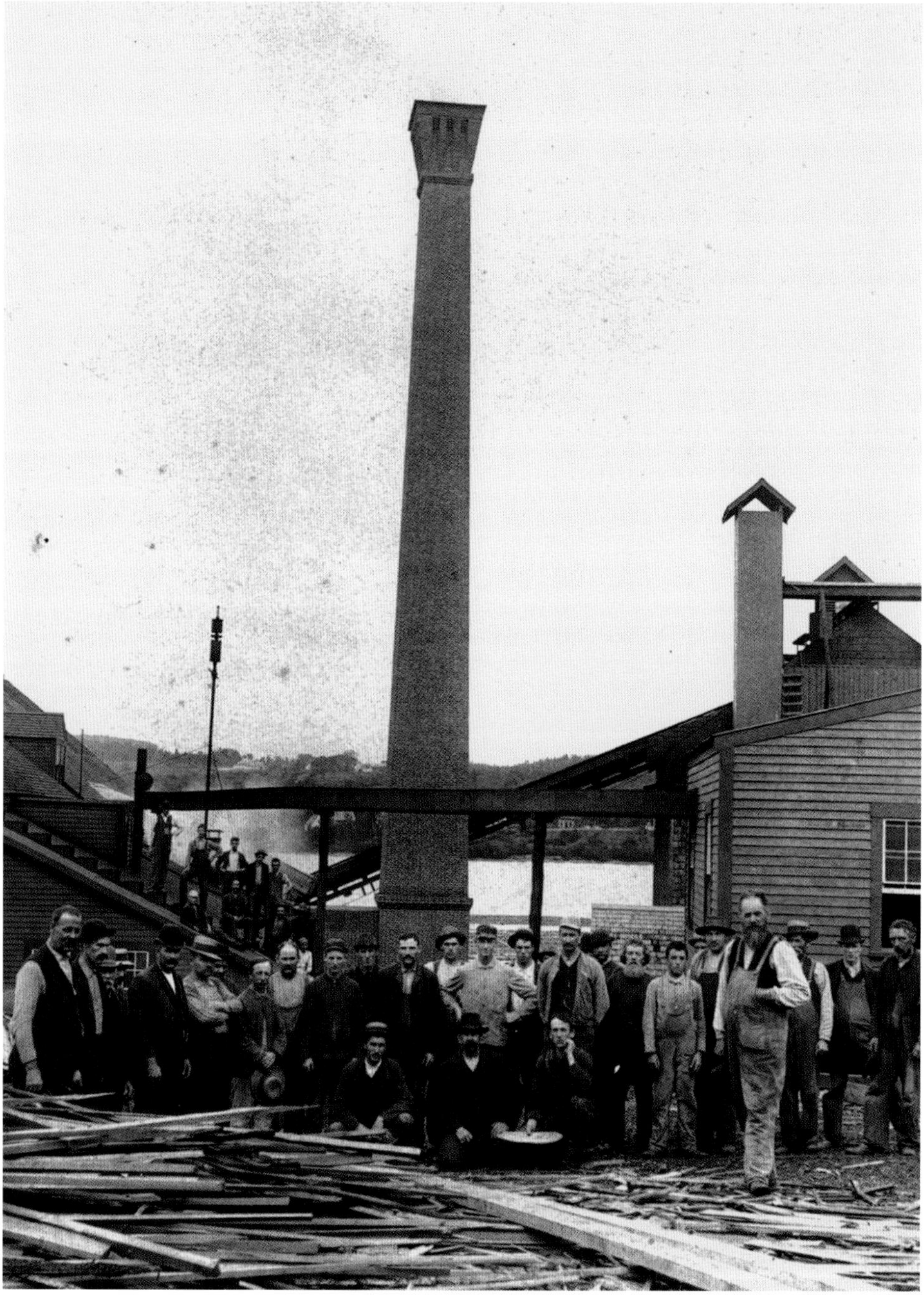

Nearly all the timber used by the shook and lumber company was towed to Meredith via the small steamers that plied the waters of Lake Winnipesaukee. About 60 workers were employed at the mill.

These photographs allow for a perfect then-and-now comparison of the shook and lumber mill on Meredith Bay. The company was purchased by Dodge and Bliss (a New Jersey company) and was in existence from about 1860 to 1912. The property later became the location of St. Charles Church. In 2003, after the St. Charles Parish moved to a new facility, the property was purchased by the Hampshire Hospitality Holdings, and the spectacular promontory that juts into Meredith Bay became the site of a fine new inn. In March 2003, construction began on the Inn at Church Landing, the fourth and final member of the Inns at Mill Falls family. In May 2004, Church Landing celebrated its grand opening.

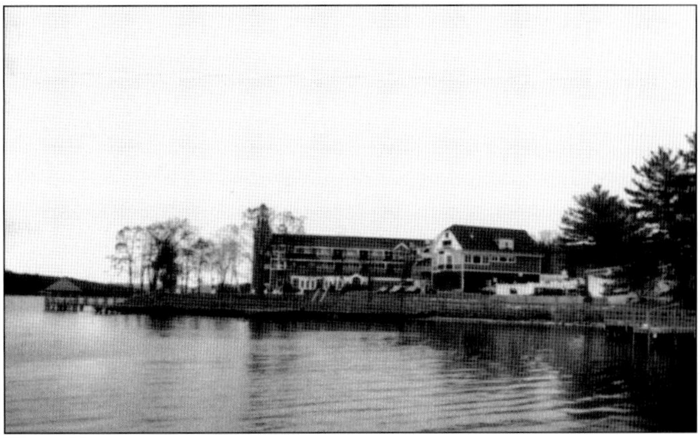

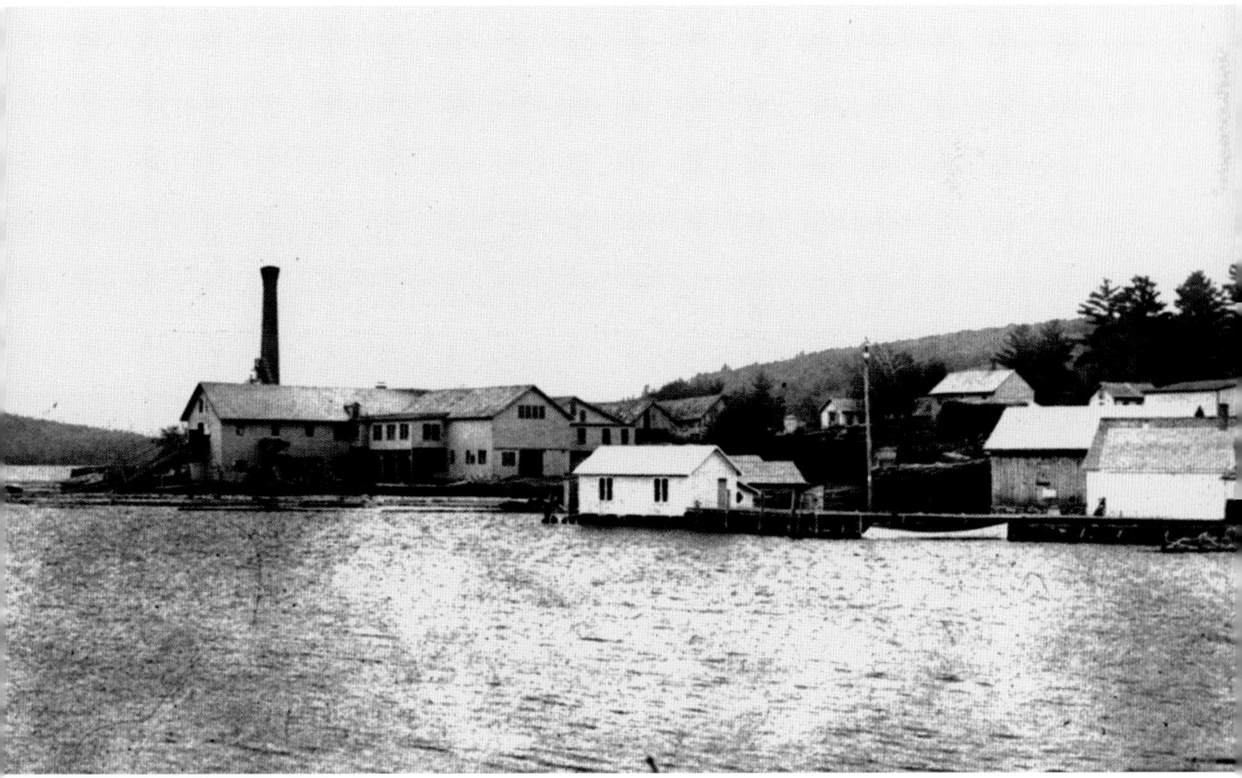

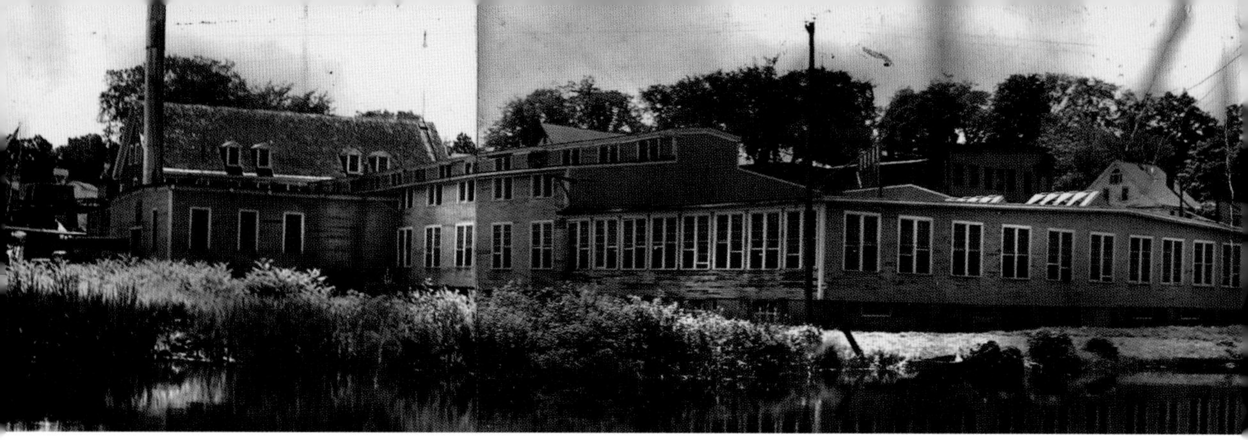

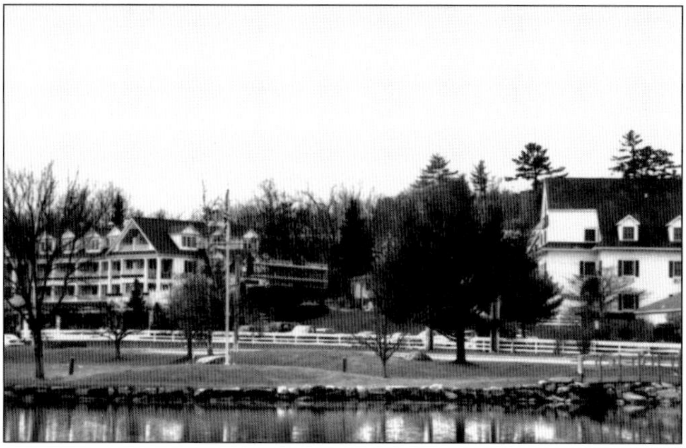

The Meredith Linen Mill was located on the shore of Meredith Bay. In the late 1800s, brothers Allie and Minot Hall came to Meredith from Massachusetts and bought the water rights for mill power. After equipping and erecting new buildings, they purchased flax from Europe and manufactured an excellent grade of pure linen in what was then known as the Meredith Flax Mill. Later, the entire business was acquired by Allie Hall, who in turn established the Meredith Linen Mill. Years later, an asbestos mill was constructed at the site, and it operated until the 1970s. The mill was located on the property of the present Inns at Mill Falls. In the early photograph, note the space between the building and the lake. The mill was located on what is now Route 3. In the distance of the present-day photograph is the Mill Falls Marketplace.

In 1919, Pynn's Garage was a landmark on the corner of South Main Street and Railroad Avenue. Today this property is owned by the Garrity Lumber Company, which has rented out space to the Cerutti Contracting Company and Sally's School of Dance.

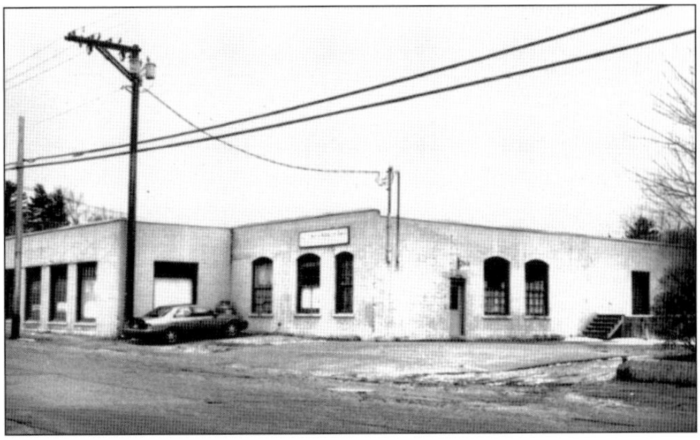

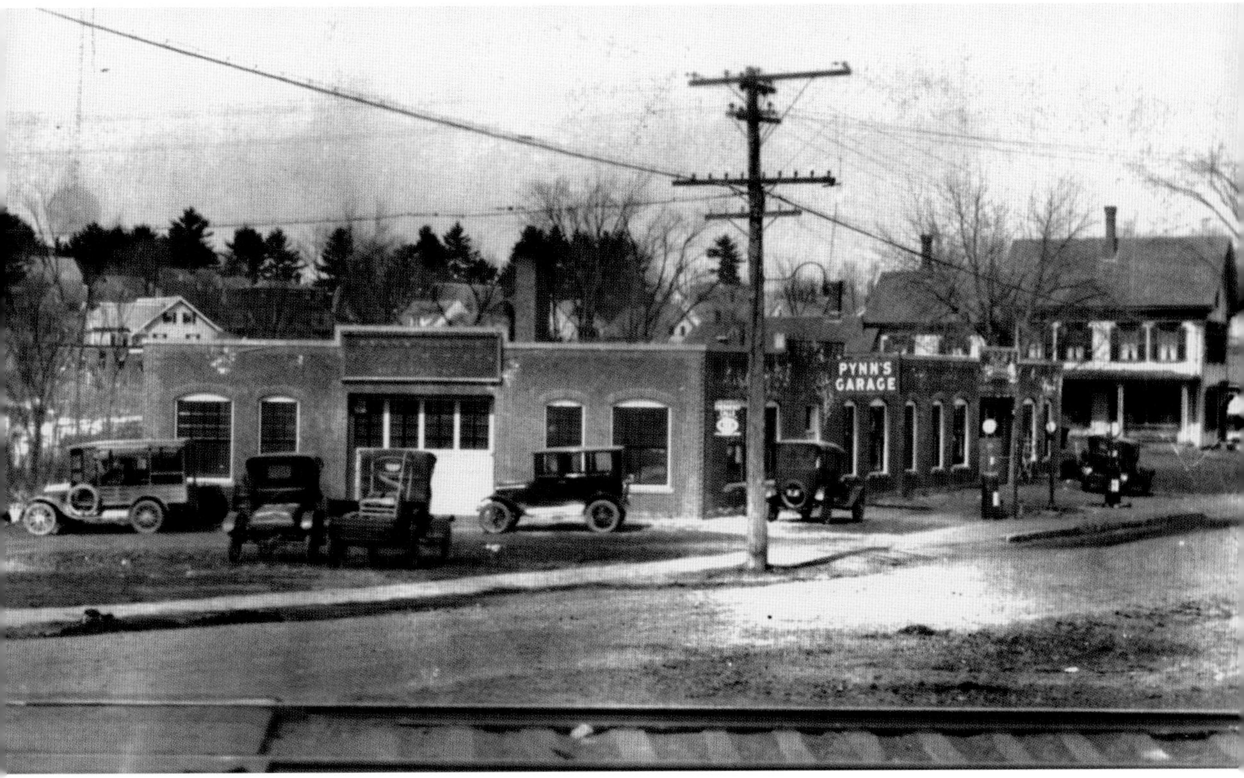

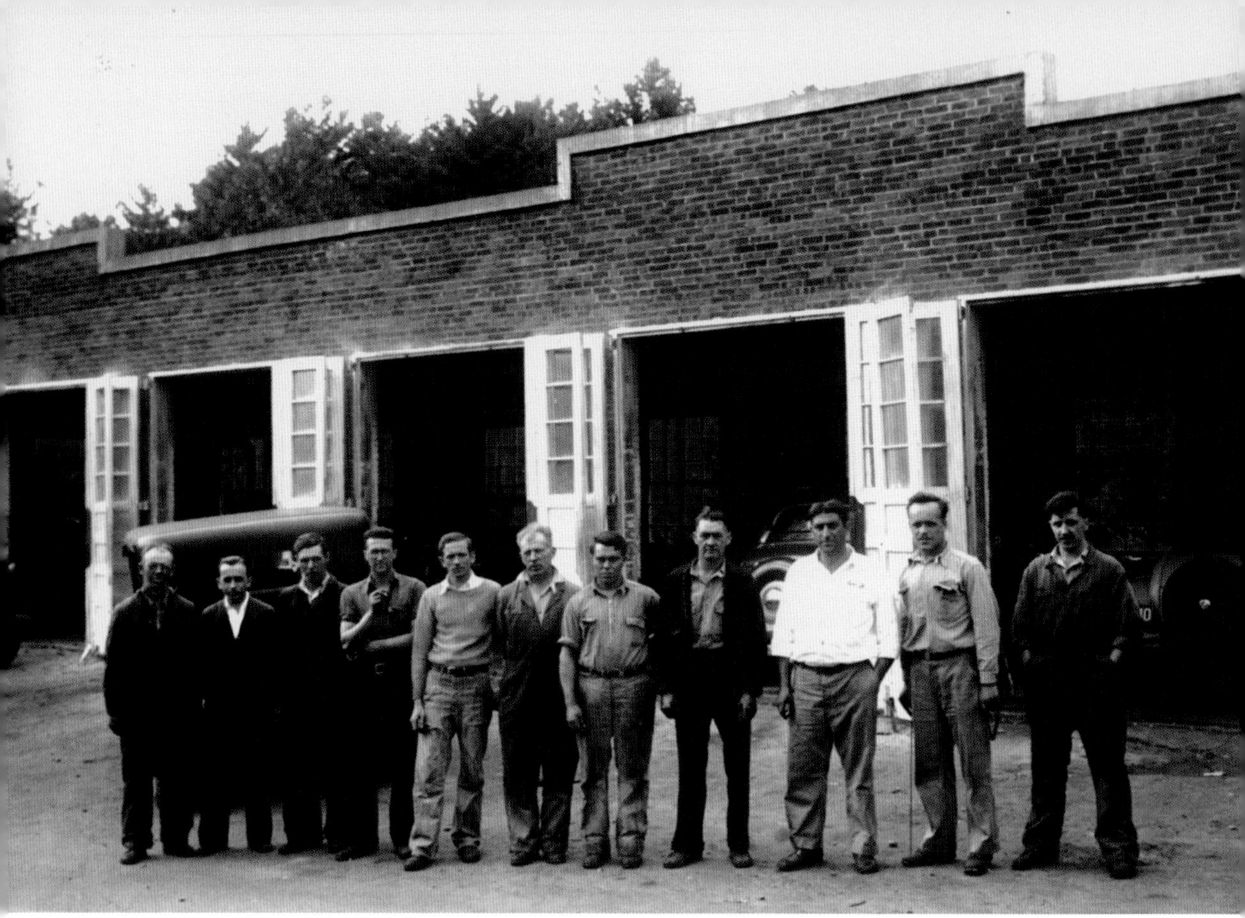

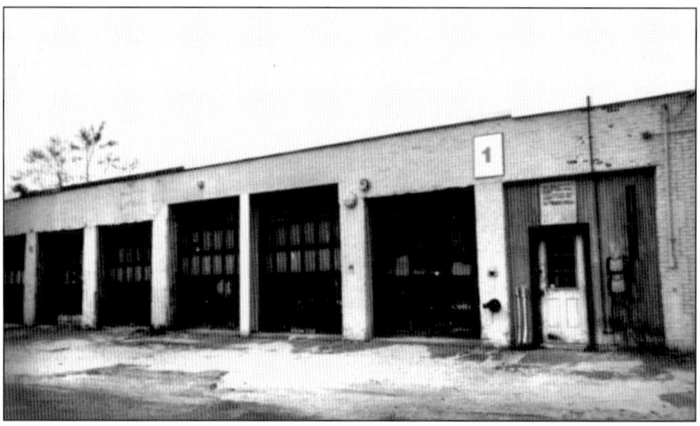

The workmen of Pynn's Garage, on South Main Street, pose *c.* 1930. From left to right are Elno Avery, Wally Bishop, Ken Nelson, Ralph Nelson, an unidentified man, Percy Estes, Ernest Valliere, Olin Lund, Fred Lamond, Sherman Carter, and Ken Vittum. The property now belongs to the Garrity Lumber Company and is used for storage.

The American gas station on the corner of Route 3 and Winnipesaukee Street (Route 25) is shown in a 1960s view. During the 1950s, Harry Wallace owned and operated the station. In the 1960s, the station was removed, and the Piper and Israel office building was constructed. In 1993, the Piper and Israel building was bought by the Hampshire Hospitality Holdings, who renovated it to become the Inn at Bay Point.

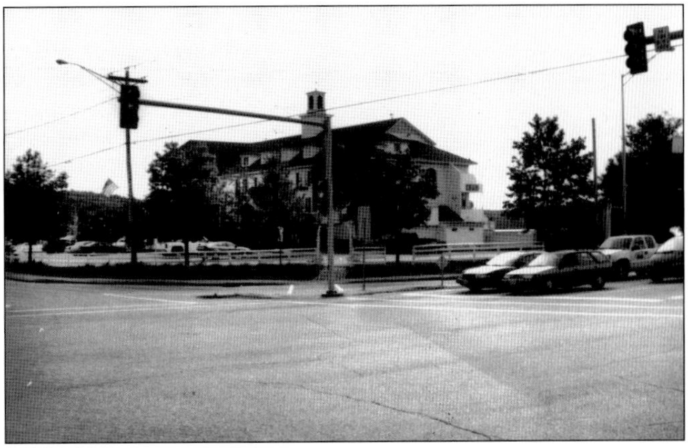

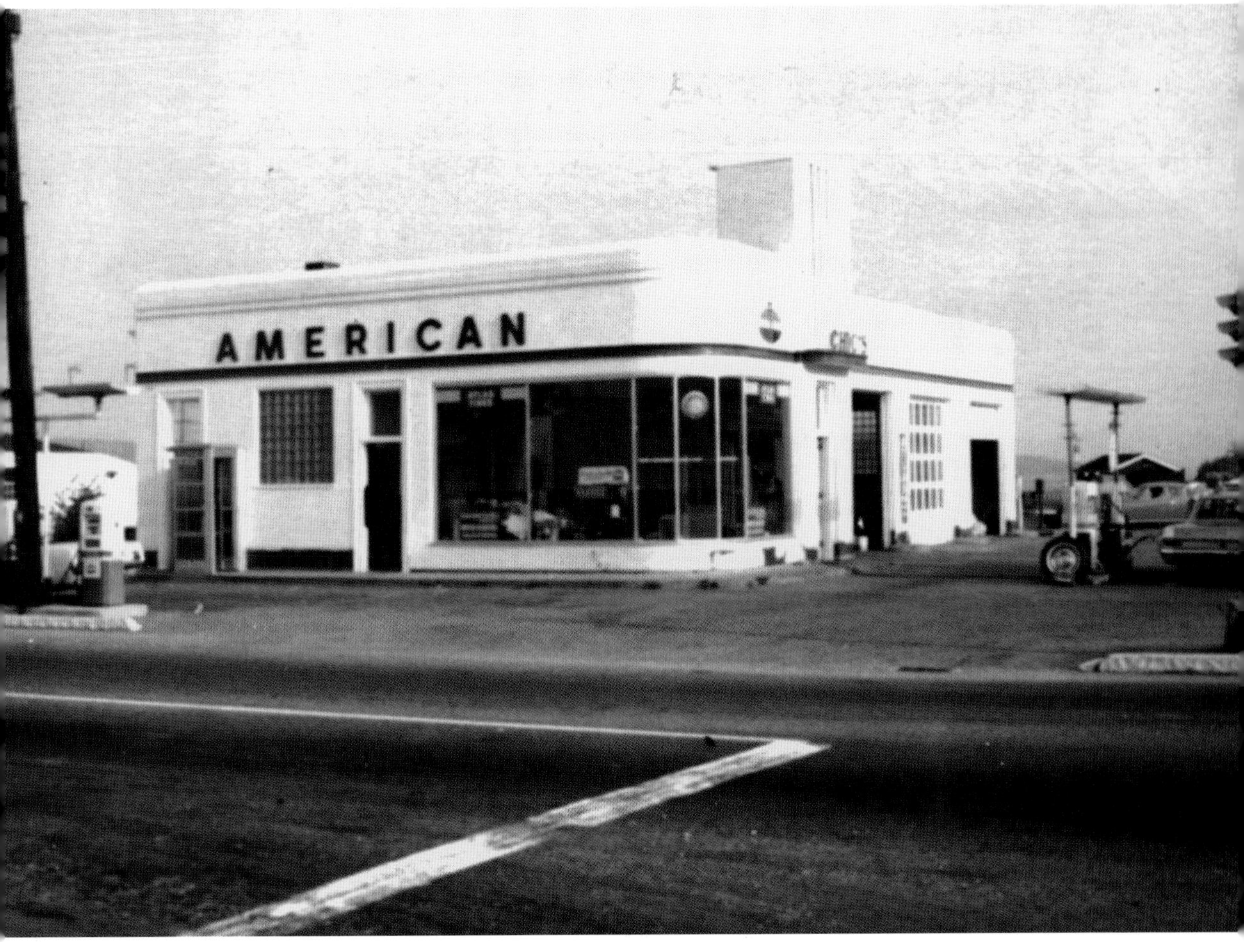

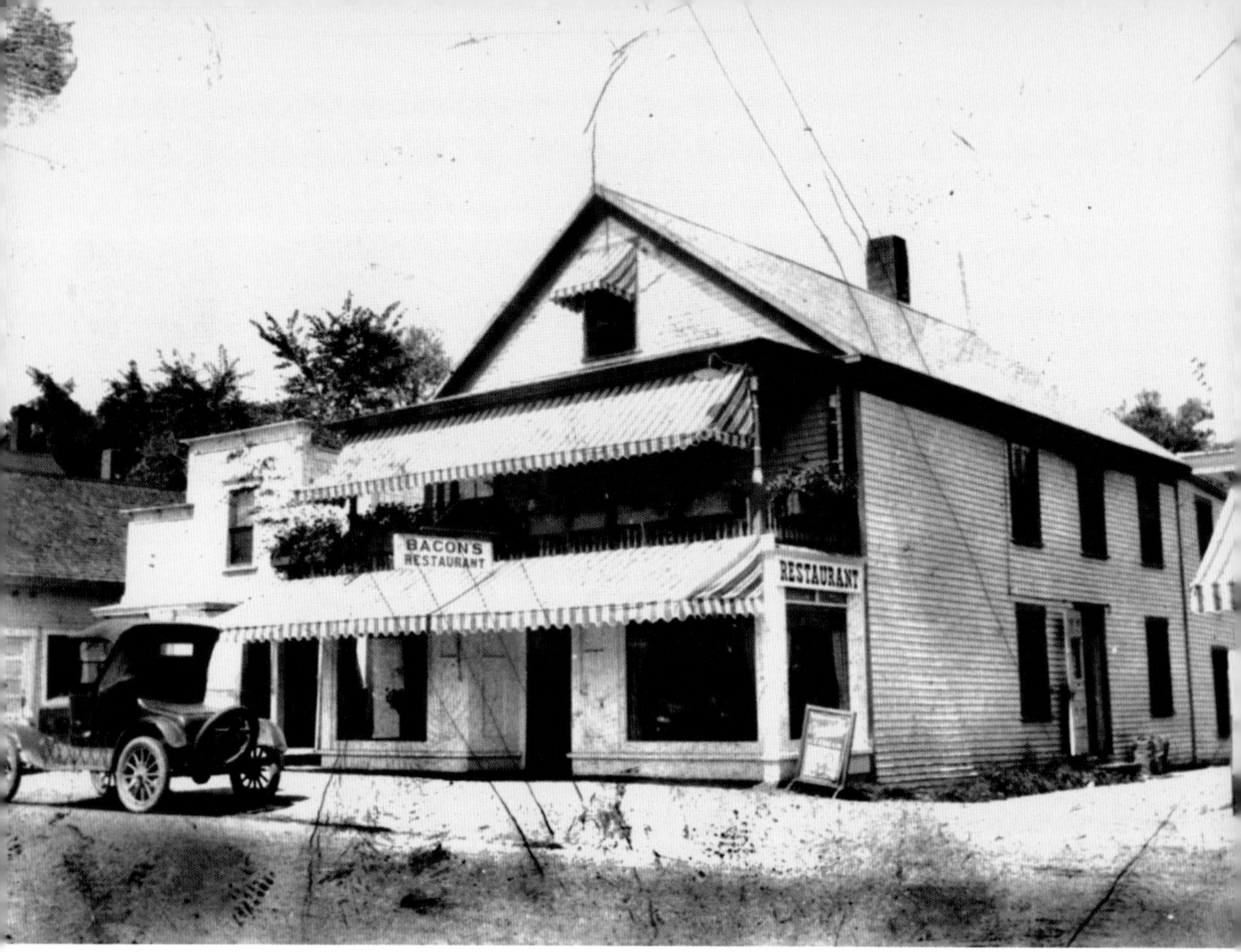

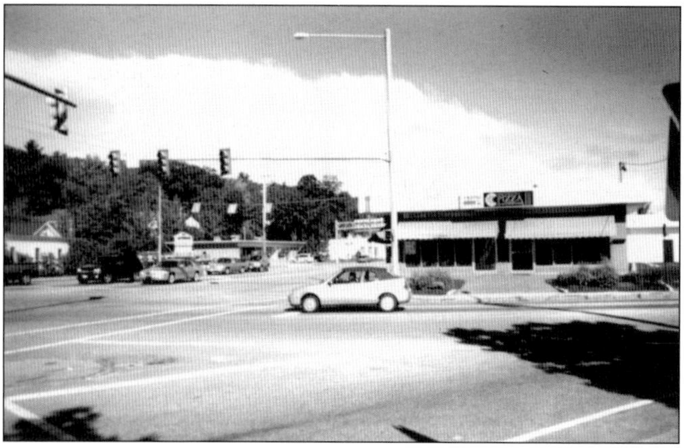

Bacon's was a popular eating place on Winnipesaukee Street during the 1920s and 1930s. This landmark was demolished in 1948 for construction of the intersection between Route 3 and Route 25.

In the late 1940s, brothers Russ and Larry Hart, along with their wives, left New Jersey to begin farming in New Hampshire. By 1953, they were raising turkeys exclusively. In 1954, they opened a 12-seat restaurant that specialized in turkey sandwiches and dinners. In 1965, the Harts discontinued raising their own turkeys after they discovered they could acquire turkeys that were equal in quality to their own home-grown birds by selectively purchasing them from turkey farms that met the high standards of the restaurant. In 1986, Russ and Helen Hart's children—Lynn, Dale, Russell T., and Glenn—purchased the restaurant and continued their active involvement in its daily operations. For 50 years, Hart's Turkey Farm Restaurant, on Ladd Hill, has been a landmark and a legend in the community.

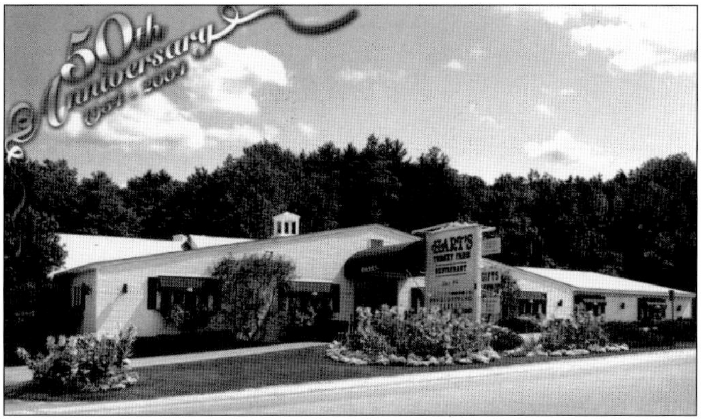

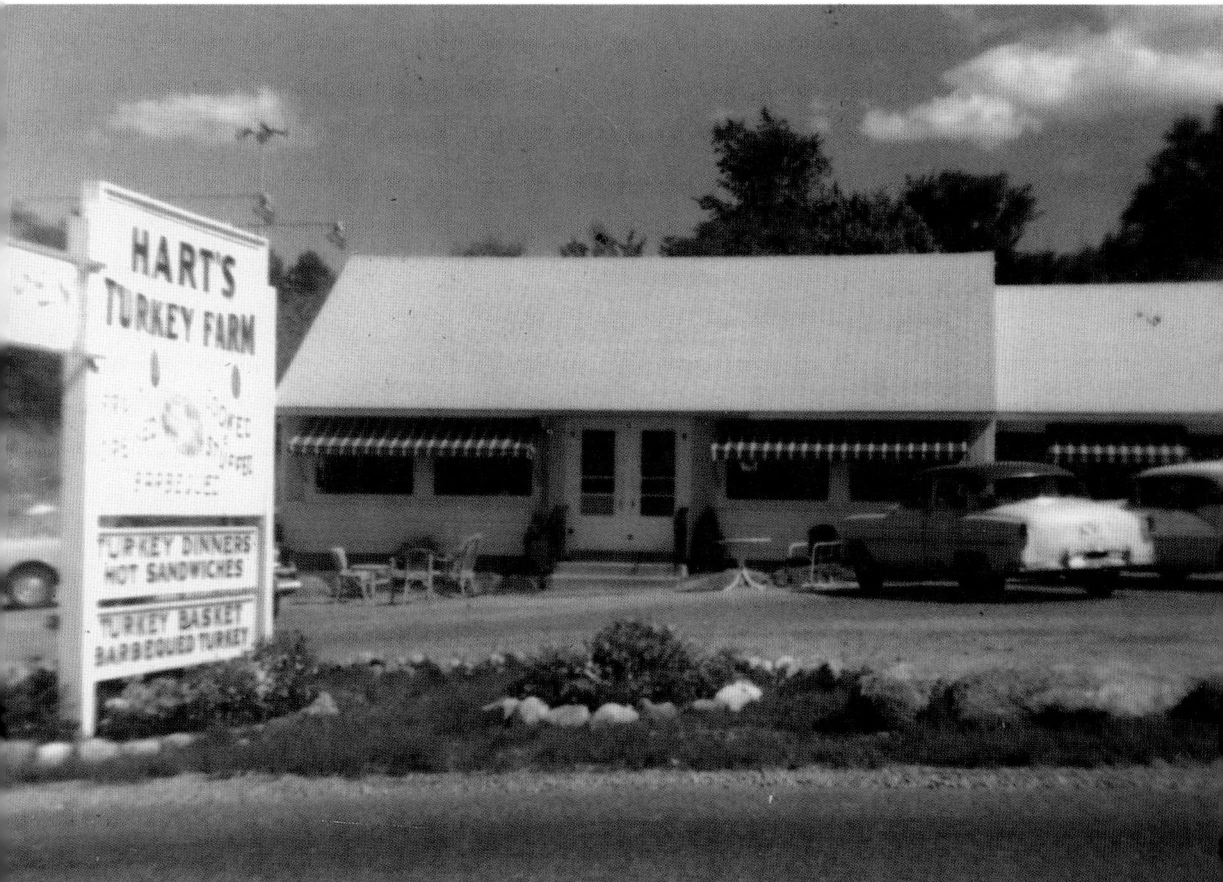

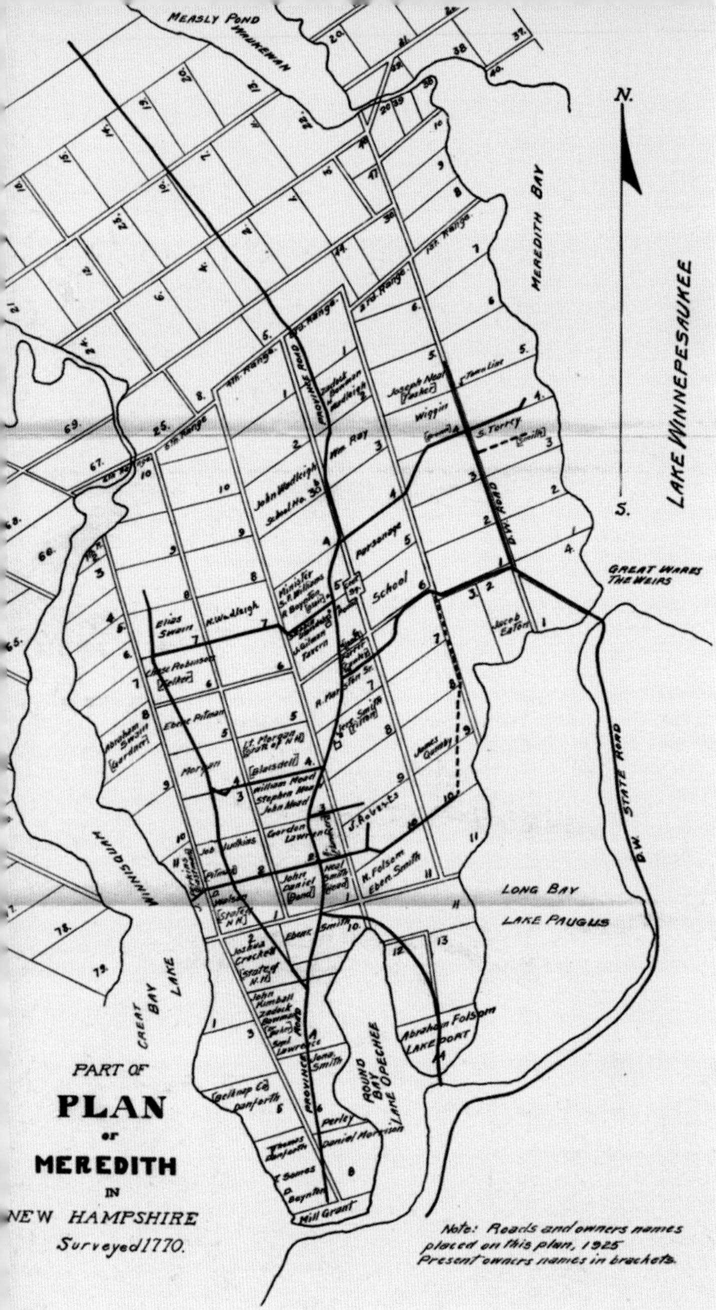

This plan of Meredith dates from 1753. A present-day map shows the entire town with an inset of the village.

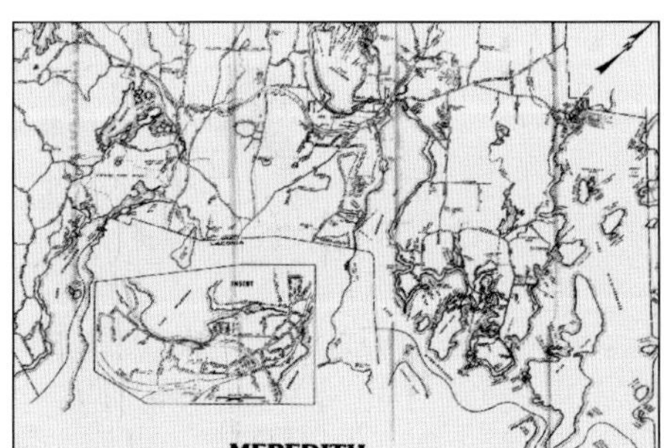